Stories behind
My Photographs

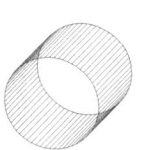

TOM OMIDI, Ph.D.
(also BA, MBA, MSMS, CGA,
and a former member of The Federation of Canadian Artists)

Copyright © 2023, 2025 by Tom Omidi

All rights reserved. No part of this book may be reproduced, translated, or transmitted in any form or by any means—graphic, electronic or mechanical, including photocopying, recording, taping or information storage or retrieval systems—without the prior written permission of the publisher or author.

Omidi, Tom, 1945-, author
Stories behind My Photographs
/ Tom Omidi, Ph.D.

ISBN 978-1-988351-18-6 (Paperback).
A copy of this book is held at
Library and Archives Canada Cataloguing in Publication

1. A Collection of Tom's Photographs.
2. Photographs' Background and Stories.
3. Photography's Goals and Psychological Property
4. Arts' Value and Outlook
I. Title.

Front Cover: A View of Downtown Vancouver in 1980's: A Photograph by Tom
Back Cover: Self-portrait by Tom in 1962

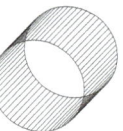

Published by Eros Books,
Vancouver, Canada

erosbooks2020@gmail.com

Printed in 2025

Author's Books
(As at 2025)[*]

Non-fictions (Sociology/Exploratory)   ISBN

The Nature of Love and Relationships 2011, 2016, 2020	978-1-988351-03-2
Doubts and Decisions for Living:	
Volume I: The Foundation of Human Thoughts **2014, 2020**	978-1-988351-11-7
Volume II: The Sanctity of Human Spirit **2014, 2020**	978-1-988351-12-4
Volume III: The Structure of Human Life **2014, 2020**	978-1-988351-13-1
Relationship Facts, Trends, and Choices **2016, 2020**	978-1-988351-04-9
The Mysteries of Life, Love, and Happiness **2016, 2020**	978-1-988351-05-6
Marriage and Divorce Hardships **2016, 2020**	978-1-988351-06-3
Gender Qualities, Quirks, and Quarrels **2016, 2020**	978-1-988351-07-0
Relationship Needs, Framework, and Models **2016, 2020**	978-1-988351-08-7
Being Better Beings[1] **2020**	978-1-988351-02-5
Humans versus Humanity[2] **2025**	978-1-988351-19-3

Novels (Amusing/Autobiography)   ISBN

Persian Moons 2007, **2016, 2020**	978-1-988351-14-8
Midnight Gate-opener 2011, **2016, 2020**	978-1-988351-10-0
My Lousy Life Stories **2014, 2020**	978-1-988351-09-4
Persian Suns **2021**	978-1-988351-15-5

Other (Artistic/Archival)   ISBN

About My Books 2016, 2022, **2025**	978-1-988351-20-9
About My Paintings 2022, **2025**	978-1-988351-17-9
The Stories behind My Photographs 2023, **2025**	978-1-988351-18-6

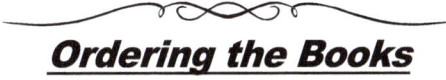

Ordering the Books
(Use the books' ISBNs for getting the latest editions)
For these books' most economical prices, order at **Amazon.ca**
Available also at Amazon.com and some bookstores,
as well as international markets

----

erosbooks2020@gmail.com (for comments and contacting the author)

---

[*] Enhanced Editions of 12 older books were printed in 2020. They were resubmitted to the Library and Archives Canada Cataloguing as well. If a book's 'print date' on the copyright page is older, the newest version is available at Amazon and bookstores.

[1, 2] These two books are complementary in terms of humanity topics.

Table of Contents

List of Photographs Painted
Introduction *1*
Welcome 3
Nature's Pervasive Glory in Vancouver 6
Magic of a Click 10
My Favourite Locales 14
Yosemite Park 15
Mosquito Creek Park 18
Stanley Park and Lost Lagoon 21
Lovely Birds 26
The Forlorn Black Swan! 33
Creating a Semblance of Impressionism 37
Lions Gate Bridge 41
Outskirts of Vancouver 47
Downtown Vancouver-Part 2 50
Trees and Leaves 53
Flowers and Fruits 59
Especially Water Lilies 63
Arts' Value and Outlook 68
A Splendid Memory 69
The Father and Son: Subtle Rivalries and Affections 71
My Gorgeous Grandma's Lost (Confiscated) Portraits 74
Portraits' Purposes 77
West Vancouver Hills and Mountains 77
San Francisco Hills 82
Horseshoe Bay and Beyond 84
Wild Flowers and Shrubs 90
Miscellaneous and Odd Pictures 95
Views of North Vancouver 102
On the One Hand… 103
On the Other Hand… 103

Appendix A: *Common Pictures Inspiring Good Paintings 105*
Appendix B: *Odd Urges to Photograph 128*
Appendix C: *Three Sentimental Photographs in Three Life Phases 132*

List of Photographs Painted

Only those photographs inspiring most of my paintings are listed below for keen readers interested in comparing them, i.e., a painting with its source or vice versa.

Photographs' Number and Name	Page	Inspiring Painting # [*][†]
19. Yosemite Tree 1	16	3
20. Yosemite Field 2	17	31
22. Mosquito Creek trail 1	18	4
23. Mosquito Creek trail 2	19	5
24. Mosquito Creek trail 3	20	16
27. Lost Lagoon 2	23	8
28. Lost Lagoon 3	24	9
29. Lost Lagoon 4	25	10
39. The Monarchs, Duck and Duckess of Stanley Park	32	10
45. Lost Lagoon Mood 1	39	120 (sold) & 121
46. Lost Lagoon Mood 2	39	7 & 110
57. Howe Sound	46	1 (front cover)
62. Vancouver Coast 4	49	87
70. Spring in BC Mountains	53	30
71. Yosemite Tree 2	54	108
73. Yosemite Tree 3	55	25
74. Yosemite Tree 4	55	(sold painting)
76. Lonesome Tree	56	15
77. Stanley Park Hills	56	14
80. Silhouette	57	29
93. Water Lily and Fish 1	64	18
94. Water Lily and Fish 2	65	19
96. Water lilies in Whistler Lake 2	66	109
98. Water lilies at Whistler Lake 4	67	21
102. A View of Pacific Ocean from West Vancouver Hills 1	78	78
106. A View of Pacific Ocean from West Vancouver Hills 4	80	(sold painting)
108. A View of Pacific Ocean from West Vancouver Hills 6	81	42
110. San Francisco Hills 1	82	12
116. Solitude 1	85	(sold painting)
120. Seagulls Flight at Sunset (a beginner's painting)	87	127
121. A View of Howe Sound from Whytecliff Park	87	6
122. A View of Pacific Ocean from Whytecliff Park	88	28
125. Yellow Field 1	90	(sold painting)
128. Yellow Field 2	91	124
138. Forget the World in the Middle of the Day 1 (Nice)	96	22 & 97
140. Lost Lagoon 5	97	(sold painting)

---

[*] This is a reference to the paintings listed and numbered in *About My Paintings* book.
[†] Sold paintings without a 'painting number' means they were sold without their pictures being taken and included in *About My Paintings* book.

List of Photographs Painted (cont.)

Only those photographs inspiring most of my paintings are listed below for keen readers interested in comparing them, i.e., a painting with its source or vice versa.

Photographs' Number and Name	Page	Inspiring Painting # *†
142. Seagulls' Contemplation at Stanley Park	99	119
145. Juliet's Balcony	101	106
149. Lost Lagoon 6	105	120 (sold)
150. Lost Lagoon 7	106	(sold painting)
151. Alberta Rockies 1	107	34
152. Alberta Park	108	20
153. Banff 1	109	36
154. Banff 2	110	35
155. Alberta Rockies 2	111	124
156. Sausalito	111	48
157. Jean Pierre's Living Room	112	37
158. My Dinning Room	112	38
159. Sneaky Tulip	113	33
160. Cherry Blossoms in Stanley Park	113	50 & 123
161. Spring in Vancouver	114	116
162. Cherry Blossoms in Mosquito Creek Park	115	44
163. Colours of Romance	116	65
164. A Cosy Corner in Gallery's Backyard	117	32
165. Fog	118	96
166. Solitude 2	119	49
167. Lost Lagoon 8	120	43
168. Colours of a Creek	121	98
169. Puddle in the Path	122	46 & 73
170. Tree Shadows in Whytecliff Park	123	80
171. A Secret Path at MC Park	124	17

---

* This is a reference to the paintings listed and numbered in *About My Paintings* book.

† Sold paintings without a 'painting number' means they were sold without their pictures being taken and included in *About My Paintings* book.

Introduction

Photography has helped me connect with nature placidly since puberty after my father introduced me to this simple form of artistry. He probably had not expected me to get absorbed in this hobby so effectively for self-expression and inner reflections, yet I always cherish his gesture and our ensuing rivalries around this shared interest. More details with regard to our amusing competitions are presented later in the book for fun. Photography also proved a great source of relaxation for managing my convoluted emotions and urges for creativity until the age of fifty when a romantic episode with nature inspired me to become a painter, as explained in *About My Paintings* book. Then, ten years later, my obsession for painting was itself dampened when I decided to concentrate on writing novels and non-fictions about our faltering social systems and family relationships.

As the title implies, this book is partially autobiographical in line with family and social dilemmas affecting us all in different, and usually difficult, ways. Although every picture is allegedly worth a thousand words, adding a variety of stories and facts of life might enrich our personal perceptions of both nature and social realties in our lost civilization. A bunch of these photos might have artistic values, too, yet the stories and memories would hopefully heighten public's interest about humans' looming demise due to escalating socioeconomic/political downfall and the absence of capable leaders to serve humanity. Combining the gloomy truth about global mayhem with the images' subtle messages around nature's glory might also goad more people reassess their phony lifestyles against life's realities and strive for radical changes required in social and personal mentalities. Our current approach to address only the symptoms of social and global turmoil at the cost of ignoring their roots, especially capitalism, is pointless and deplorable. Perhaps some readers would also check out my books that discuss many details about the depressing facts of living in our so-called modern world.

At the same time, the privilege of communicating with thoughtful readers has now turned into a new mission for me after giving up painting, my marriage, and my tedious job with the government to delve into writing fifteen years ago. Some readers might also learn why and how my peculiar curiosities (possibly driven by my busy muse) make me whine so much in my books about our modern, whimsical lifestyles and family values, while also exposing my convoluted mentality so readily. They might now gather a fairer view of my cynicism as well, instead of relying merely on people's crude judgments about a cynical (or lost) human with a bizarre, radical attitude! In fact, they might agree that no amount of nagging about humans' inherent idiocy is ever enough!

The idea of writing this book emerged in 2022 rather abruptly when preparing the book, *About My Paintings*. As much as those paintings deserved archiving for varied reasons, they had been mostly inspired by many thousands of photographs I had been taking around the world for decades, especially in Vancouver. The value and relevance of those photos also became clearer as I recalled the stories behind the paintings I was photographing for the paintings' book. Many poignant stories encouraged me to revisit my neglected pictures of nature that I had printed painstakingly in my colour dark room in Vancouver. Some of those stories, including my personal ordeals, were narrated in the paintings' book and some are included here along with my sentimental memories of related incidents and individuals during my long photography adventures. However, they are mostly for stressing on the acceleration of social and family troubles like a global plague—an immensely urgent topic that now comprise the main tone of most of my books. It is also for discussing the meaning and value of art now that humanity itself is running out of options for survival.

Sadly, justifying even our artistic efforts and books is getting harder in societies laden with colossal deformity after millenniums of severe mismanagement. In fact, now all our efforts and leisure, especially those related to sports, movies, and art, or even futuristic scientific research and space explorations, feel futile and selfish if humanity itself is doomed. They merely indicate our dire nonchalance about the horrifying social climate, instead of trying to understand the vulnerability of the world we have created for ourselves and the role we are, or ought to be, playing in that regard. It is vital now that everybody feels the gravity of situation due to the fast downfall of social structures in line with humans' growing idiocies that transpire clearly in my weird personality, too, especially regarding my vain hopes about a minute chance of salvaging humanity. Glumly, I explore every occasion to fathom and outline the basic facts behind growing global unrests, humans' sufferings, and need for mass immigrations, which all point to one conclusion: That all this mayhem is merely due to humans' misled mentalities, vanity, and power struggles throughout history in line with ineffective socioeconomic systems and values driven by greedy, ignorant leaders towards irreversible global and natural calamities.

For me, luckily, my passions for photography and painting over five decades have been instrumental, like major blessings, for balancing my zeal for grasping and coping with social mandates, expressing my artistic and academic perceptions, and releasing my tensions by exploring the enigmatic truth of existence through self-realization.

This book's 180 images were selected out of 400 large photos I had printed in my colour darkroom painstakingly for getting the best results in terms of colour and quality, while performing some experimentations as well. This was before digital photography and printing made my large collection of negatives and slides (around 10K) obsolete along with the darkroom I had built for printing many more negatives. This setback was probably another reason I was drawn to painting mysteriously, as outlined in *About My Paintings*. Still, my last minute opportunity to work in my darkroom—those 5-6 years—feels like another timely blessing when I view the large prints on the walls or hoarded in the closet. Those efforts have proven even more worthwhile now for preparing the images printed in this book.

The pictures have been chosen mostly by the way they inspire a memory or mood for me, but hopefully also reflect the glory of nature, artistic intonations, or interesting notions. Hopefully, some of them can also help others relax and reflect on existence deeper to fathom humans' real needs and humanity's ultimate objectives beyond the horrid mandate of living in our dark societies driven by too many lame leaders.

Pictures are numbered mainly for reference in this and other likely books, as well as the corresponding paintings in *About My Paintings* inspired by those photographs.[*] Accordingly, my painting and photography books are complementary and follow similar sentiments about the role and meaning of art in a dying society. The Table of Contents can also help in finding topics and stories that might grab the readers' interests.

Recalling the dates and locations of some pictures taken ages ago became a challenge and made the task of naming the photographs even harder. Thus, please forgive any likely error regarding a location, while naming all images with a hint about their backgrounds had weirdly felt essential. Nevertheless, as noted before, this book is mainly about the stories behind the photographs than the images per se. Hopefully, some of those pictures might be inspiring or artistic as well. Most of all, understanding the role and future of art at this depressing historical juncture has been a big incentive for preparing this book—since even art is now becoming less justifiable daily.

---

[*] Photographs on the front and back cover of the book are numbered 1 and 2 respectively.

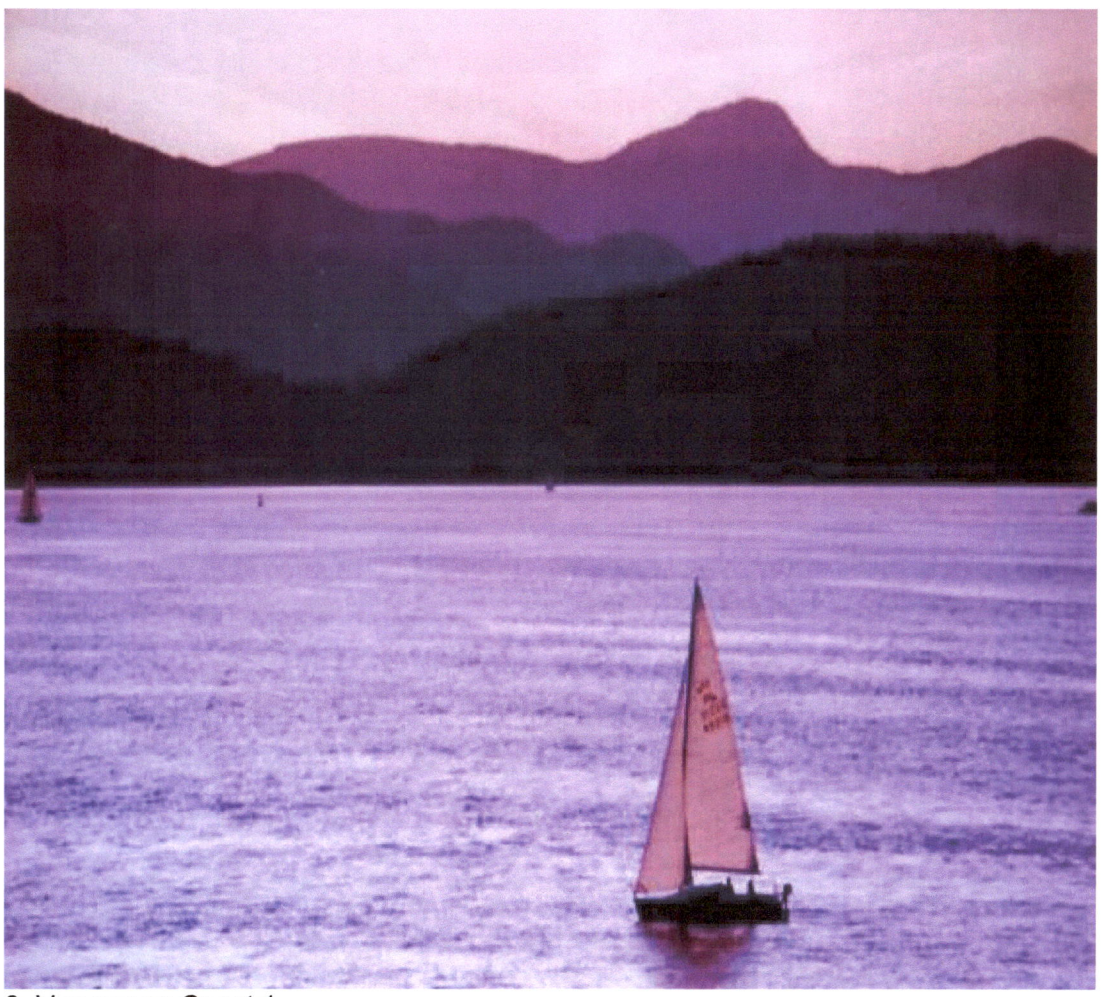

3. Vancouver Coast 1

Welcome

Welcome to my sphere of imaginations, ideals, and semi-philosophical outlook in line with my lifetime endeavours to connect with nature, grasp a finer sense of reality, and minimize my burdens of living and socializing. Unfortunately, the contrast between nature's splendour and humans' evil is growing faster every generation with lesser prospect for us gaining enough intelligence and humility to develop viable societies. Besides the sadness of this horrific reality, it astonishes me too deeply and intimately —for some odd psychological reason perhaps—about the horrendous absurdity of our arrogant claims about human intelligence! The mix of our negligence and ignorance just looks too rooted and embarrassing when we witness nature's divine harmony and animals' extraordinary genetic sense about their priorities and plans. In fact, it feels magical (both mysterious and thrilling) that the more heartedly we study nature and animals' life, the more we learn about ourselves as a confused, desperate species with a beautiful brain wasted so much on trivia and fantasy. Especially, the recent historical compilation of idiotic ideologies and socioeconomic structures to fulfil our selfish goals for prosperity and pleasure have ruined humans' mentalities and made them lose track of their real priorities for sustaining their existence and humanity.

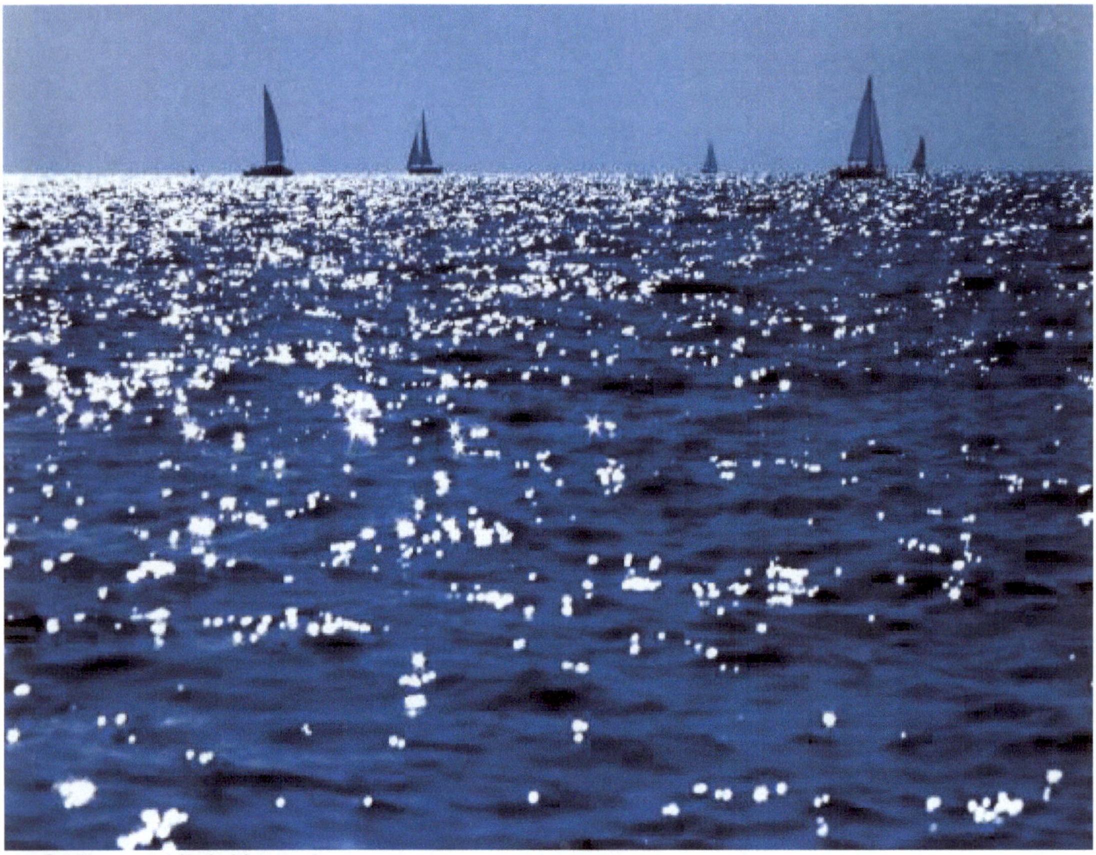

4. Sailing at High Noon 1

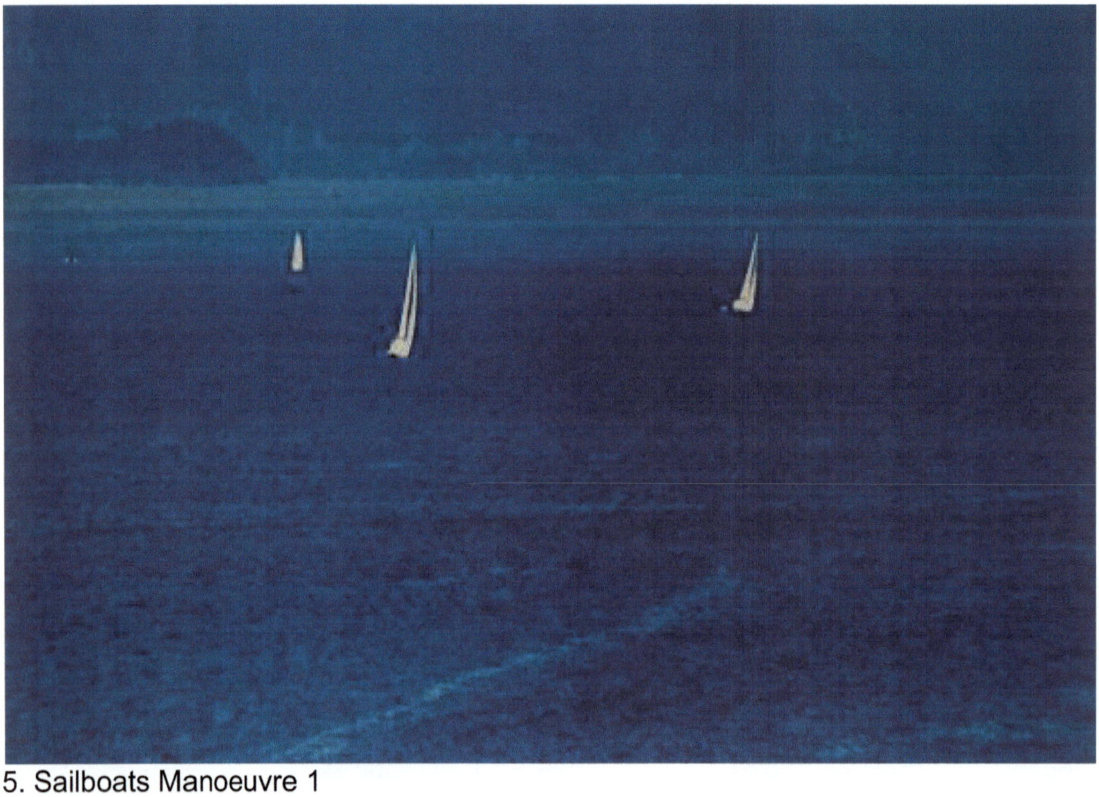

5. Sailboats Manoeuvre 1

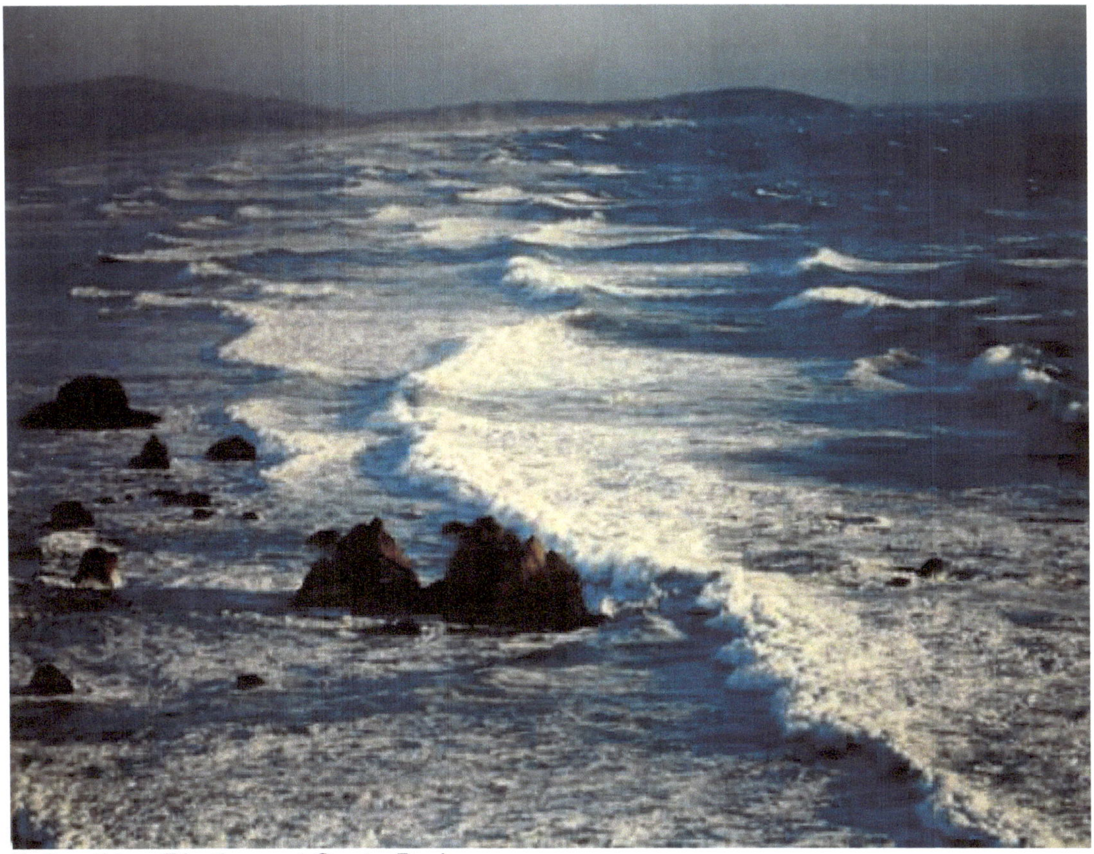

6. Soothing Rhythms at Santa Barbara

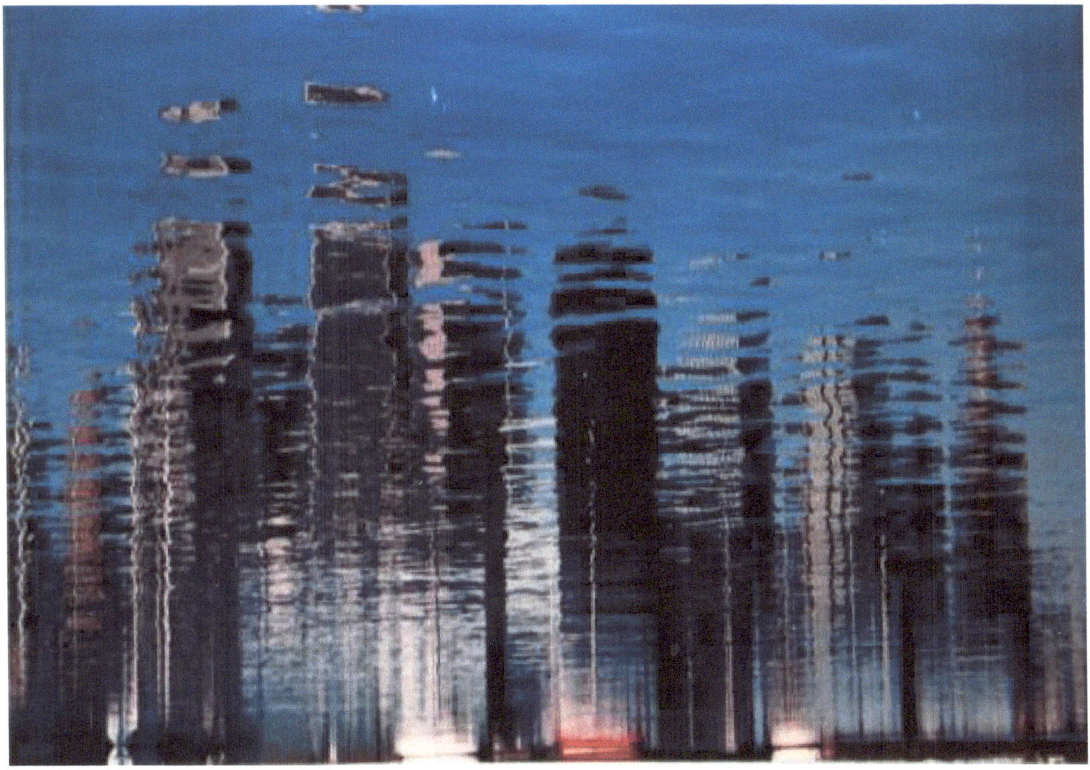

7. Sail Boats Imagery in Burrard Inlet

Nature's Pervasive Glory in Vancouver

My photography had not stressed on nature as much until we arrived in Vancouver in 1982 and basic natural beauties and landscapes enthralled me spiritually—or maybe even sentimentally due to my pensive mood at the time. I had always strived to take expressive photographs of various subjects, including people and limited landscapes around me in Iran, Europe, and the United States. Yet, only random opportunities for capturing nature's majesty had rendered unique photographs, mostly in slides, which I never got the facility to print in large formats or include in this book, anyway.

In Vancouver, my photography was rather monopolized by nature, as evident in the images printed in this book. The photograph of downtown Vancouver on the front cover was taken in the early 1980's before the Canada Place and more high-rises were developed in the core of the city. The Seabus shown on Burrard Inlet carries passengers between downtown and North Vancouver.

A few pictures of downtown Vancouver and Burrard Inlet are offered in this section and some more are depicted on pages 50-53 to avoid monotony. Even these general images manifest nature's glory due to romantic moods that lights, rays, and clouds spawn around man-made facilities. In the upcoming parts, we also traverse westerly on Burrard Inlet towards Lions Gate Bridge and beyond on the Pacific Ocean to exhibit nature's widespread glory in Vancouver and British Columbia. Other categories of photographs, including portraits and still life, complement nature's majesty by raising our moods and curiosities in line with general beauties that birds and plants, and even humans, bring to our lives in every corner around us.

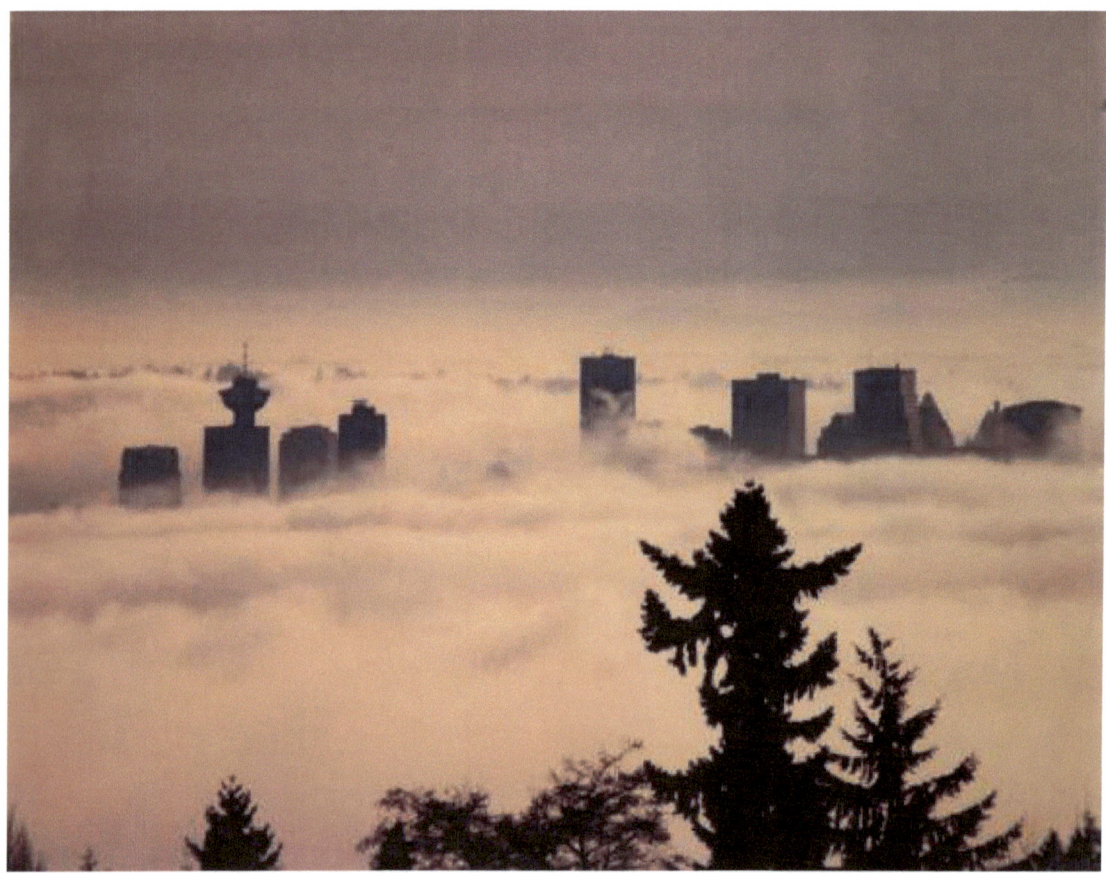

8. Downtown Vancouver 2

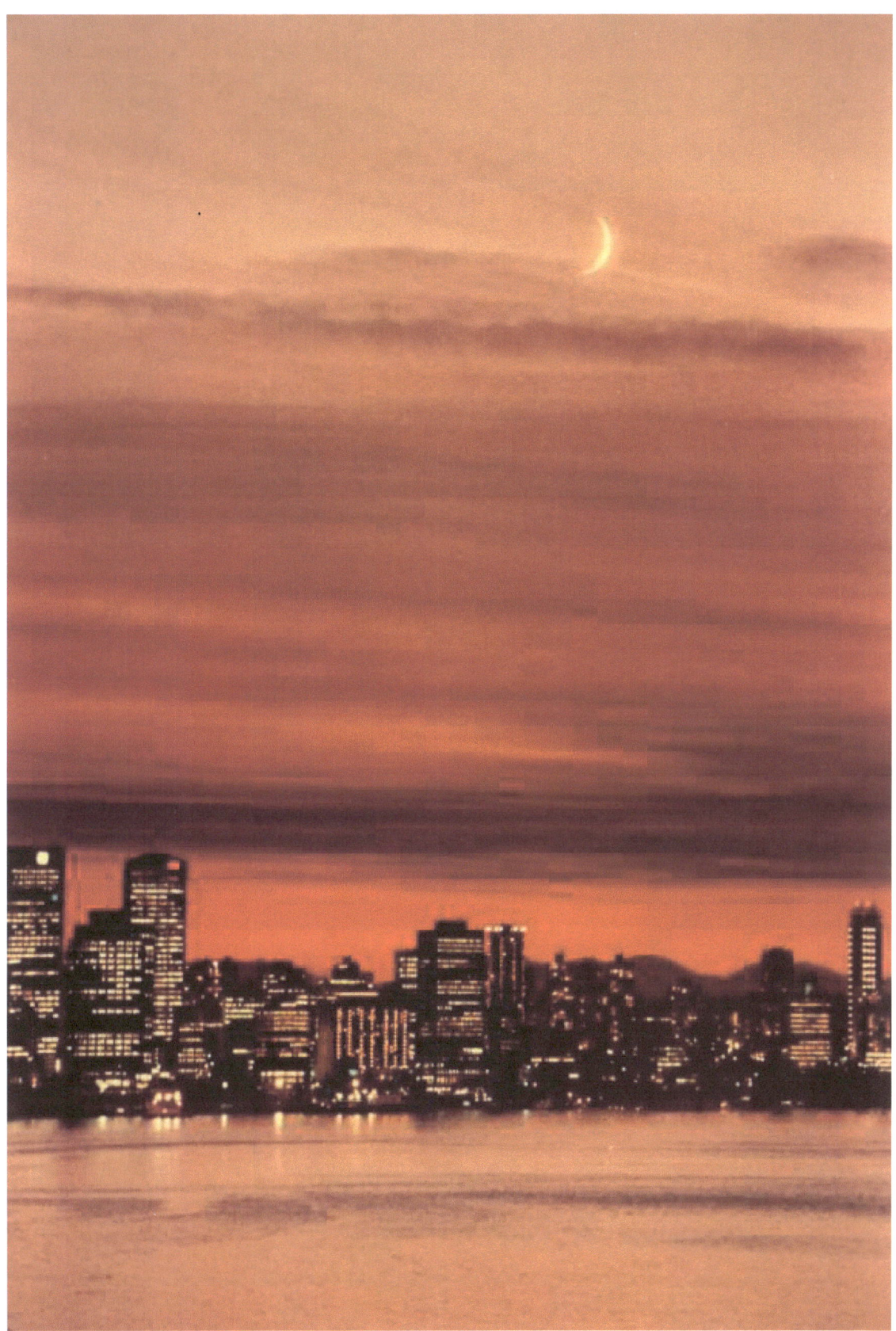

9. Downtown Vancouver 3

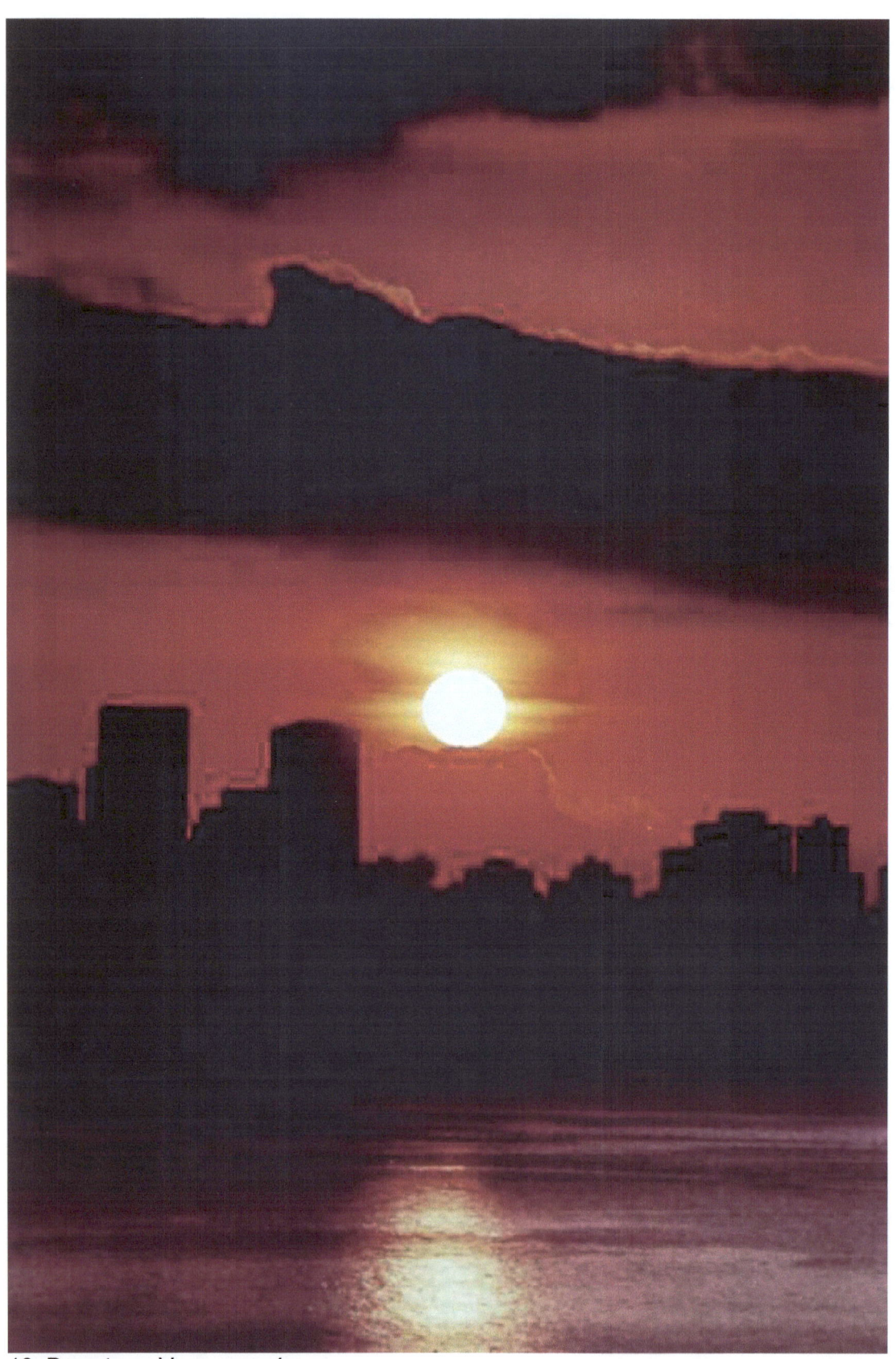

10. Downtown Vancouver 4

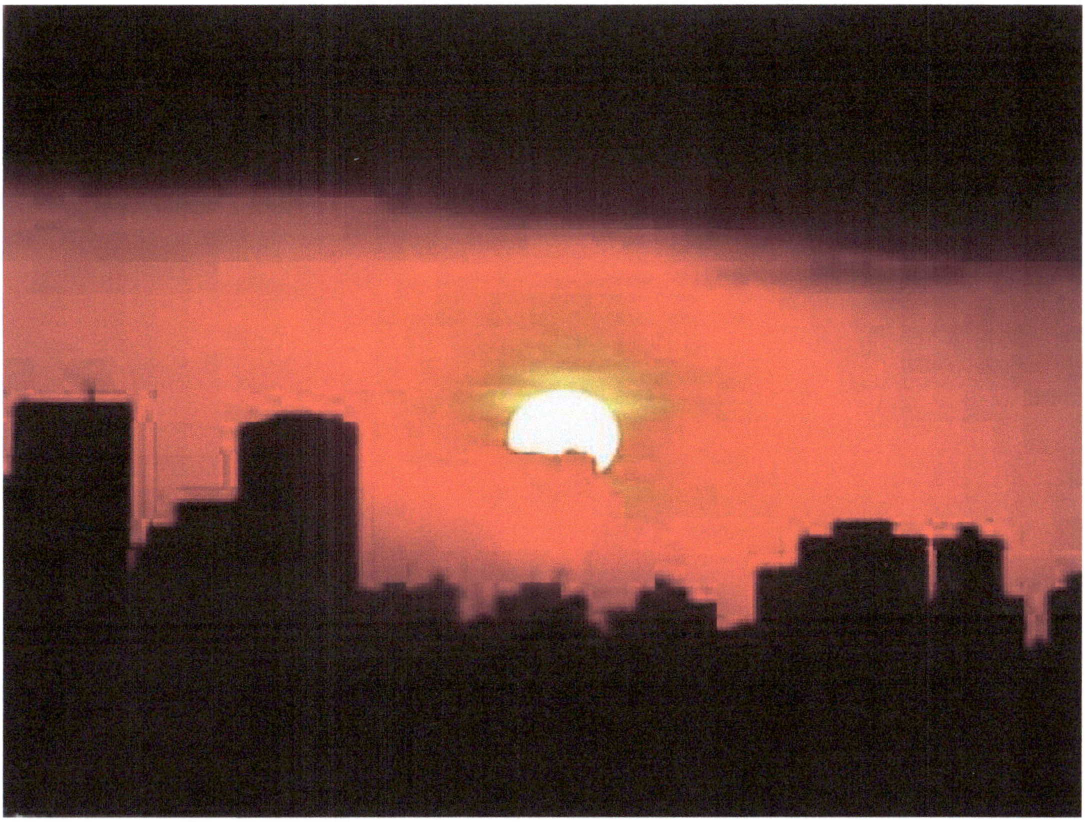

11. Downtown Vancouver 5

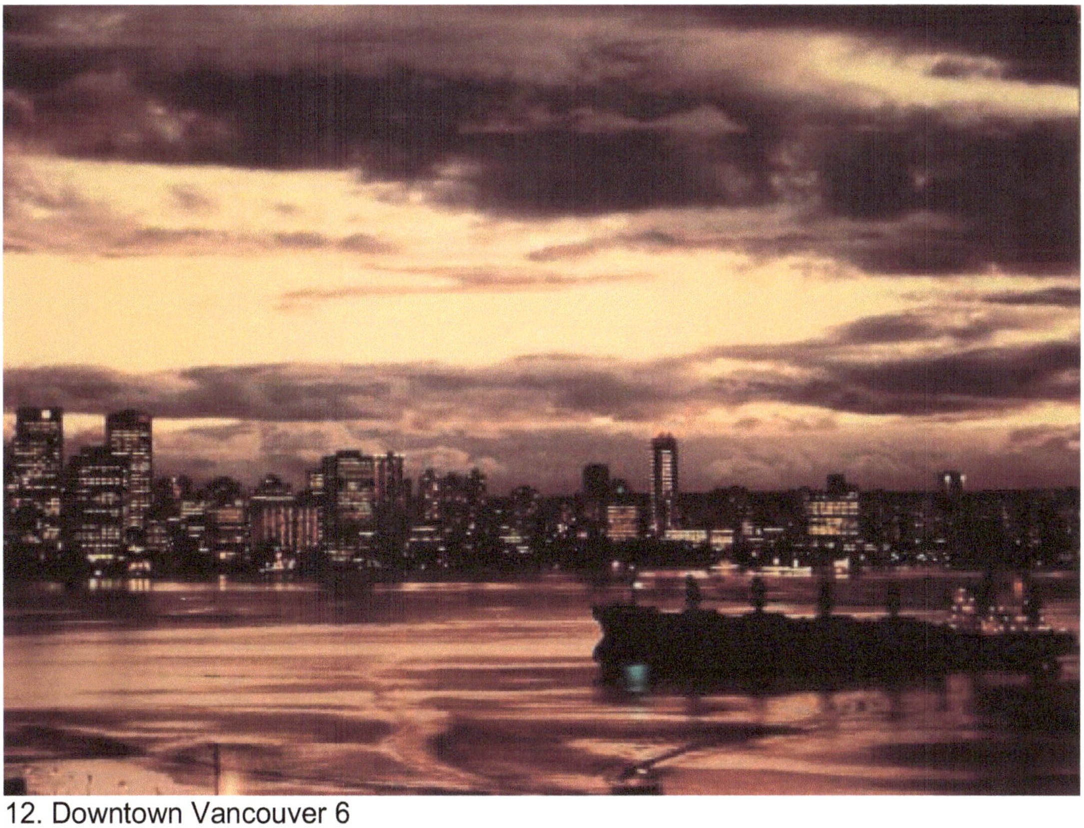

12. Downtown Vancouver 6

Magic of a Click

As a long devotee and experimenter of both photography and painting, knowing their differences has felt interesting to me, thus discussed in this book sporadically as well. In particular, the unique psychological benefits of photography, despite its lower artistic prestige, feel substantial to me, although only a tiny fraction of pictures usually prove momentous. Actually, this merely sentimental property of photography will feel more precious as the importance and purpose of art in general become more questionable every year in line with humanity's shakier future. This topic is reviewed further in an upcoming section about *Arts' Value and Outlook*.

With a click we try to capture nature's glamour or an emotional notion in a special moment. We strive to stir the same or even more feelings through paintings, but the big difference is that pictures reflect the essence of nature, people, and objects more sincerely. In return, paintings usually absorb and amuse us better with higher effects due to artists' drive to make them appealing by all kinds of exaggerations, especially lots of warm colours. We might stare at powerful paintings serenely for hours, since our psyches crave too much fantasy these days. Even Monet has mastered this liberty and privilege of painting. Actually, nowadays, some painters just pour lots of vibrant colours on canvas to flaunt their creativity and people seem to love those meaningless paintings without even caring about their artistic or other fathomable purposes.

I have tried to elude the lure of warmer colours somewhat and keep my abstract or artistic experiments in some balance with realism, too, to avoid absolute subjectivity with regard to their meanings. Painting #63, *I Scream 2*, in *About my Paintings* book is a good example. Still, realism is often compromised in my paintings as well mainly by mixing two or more of my photographs to craft *partially* imaginary scenes. Creating semi-abstract photographs has also felt exciting and satisfying due to the calculated efforts needed to challenge realism subtly with some kind of special effects, such as the birds' images on pages 29-30.

Clearly, photography is much less complex and time-consuming than painting, but harder for getting good results and reflecting an artist's unique imagination or a novel concept. Paintings demonstrate artists' feelings, talents, and impressions better, while we relate easier even to common paintings than we do even to artistic photographs.

Conversely, photographs' realism gives us a precious opportunity to manage our psyches and daily routines in line with the essence and messages of nature without necessarily grasping or fussing over photographers' intentions or sensations per se. Photographs' veracity is vital for curbing our psyches' relentless exposure to fantasies as a normal feature of modern lifestyles at the cost of ruining our identities and senses of life's realities. Plenty of odd urges also drive our adventures in photography, some of which are noted on pages 95-101 and Appendix B, page 127.

Now, which one—the higher realism of photographs or artists' crude impressions of reality—serves our psyches better is hard to conclude swiftly. They are probably both valuable somewhat for teaching us the truth versus rendering a chance to soothe our depressed spirits and psyches during our incessant struggles for living around our naïve visions of reality. Ironically, this seemingly primitive point with regard to the value of truism applies widely and deeply to all human encounters, especially among close individuals, as we seek and value at least a basic level of decency and integrity. We cannot trust one another, nowadays, not only due to humans' historical urge for evil and conceit, but also their zeal to look modern and tactful, which often dilutes, if not ruins, their abilities for authenticity and honesty. In all, while a small dose of dreaming and hopefulness might help us manage our ambitions, curbing our psyches' exposure to fantasy, contrary to our current practice, would be a finer strategy for humans' and humanity's health in the long run.

Nevertheless, we click our cameras a lot for various reasons with limited chance of capturing arty pictures. The 180 photographs chosen for this book from nearly 400 images printed in my darkroom represent around 10,000 clicks to record many scenes with mixed outcomes during my forty years of devotion to photography. Showing only two percent of my photographs feels like an immense contrast to the idea of putting all my paintings' images in *About My Paintings* book, including even those *beginner's masterpieces*!!! This big leverage in photography, i.e. the luxury of trial and errors or relying merely on nature's beauty and accidents to produce a few masterpieces, gives painting a higher esteem in our minds, since we must do every brushstroke nicely and carefully with deep concentration, huge efforts, intention, and unique talents in order to produce worthy paintings.

Then again, some simple photographs make us pause and ponder nature deeper, learn, and satiate our psyches' craving for connecting to our spirits. This shows the power of a click, which the following four photographs are chosen to demonstrate, too.

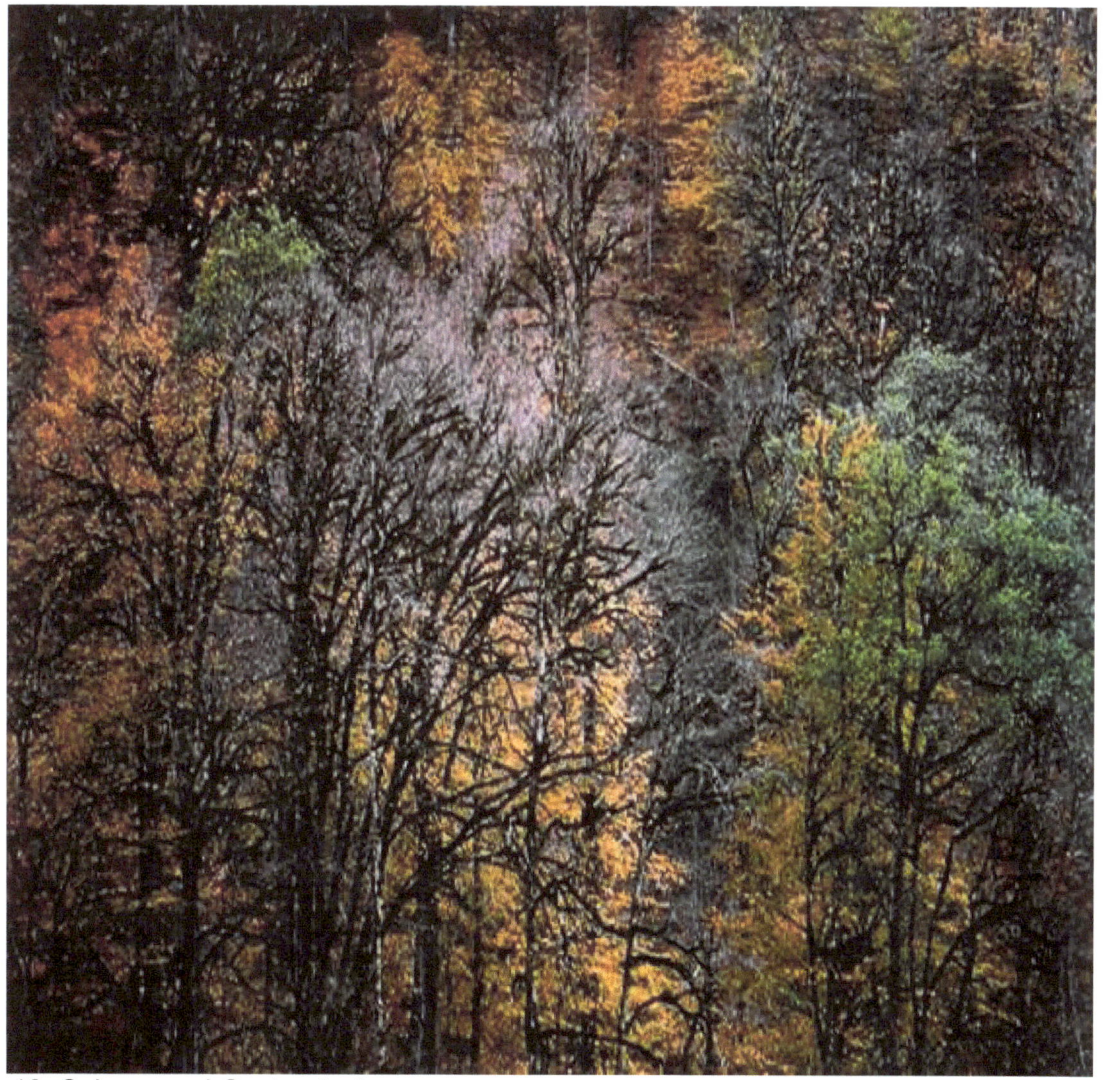

13. Colours and Contrasts 1

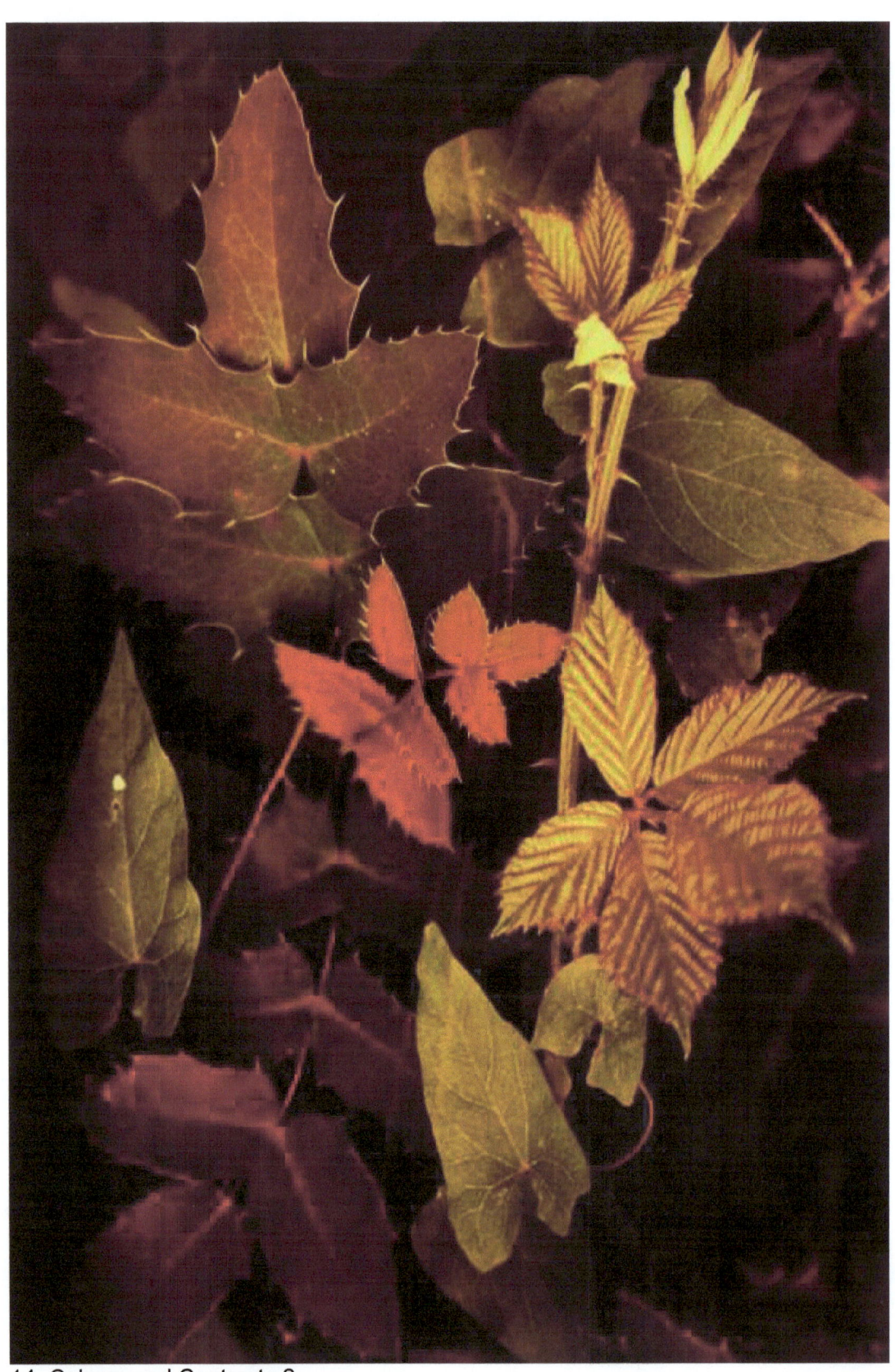

14. Colours and Contrasts 2

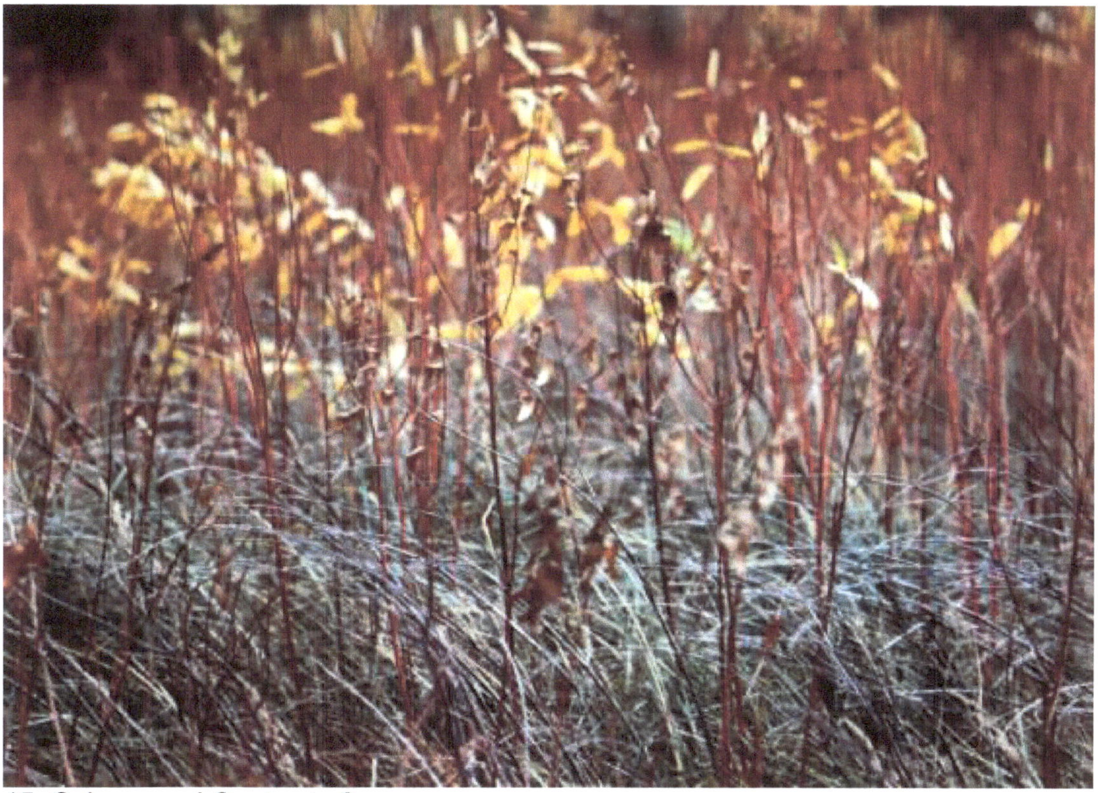

15. Colours and Contrasts 3

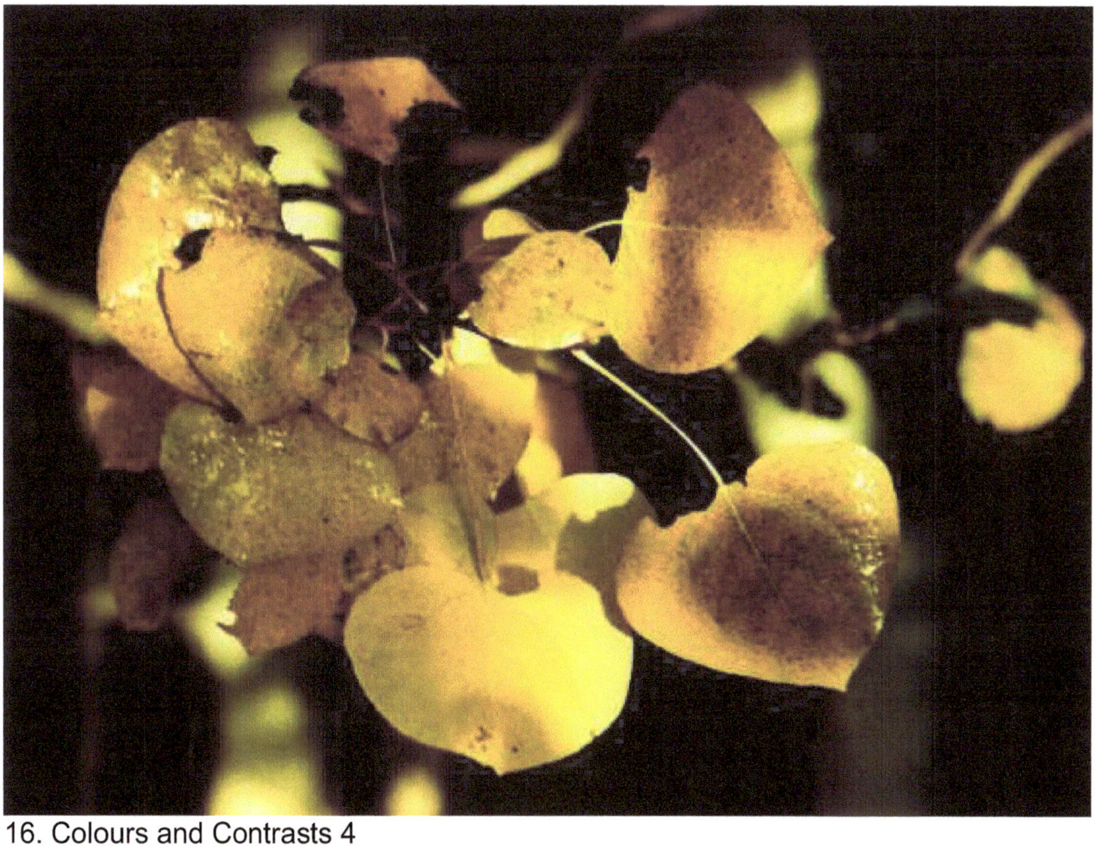

16. Colours and Contrasts 4

My Favourite Locales

This book's photographs were captured mainly during the 1980's and 1990's in North America and printed in my colour darkroom. Accordingly, a large number of precious, older negatives and slides prior to this era have not had a chance of reflecting my sentiments in the young ages. Thus, perhaps another book is prepared later by using that group particularly.

Meanwhile, most of this book's images are the products of my routine exploration of Mosquito Creek Park, which has been so conveniently near my house for afternoon walks, and Stanley Park in downtown, where a big variety of birds are busy with their purposeful lives, especially around the exciting Lost Lagoon. Yosemite Park has been another serene environment I had visited during the 80's and 90's, thus the source of many of my photographs and paintings. More about these locales are explained later in this book as well as in *About My Paintings* book along with the images of related paintings. The 'List of Photographs Painted' in the beginning of this book provides references to some of those paintings.

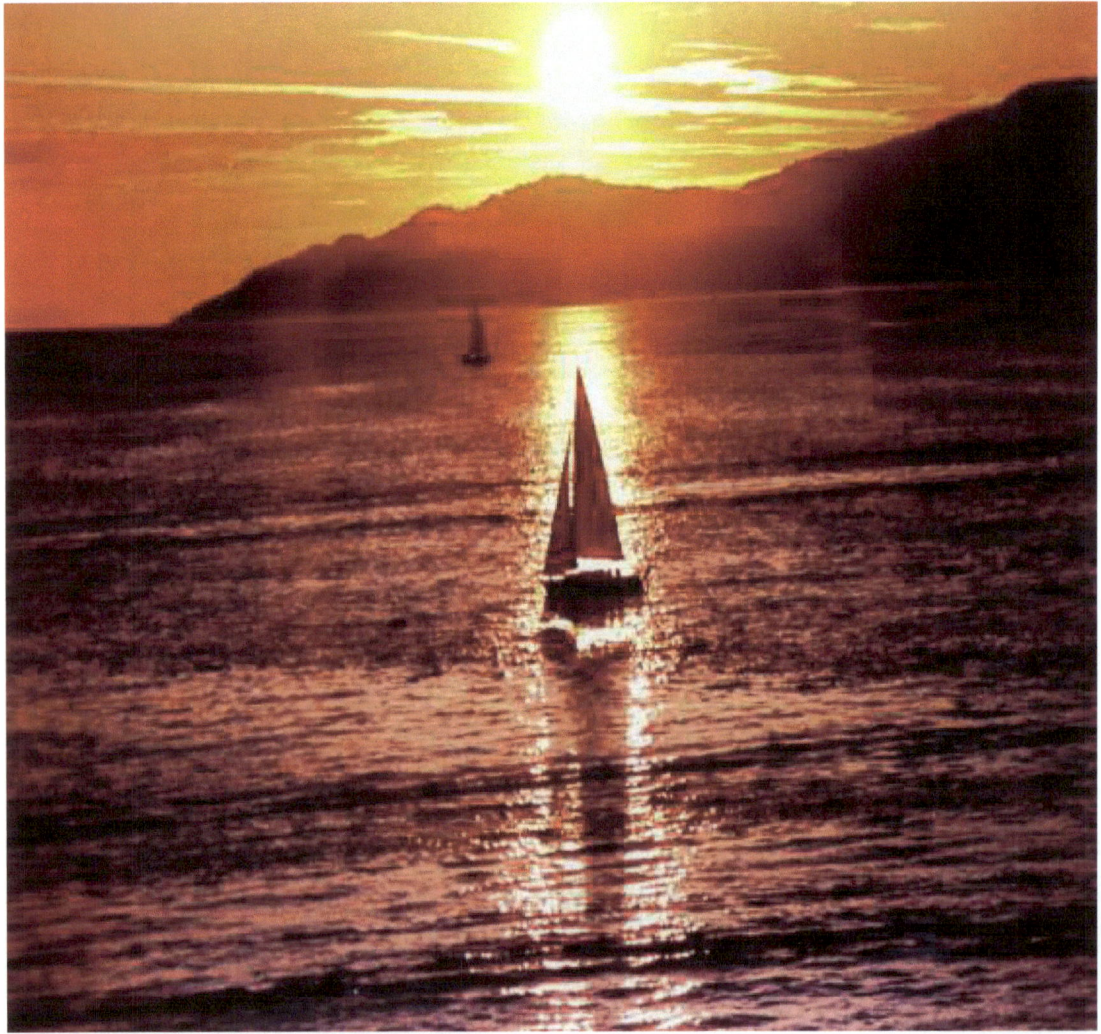

17. Last Light at English Bay (Vancouver)

Yosemite Park

Ansel Adam's famous pictures at Yosemite, especially Half Moon, encourage people, especially a curious photographer, to visit the park and maybe take a few pictures of that splendour, too. Still, I never found time and priority to visit Yosemite during the ten years I studied and taught at various universities in California. At last, this opportunity presented itself during 1980's and 90's when my ex-wife and I visited our relatives in California and she agreed to go to Yosemite together, too. Seeing Ansel's noted sites was probably my main reason for visiting the park, but then I was mesmerized by the fields and trees that make Yosemite such a popular place for touring and camping. My memory of those beautiful vistas during a few camping experiences that my fussy ex-wife shared with me are still precious. I miss those old good times, not only for my obsessive zeal for nature and artistry, but also the warmth of belonging and family values, which now feel too naïve and a waste of our sentiments. Luckily, I also took many landscape photographs during our few trips to Yosemite and printed a bunch of those negatives personally, some of which are offered below.

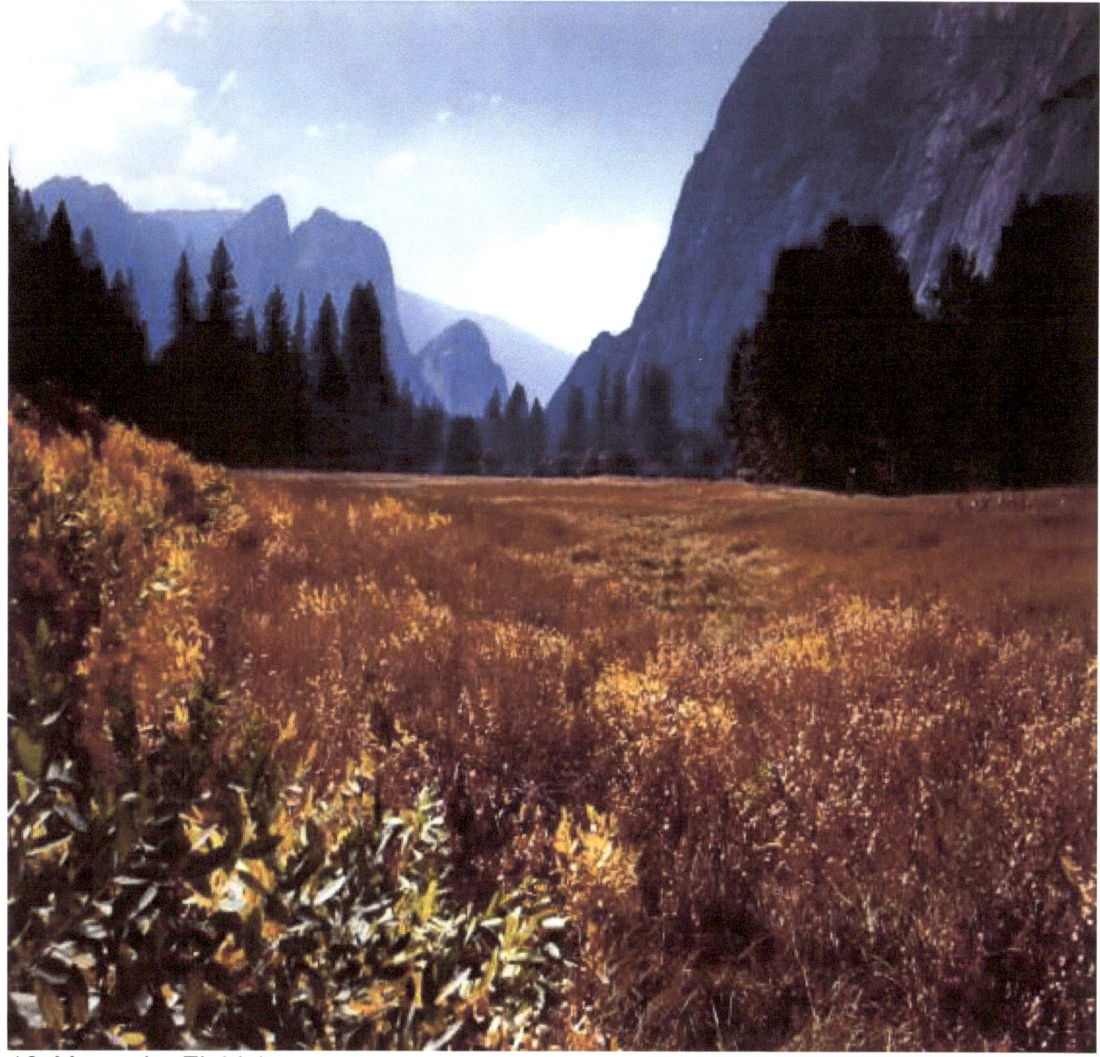

18. Yosemite Field 1

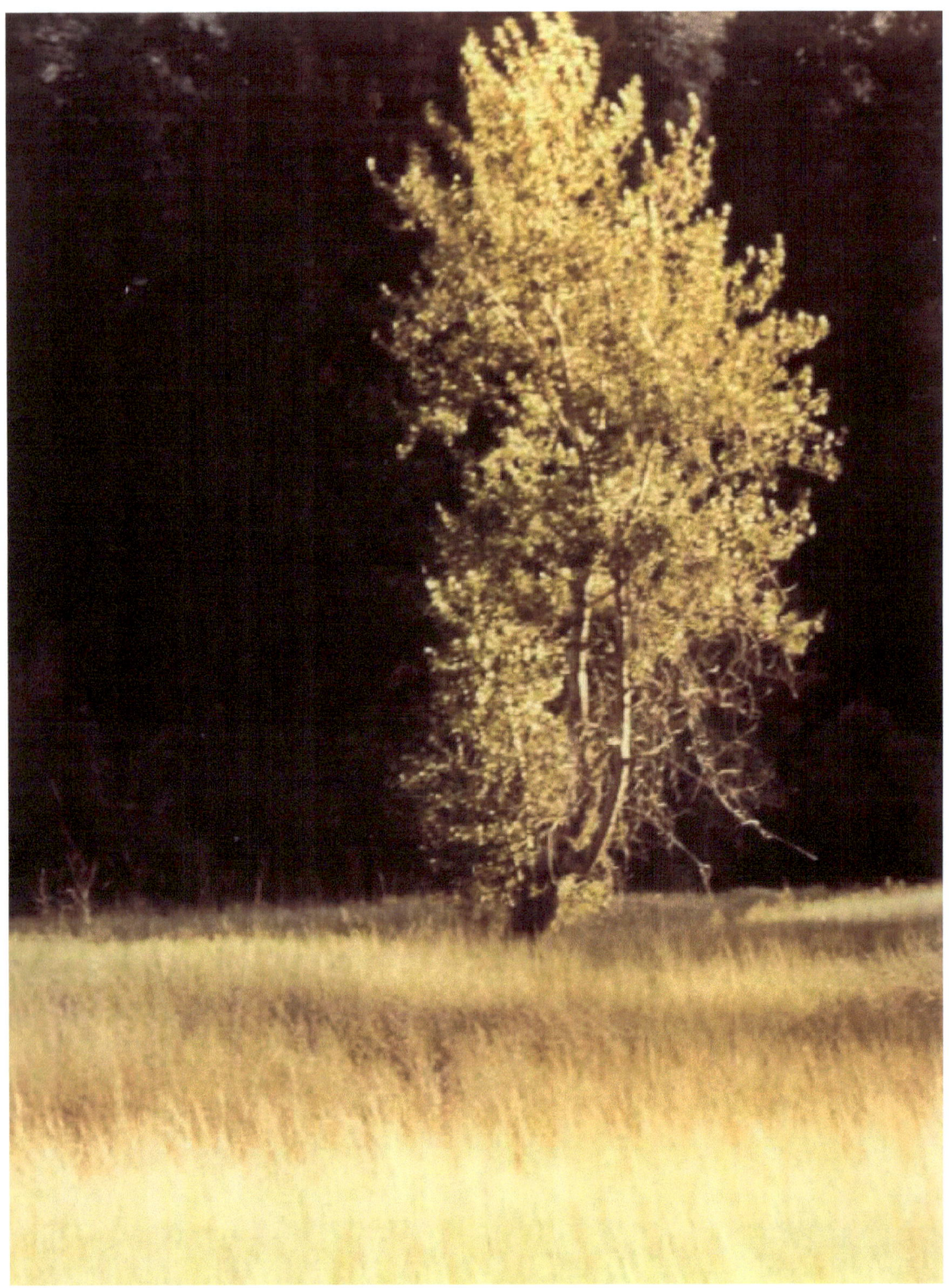
19. Yosemite Tree 1 (used for painting #3, which is one of my favourites.)

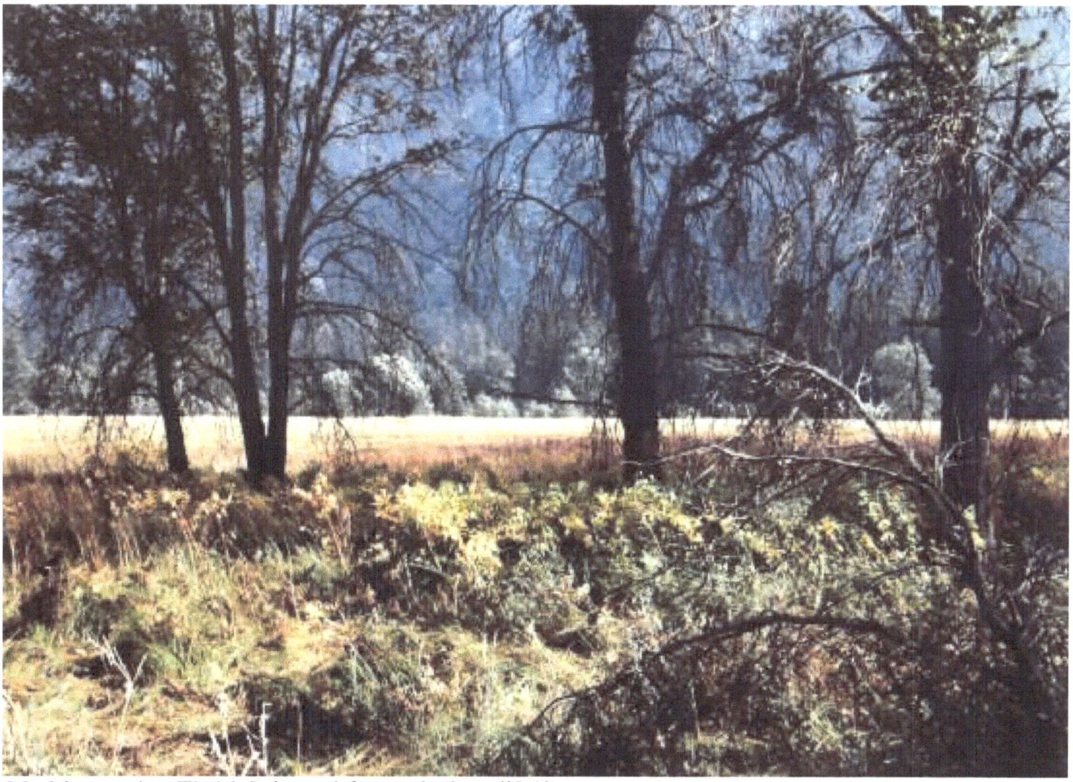

20. Yosemite Field 2 (used for painting #31)

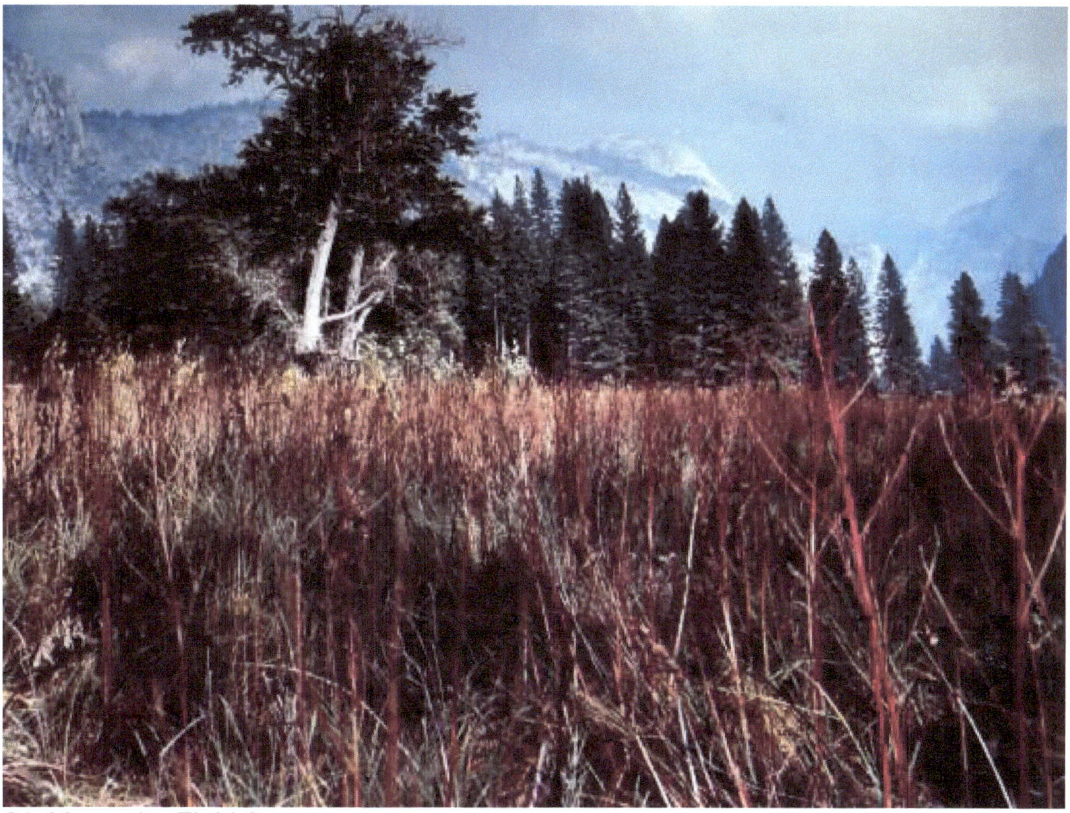

21. Yosemite Field 3

Mosquito Creek Park

Photography had helped me since adolescence to keep my life in some manageable perspective, but my urge to discover nature and reflect on life's dilemmas had grown vastly after we arrived in the scenic Vancouver forty years ago. Our calm setting in North Vancouver had simply enthralled me, plus the chance of taking many landscape photos during my afternoon walks in Mosquito Creek Park. Then, the opportunity to print many of those photos in my home's basement brought me even more joy.

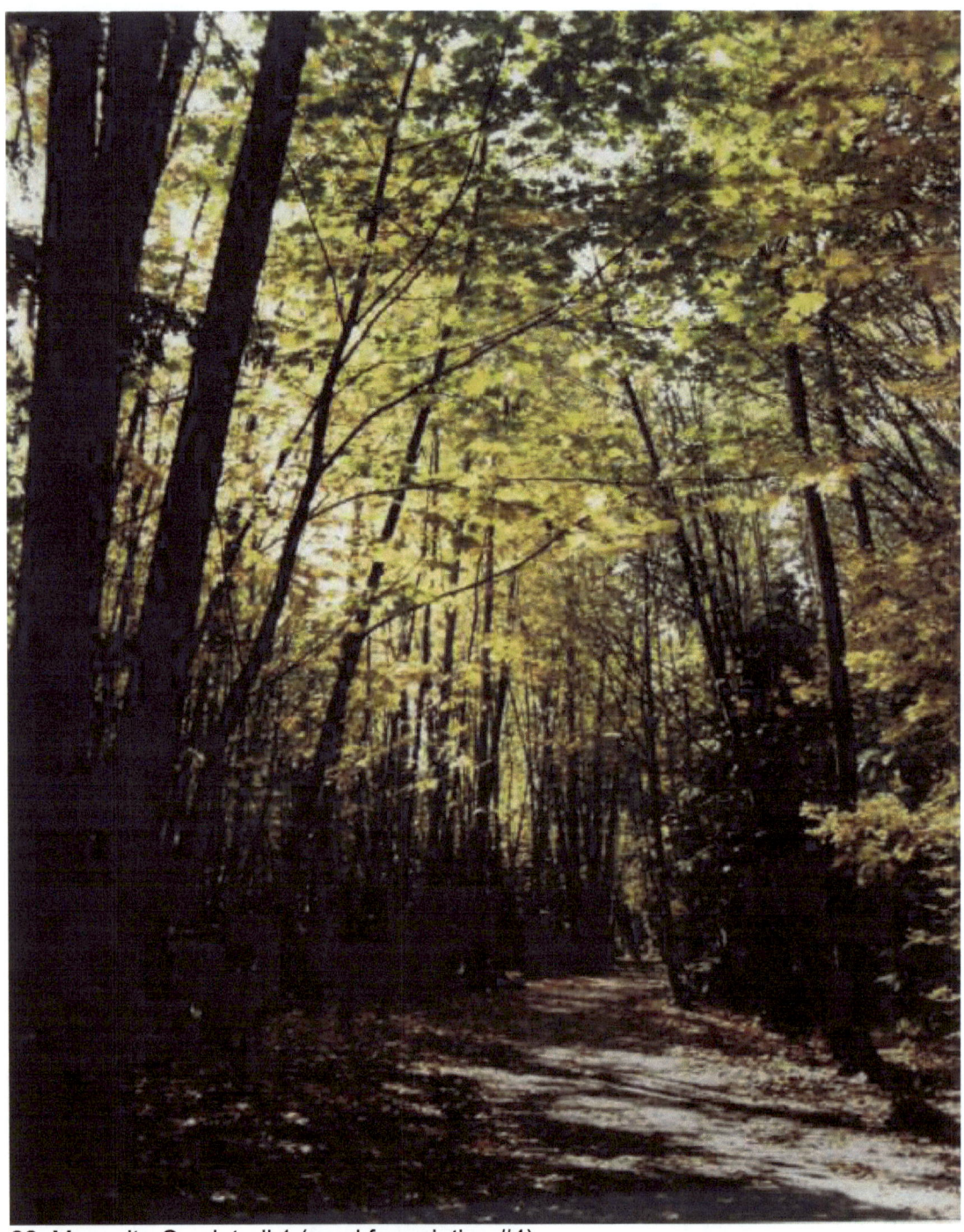

22. Mosquito Creek trail 1 (used for painting #4)

Hiking in Mosquito Creek Park and taking photographs also helped me relax and reflect on my tedious employment and faltering marriage. At the same time, those ultra pressures at the time had most likely also augmented my sudden urge to embrace a tougher challenge at the age of fifty, i.e., painting, to forget myself and life in general better, which also reduced my chances and craving for photography or walking in the nature at the same rate I had enjoyed in the past.

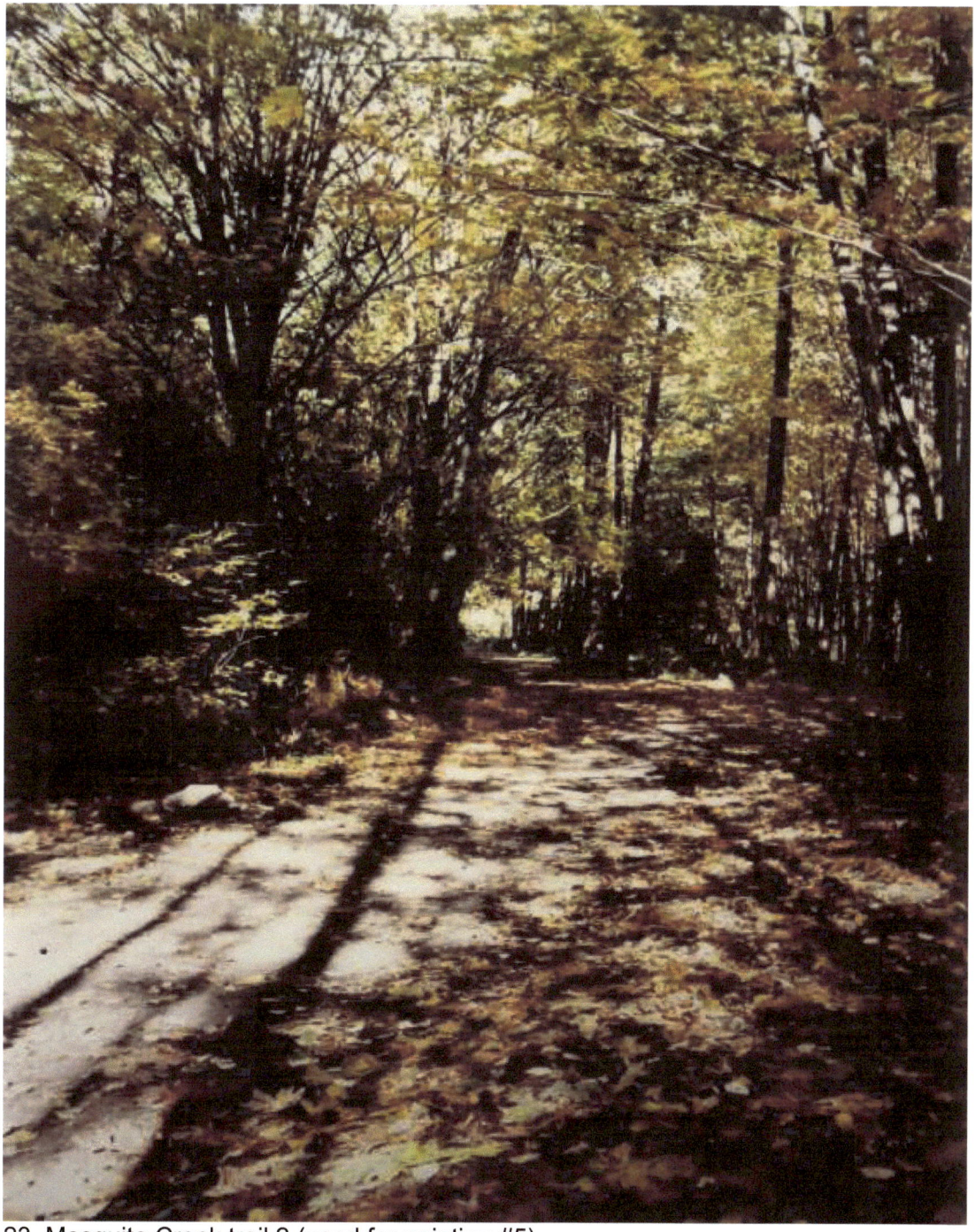

23. Mosquito Creek trail 2 (used for painting #5)

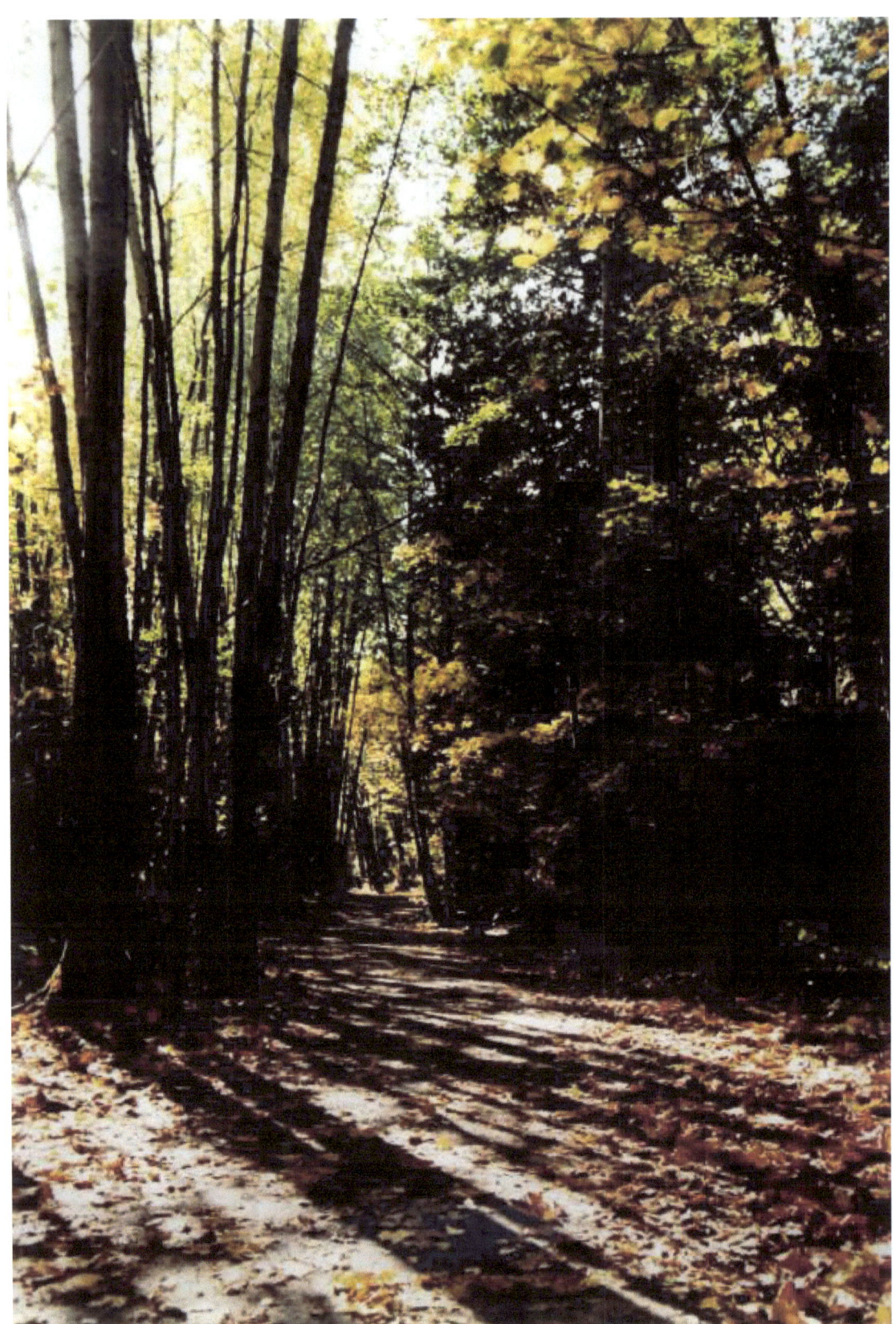

24. Mosquito Creek trail 3 (used for painting #16)

Stanley Park and Lost Lagoon

Many corners in vast Stanley Park offer picturesque views of trees, fields, mountains, and the Pacific Ocean for relaxation and photography. Thus, it had become a sacred place for me to visit regularly and take lots of pictures. Especially, Lost Lagoon availed the chance of observing and learning about birds' busy, purposeful life. Sometimes, I was thrilled by those birds sudden orchestrated plan to take a break from their routine, serious search for food and love, e.g., by taking a nap right in the middle of the day like a dire necessity, as shown in photograph #26. I always wondered wittily how a group of them decided and communicated to the whole gang that it was *suddenly* time to stop everything right away for a quick snooze without caring or worrying about all the humans walking around them! As picture #26 shows, another group is still continuing their serious plans in the lagoon. Those birds often appeared much wiser and more organized than we usually imagine about them, which made me ponder how to build more discipline to give my brain systematic breaks as well; instead of thinking and worrying so much about too many things most of my waking hours. How could those beautiful, diligent birds be so carefree and thoughtless suddenly whenever they wished before going back to their ultra busy lives again quickly—so unlike humans who are either too preoccupied or lethargic with little intuitional or systematic drives?

Overall, visiting those birds' sanctuary both soothed my gloom and satiated my artistic curiosities, yet it also made me ponder humans' mentality deeper and question the validity of our huge, idiotic assumptions about our high intelligence! Some of those corny thoughts are briefly noted in the next section that is about *Lovely Birds*.

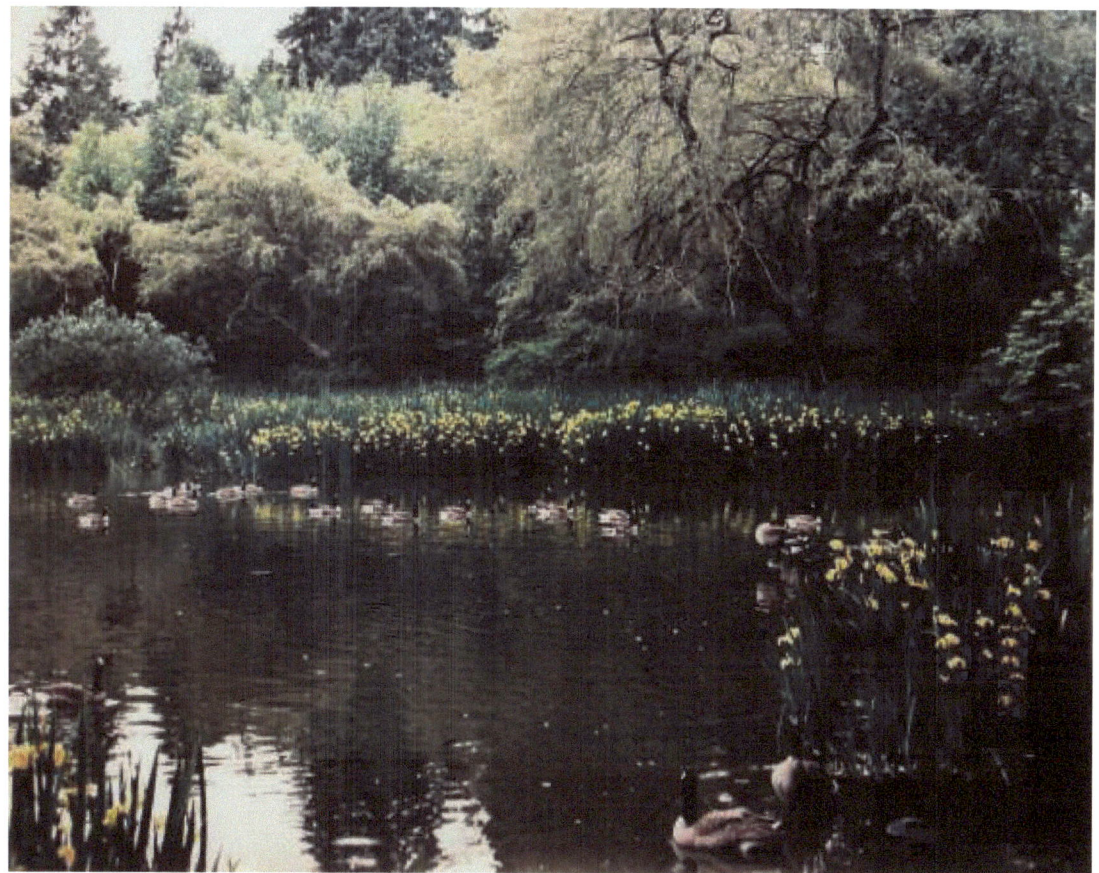

25. Lost Lagoon 1

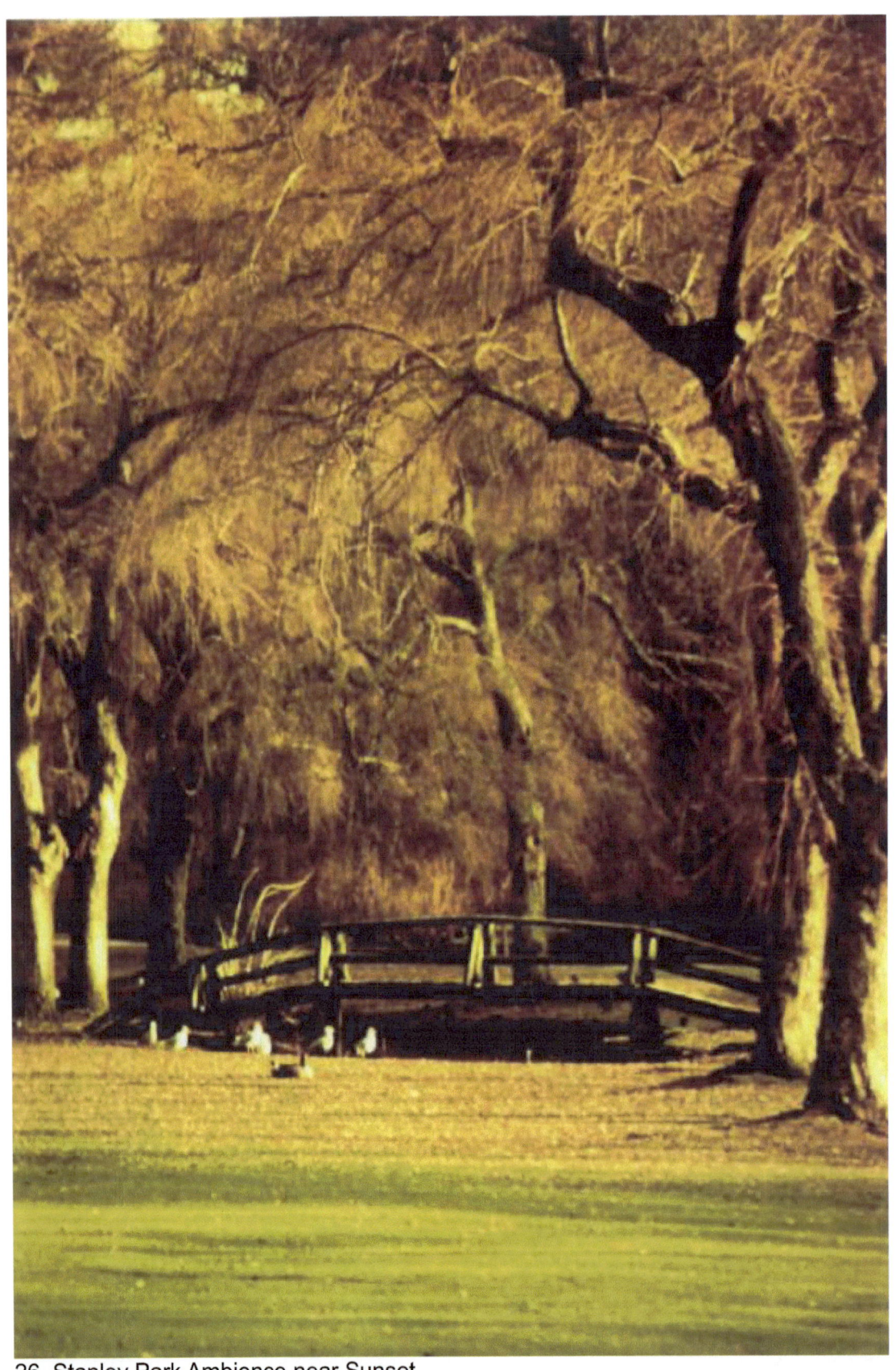
26. Stanley Park Ambience near Sunset

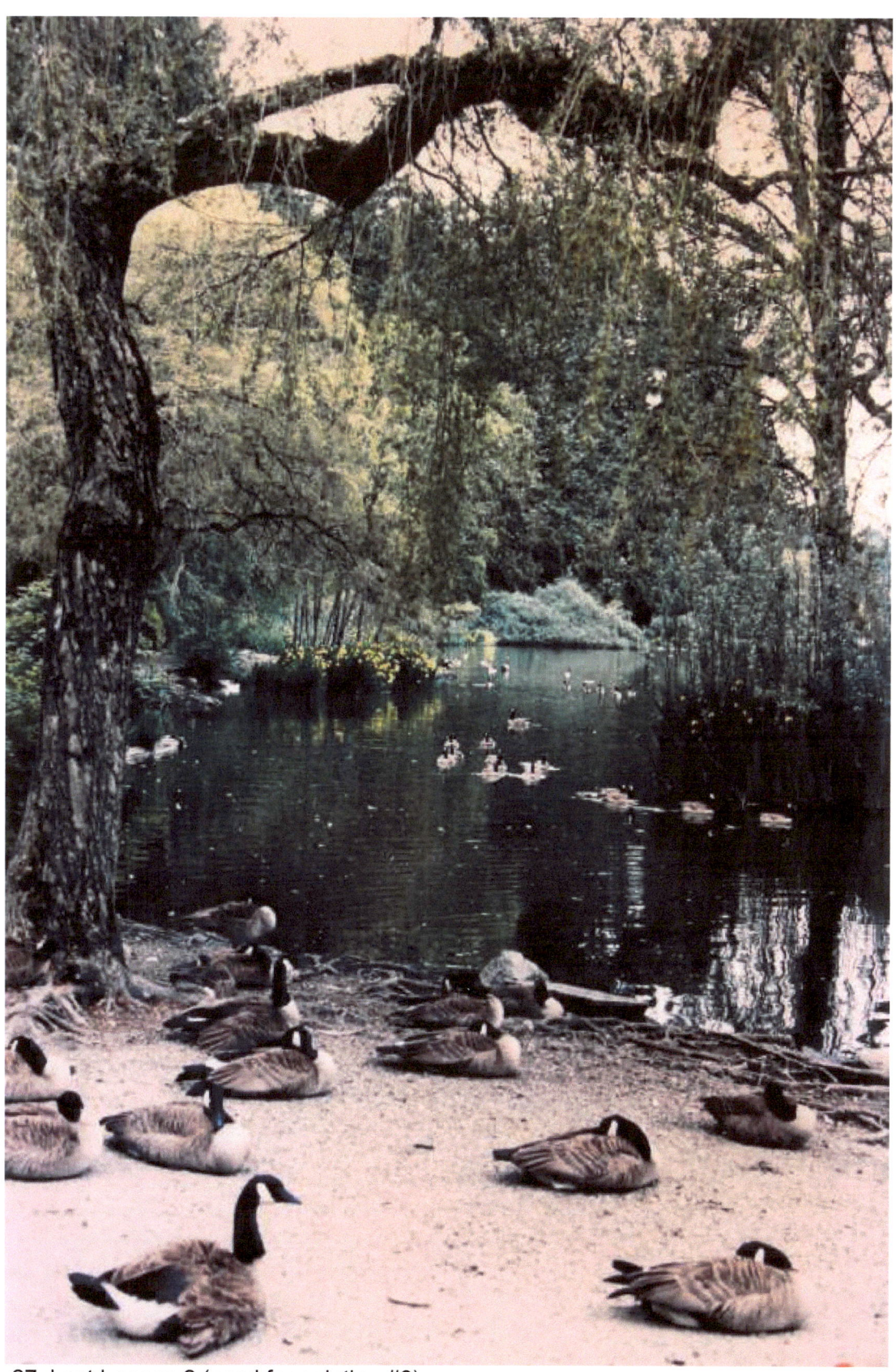
27. Lost Lagoon 2 (used for painting #8)

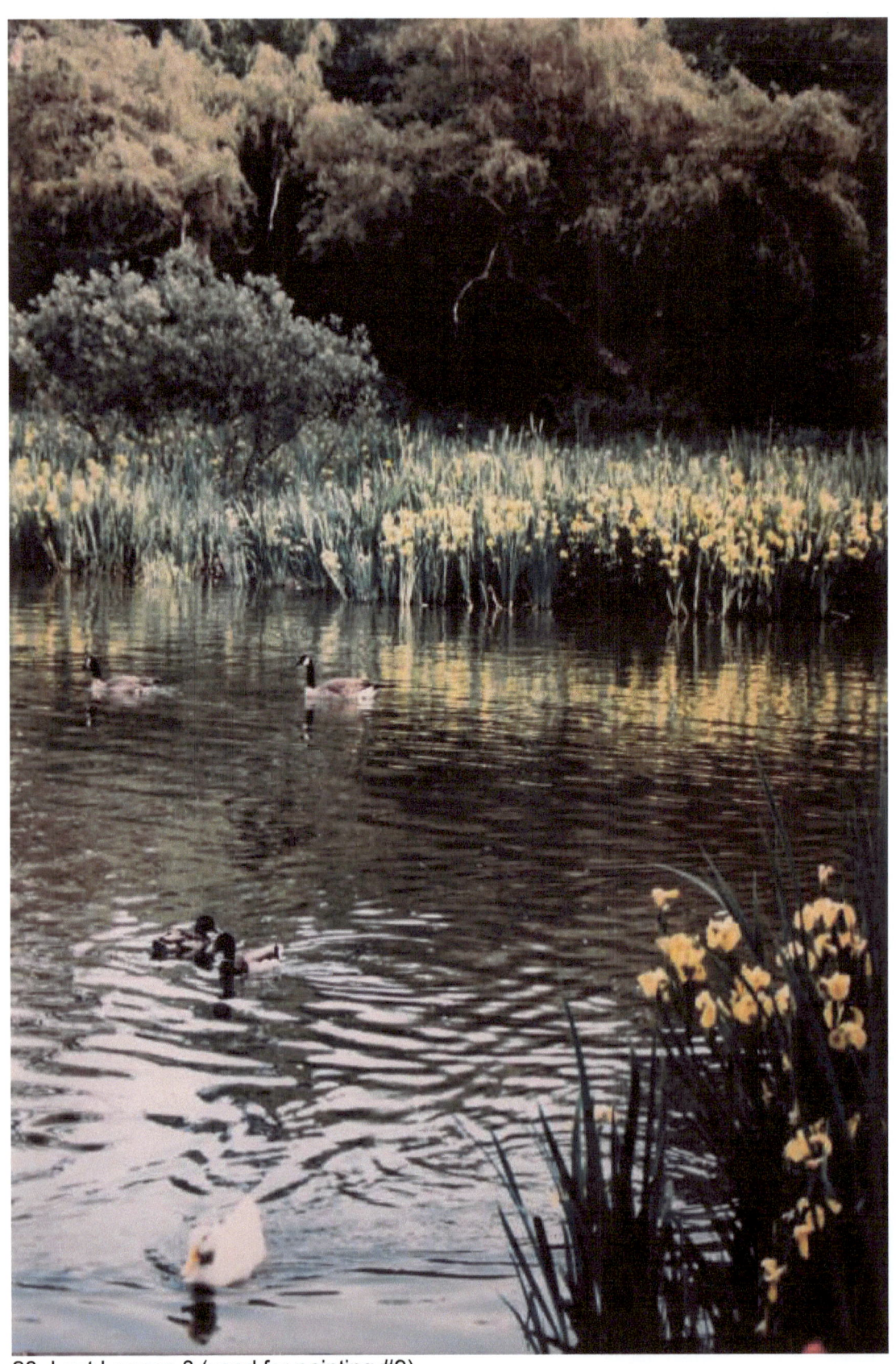
28. Lost Lagoon 3 (used for painting #9)

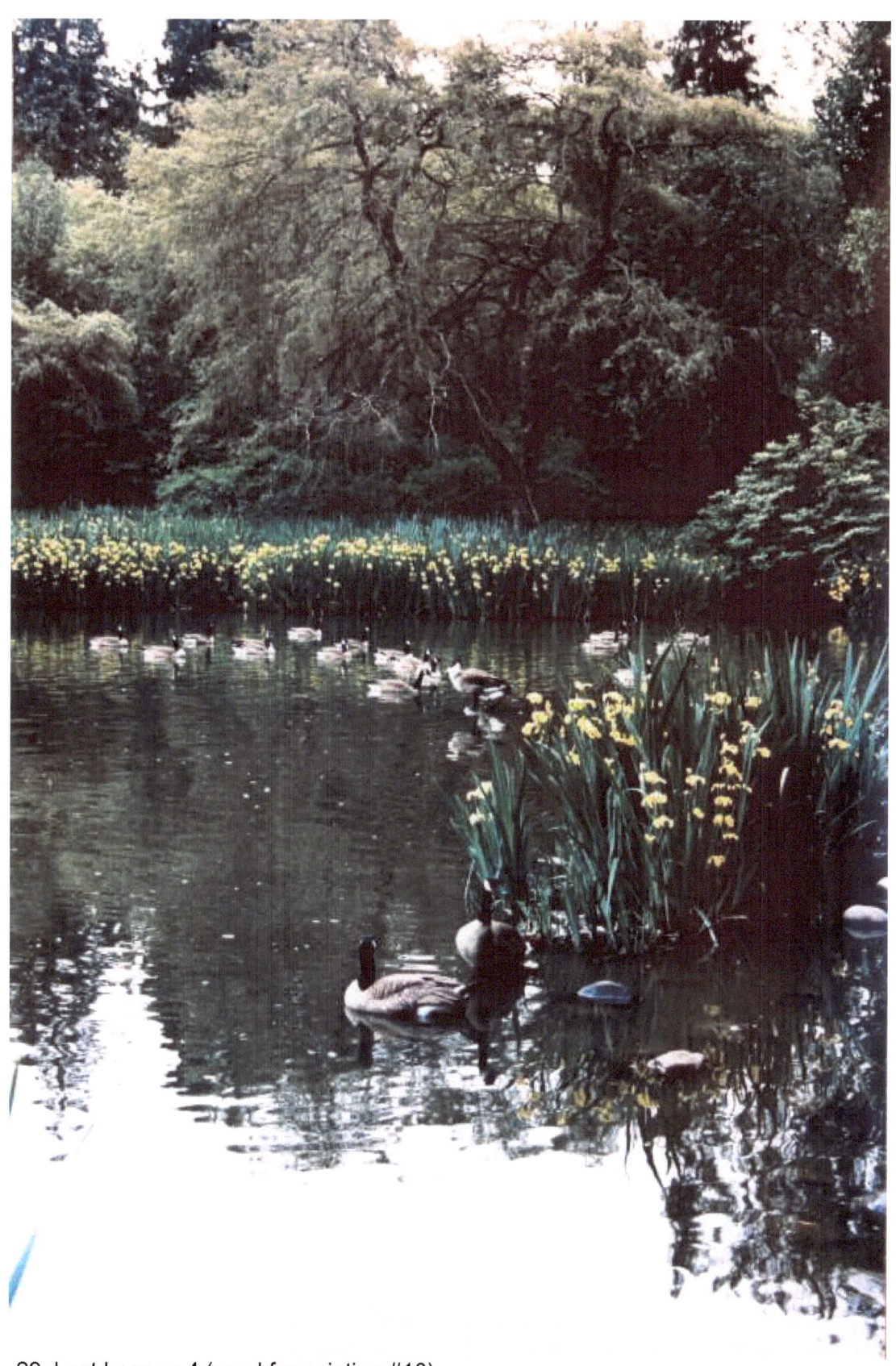

29. Lost Lagoon 4 (used for painting #10)

Lovely Birds

My regular rambling around Lost Lagoon and watching those beautiful birds' constant sense of life and purpose were turning me into a philosopher, too—the last thing my already confused brain needed! I wondered about the way we humans thought, felt, and behaved in our presumed civilized societies with so little sense of reality. Not only those birds' zeal for existence, reproduction, and love, but also their unity, stamina, glamour, and focus felt enviable to me. Most animals and fish seemingly share most of these qualities as part of their DNA and innate touch with reality. Accordingly, this basic observation makes some of us wonder why humans are at the bottom of the list in terms of recognizing their real needs and means of survival, and instead insist on adopting so much vanity and needs to manage their routines and brains around so many crude ideologies like individualism, freedom of speech, capitalism, and on and on! Too much reflections and analyses during my Stanley Park outings, especially around those mindful birds, had begun tainting even my sense regarding the purpose of art and my supposedly artistic efforts! Perhaps those birds' subtle manoeuvres and messages were also goading my psyche to focus on serious writing about life realities that we insist to ignore, instead of artistry, for bearing and defining my existence better.

Ironically, not even the pains that some crows nesting in one of my backyard trees caused me one spring deterred my love for birds, although I arranged with big hassles to prevent crows' rude occupation of my backyard in the following years! Every year in the spring, they still build their fancy nests in my neighbourhood with lots of efforts and noise, which makes my afternoon walks somewhat vexing, but at least they do not attack me as closely and fiercely as they did in the spring of 2019 to create and protect their chicks. I had lost the use of my backyard for a few months until they decided at last to vacate their luxurious premises. I wore a hood and carried a long stick to defend myself whenever I had to go to my backyard fearfully for an urgent errand.

Still, my admiration for birds, even those tenacious crows, grew as their routines and innate sense of well-defined purposes felt so remarkable and respectful compared with humans who have no valid notions about their deeds and sentiments or a plan for humanity, not even for their own children's welfare, sadly.

Certainly, I do not wish to blame only those lovely birds for my growing cynicism about humans' shoddy mentalities and ambitions, *even though those birds had played a huge role!* Ironically and embarrassingly, mainly humans themselves should be blamed for their immense failure to define and teach a practical mindset and develop proper social mechanisms after all these centuries. Only we are guilty for such a lame impression of civilization and our strenuous persistence to justify and protect it, too! Still, those birds' simplicity and easy use of intuition had made me reflect much more than usual, and thus feel deeply sad and embarrassed regarding humans' intelligence along with our futile ambitions and struggles to run and fit in such crooked societies.

Now, even the mere concept of existence feels too obscure in the current social setting with no way out of this irresolvable human foolishness and entrapment. Thank God, at least some artistic passions have kept me busy all along until I can possibly fathom a more rational reason for being or exit with dire confusion, which has a much higher likelihood!

I'm afraid I'll be entering the heaven as confused and sad as ever regarding my inability to fathom society and humans! This concerns me, of course, only because it could possibly make me look not absolutely thrilled for being in heaven like all other privileged humans blessed by god. Let's hope all these oddities of existence become clear to us at least when we arrive in the god's kingdom.

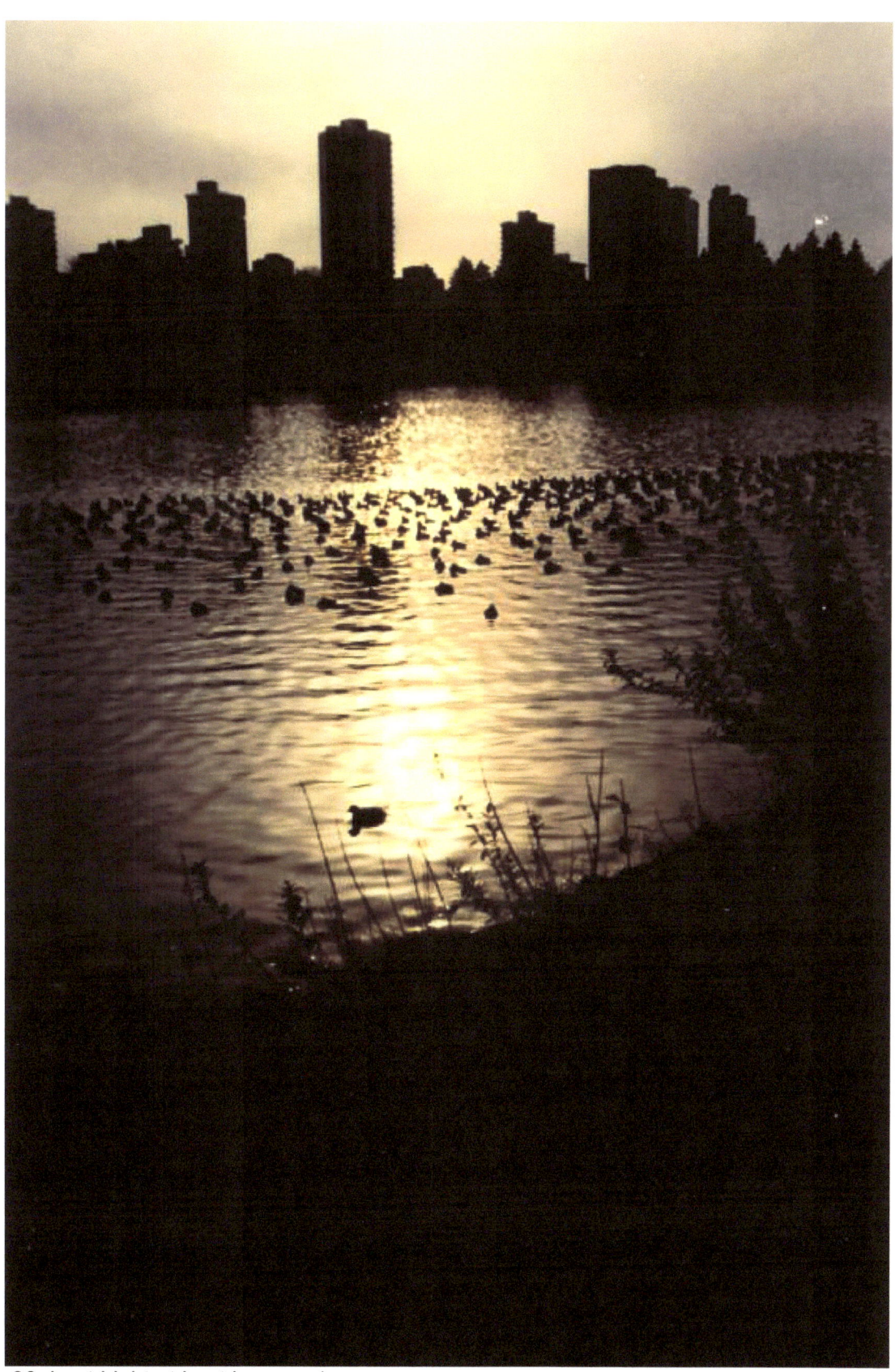
30. Last Light at Lost Lagoon 1

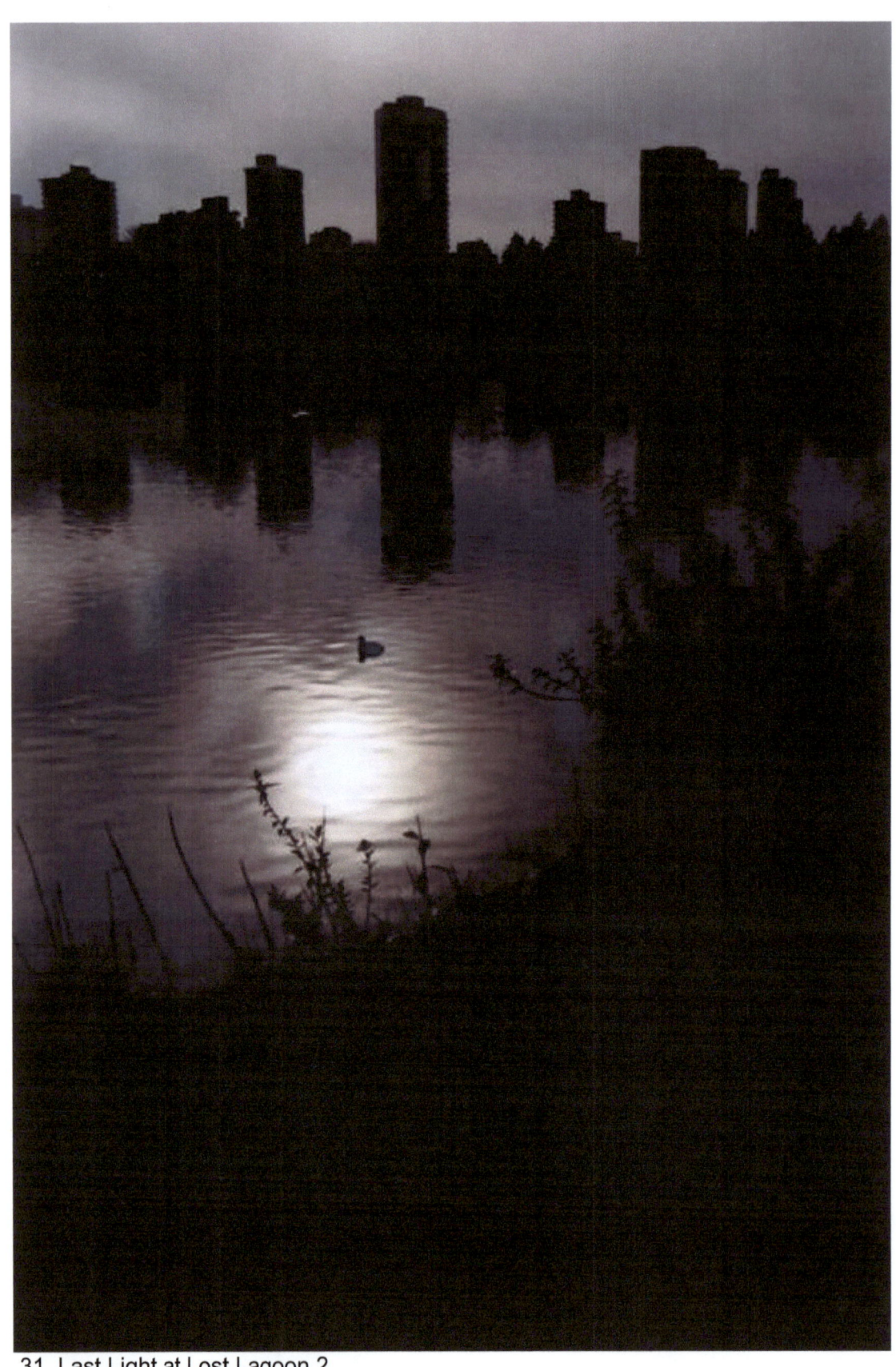

31. Last Light at Lost Lagoon 2

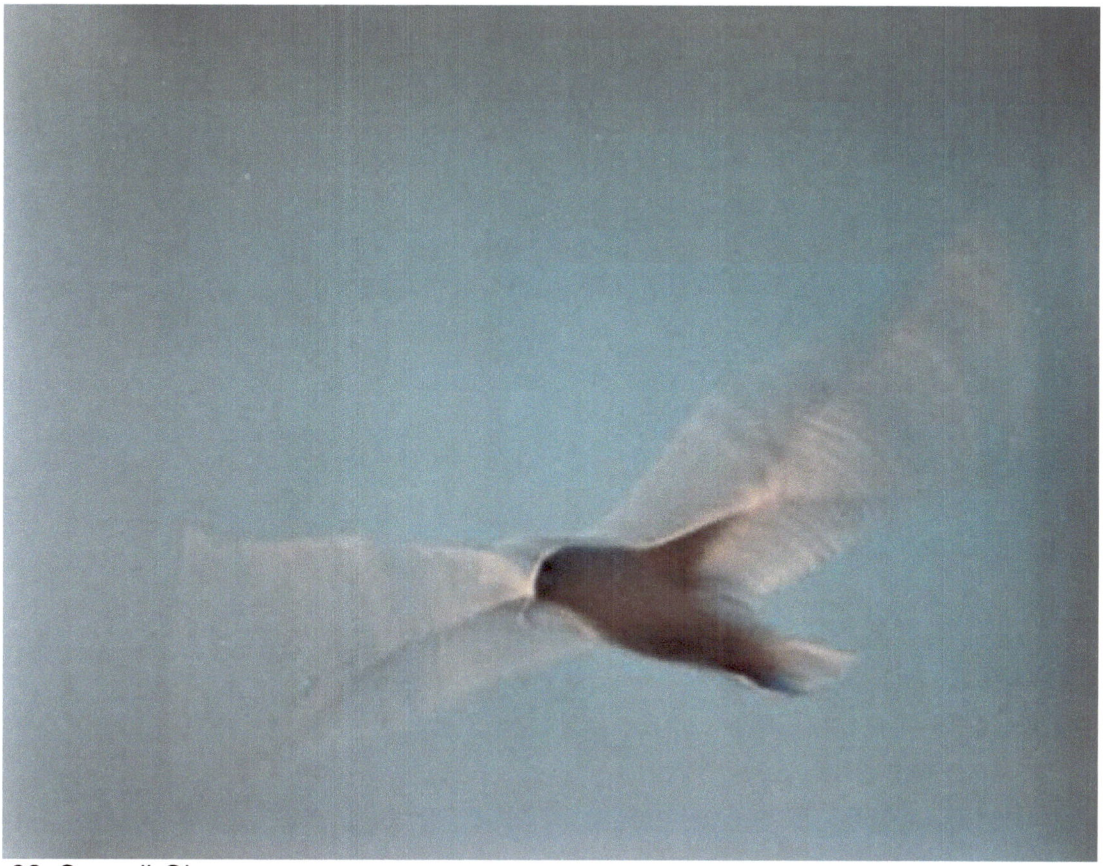

32. Seagull-Glamour

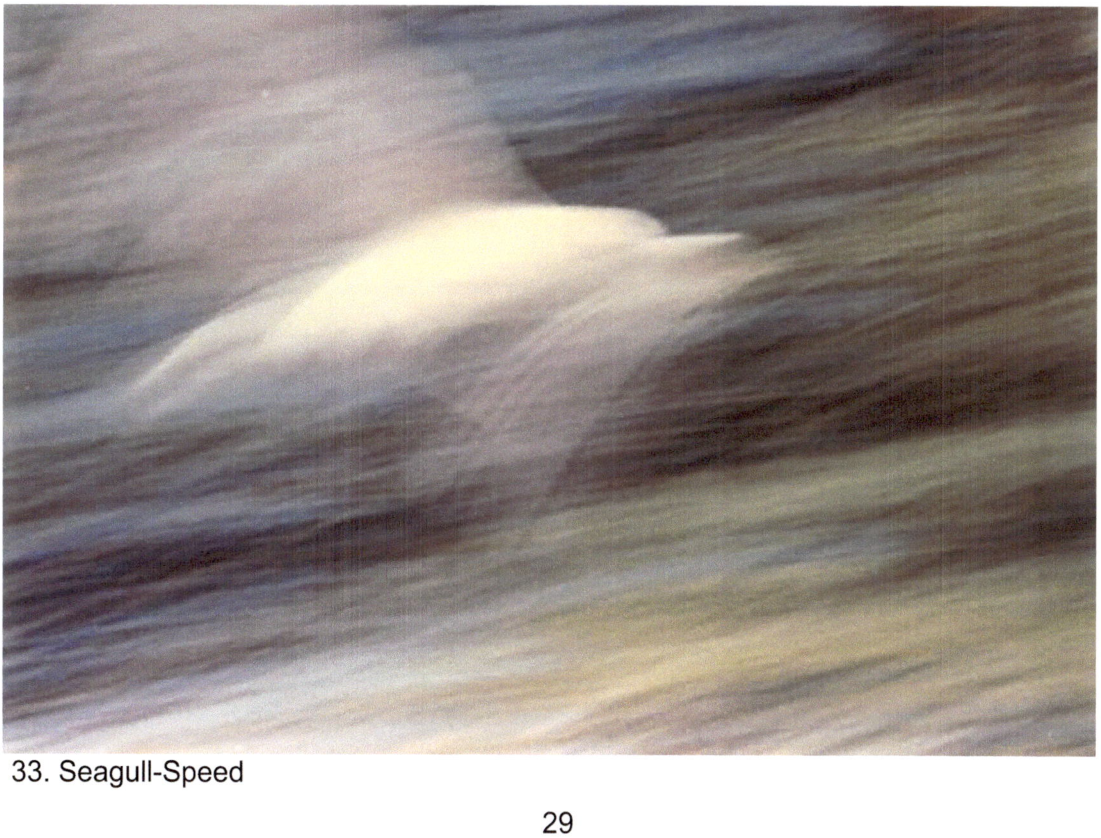

33. Seagull-Speed

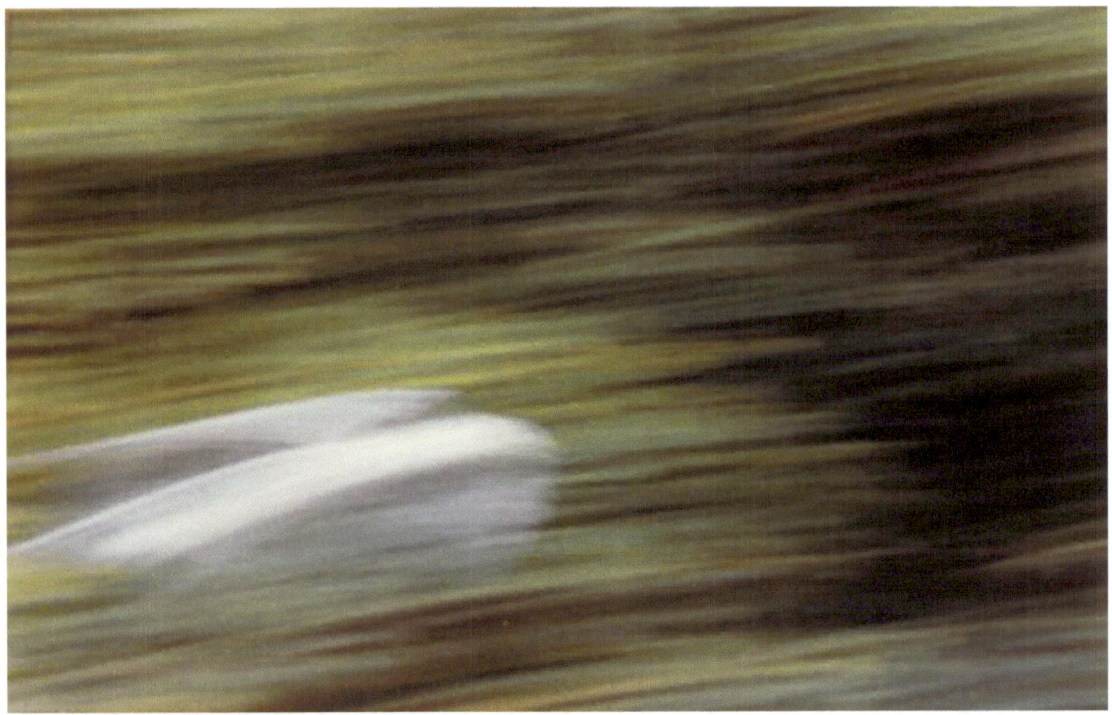

34. Seagull-Solo Flight

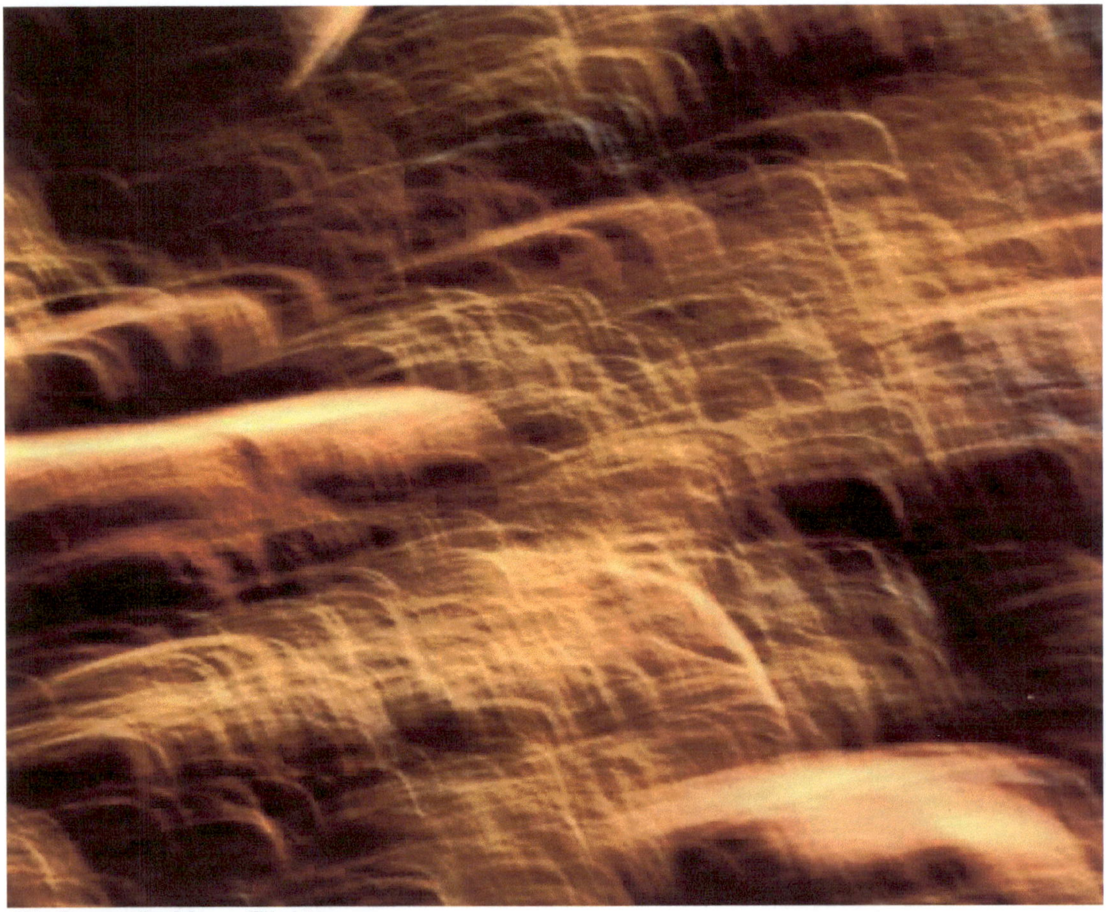

35. Seagulls-Mass Flight

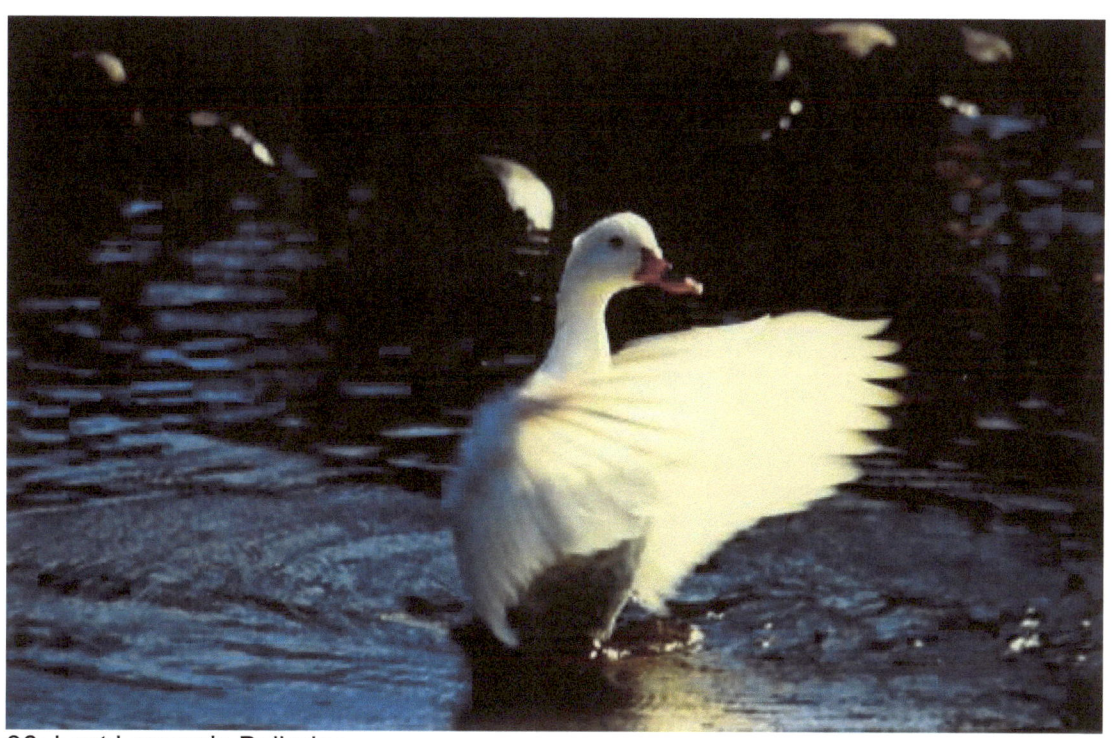

36. Lost Lagoon's Ballerina

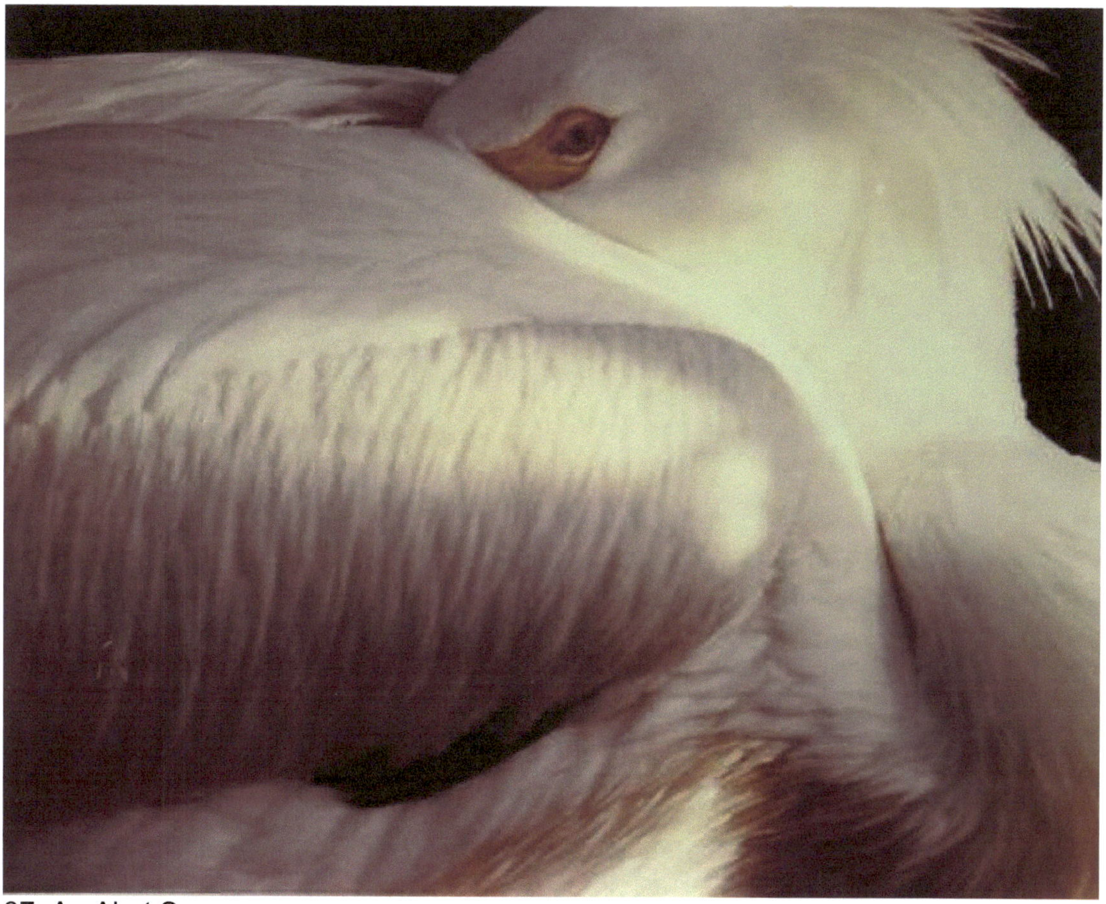

37. An Alert Snooze

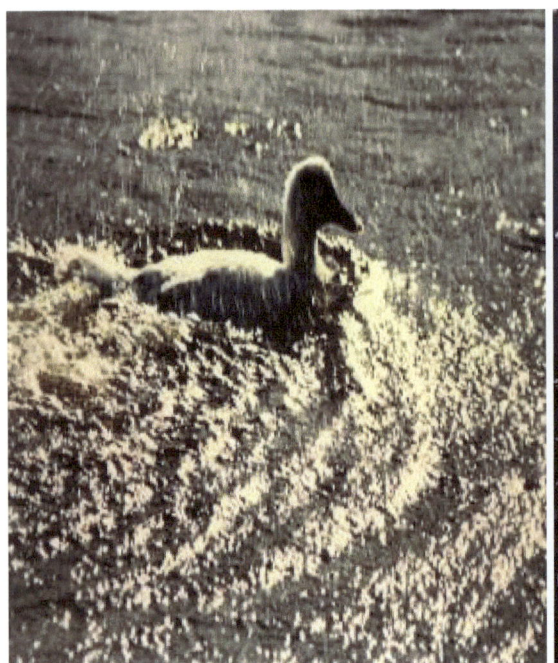
38a. Swimming in the Rain

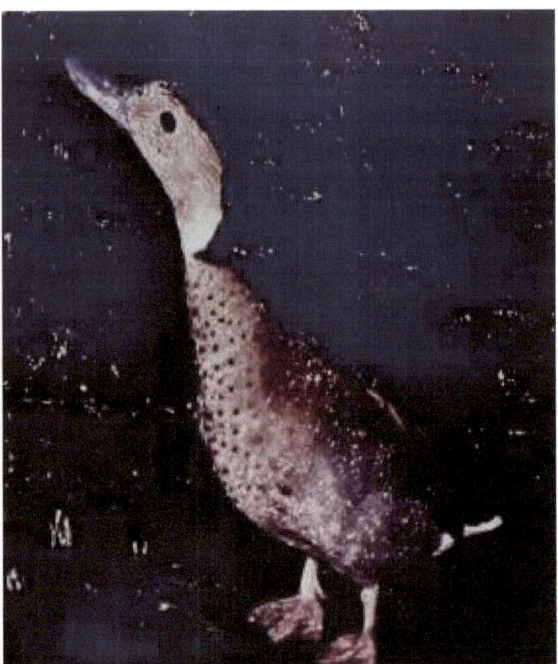
38b. Walking in the Rain at Night

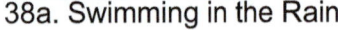
39. The Monarchs, Duck and Duckess of Stanley Park (used for painting #10)

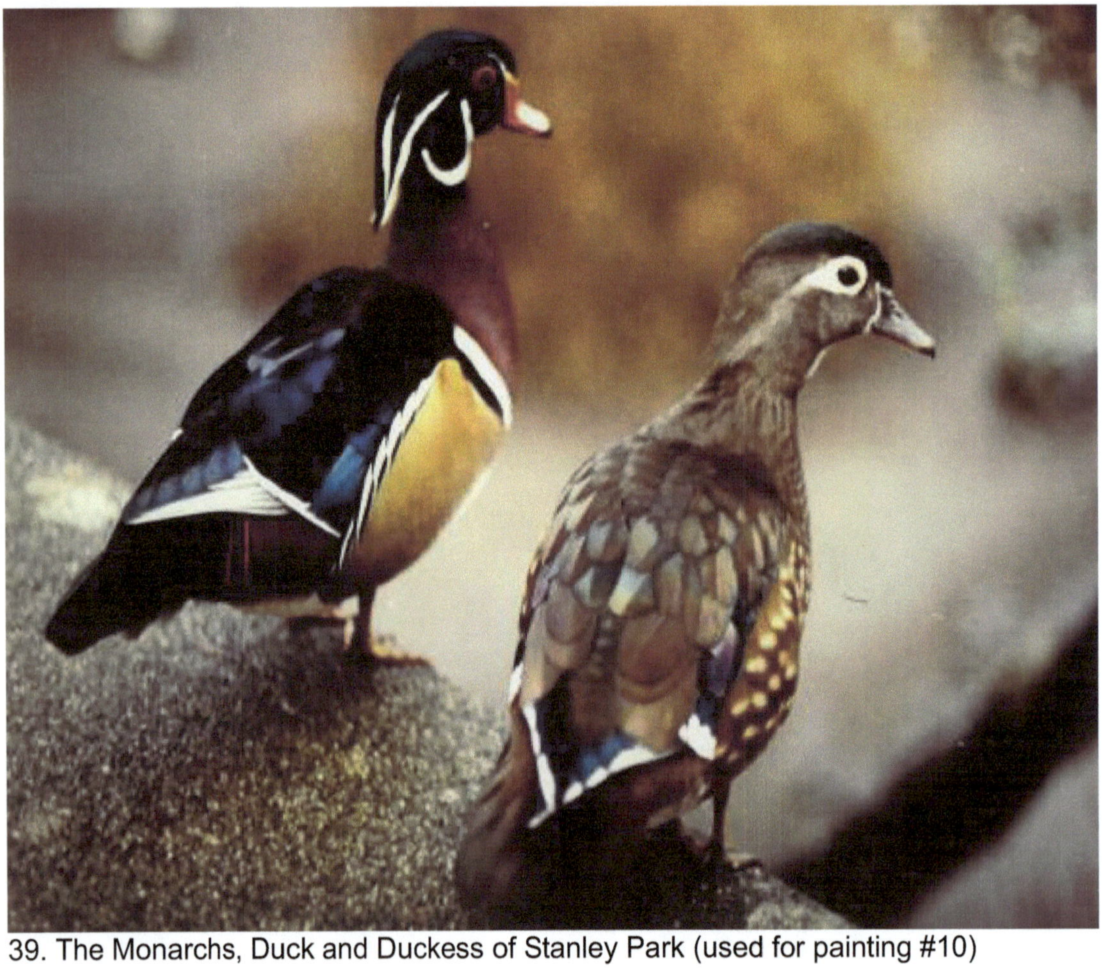

The Forlorn Black Swan!

A black swan always seemed to be ambling around me anytime I went to Lost Lagoon. It looked lonely, too, especially since a couple of showy white swans were always necking around the pond. Soon, we seemed to grow a special bond, as if we sensed each other's anguish when my marriage was falling apart and I sought any venue, including a possible bond with a swan, to boost my stamina and hopes. Actually, our bonding had felt sincerer and easier than I have ever been able to accomplish with humans on a long term basis. I even wrote a witty account of this bond in my novel, *My Lousy Life Stories*, under the heading of *Pink Dove*. An excerpt of the story, pages 277-280, is included below for humour, but also showing my respect for birds, even vengeful crows.

This rather long excerpt is included also for depicting my gloomy state of mind during those saddest years of my life. Luckily, I could defeat that pathetic mood by resorting to photography, painting, and writing—all as great venues for self-reflections and analyzing life's realities.

*****

"Entering Stanley Park through an elaborate archway, which I am noticing for the first time, a mysterious surge of serenity besieges me this morning. It is an odd feeling considering my chronic melancholy—like a sudden relief from a persistent migraine. Only some obscure flickers of daunting dilemmas flash in my head—merely resembling the fading residue of that imaginary migraine. What is so different about the park today? Besides that peculiar archway, of course, which seems to have come from nowhere overnight! Ecstatic by the esoteric experience, muttering life is a very splendid thing in tune with the old song, I proceed toward my favourite spot where I often relax on a bench near the rose bushes and admire their colourful variety and mesmerizing fragrance.

But the echo of ducks quacking and flapping their wings near the water lures me toward the lagoon where my freaky friend, the black swan, sometimes swims along the bank searching for food. The bad big bird usually hides inside the tall undergrowth and only seldom sneaks out to startle me by its appalling appearance. Its glossy black down stirs a sense of darkness and death in me. Yet, obsessively, I crave its arrival and exquisite cervical dance—the long narrow neck twirling around rhythmically and steering the bright red beak on the water surface to munch flower debris floating over the lagoon with an endless appetite. Its timid eyes betray its brave, showy manoeuvres near eerie humans like me. The poor bird must have felt enough of my fury recently, about to erupt and engulf everything and it.

Gazing over the lagoon for a sign of the wily black swan, I spot the two regular white ones that sail around and across the banks, caressing all day. With their velvety white statures, reeling peacefully in unison over the cobalt waters of the lagoon, they seem in love. They appear friendlier toward people, too. Still I look around and behind the shrubs hypnotically for the black swan. Like a possessed fool, I feel restless when I cannot locate this dubious bird, wondering whether its doomed existence has finally expired. I somehow relate to its fate, which seems full of bleak episodes similar to mine; and no companion to soothe its suffering and loneliness, either. Oddly enough, this curious bird sometimes appears to appreciate my anguish, too, maybe even better than my beloved Jasmine.

But why am I insisting on finding this black loner now that my mood has rejuvenated so miraculously this morning? Why not instead befriend those elegant white lovers inching toward me intently with their long necks erecter than ever? A premonition strikes me swiftly: That my fate will change today, as confirmed, or symbolized, now by the black swan's absence and the graceful approach of the white ones... Yes, some wonderful revelation will perpetuate my sudden jolly mood today and eradicate my worries forever... *Forget the damned black swan.*

I watch the vivacious white swans reaching me boldly, as if carrying a sacred message for me; or maybe because nobody else is around to feed them. They are now used to people bringing them bread or fruits regularly, though they often have to compete quietly with the greedy ducks and geese for their share of the loot. They linger near me patiently but curiously, which is a novel, perplexing gesture all by itself. Their sudden interest in me, or mere curiosity even, is precious this special day, though I feel guilty for not having any food for them. They are always polite and calm unlike those noisy, vulgar ducks and geese. I murmur, 'I am sorry,' as they keep gazing at me fixedly. I wonder again if my guardian angel has dispatched them as a sign, to affirm my premonition. So I keep nodding to them appreciatively and they start bobbing, too. All along, I wish the ominous black swan would never show up to spoil the serene mood and my growing friendship with the loving white swans. I promise to myself to bring them food next time and murmur my pledge to them, too.

Glimpsing one last time across the lagoon—the loverly white swans swaying away cheek-to-cheek and still no sign of the lonely black one—it is all definitely a clue about the good omen approaching. Yeah... it has all been about finding Jasmine and thanking her. Forget the black swan... Forget the pink Dove..."

*****

There was a huge difference in the ways the black swan and I reacted to loneliness, though. It seemed so cool about the matter, as if intuitively familiar with the reality of loneliness as a fundamental feature of its existence. It simply went on munching the shrubs with no regard for the showy white swans manoeuvring around us with pride about their well-deserved, eternal joy of love. Conversely, it felt so difficult for me to accept that everything I had believed to be necessary for building a family had been in vain and totally miscalculated. The black swan's nonchalance felt especially admirable when my cynicism was escalating about the sincerity, value, and meaning of love and happiness that many couples, especially the youths, kept flaunting around me with total innocence.

More than pitying my likely psychological impotence to fathom life and marriage, I wondered about the way we allegedly intelligent humans make such a big fuss about companionship and love, yet have so little grasp of what they really are and how (if ever) we can apply the true meaning of love and compassion for bettering our personal and social lives. Why cannot we admit, like all birds and animals, that all creatures, especially humans in current corrupt societies, would feel lonely, at least mentally, unless compassion and honesty become innate human traits, which sounds dreadfully unlikely? Actually, we have only made the matters much worse for ourselves and one another with our naïve slogans and increasing superficial needs, especially regarding love, individualism, and happiness, instead of trying to learn some fundamental facts about the harsh reality of existence!

Why does it feel so difficult and unnatural for us fanciful humans to build proper mentalities and lifestyles in order to cope easier with the rising tough requirements of social living? Is this basic fact too complex to fathom or implement? What is so horribly wrong with our intelligence?

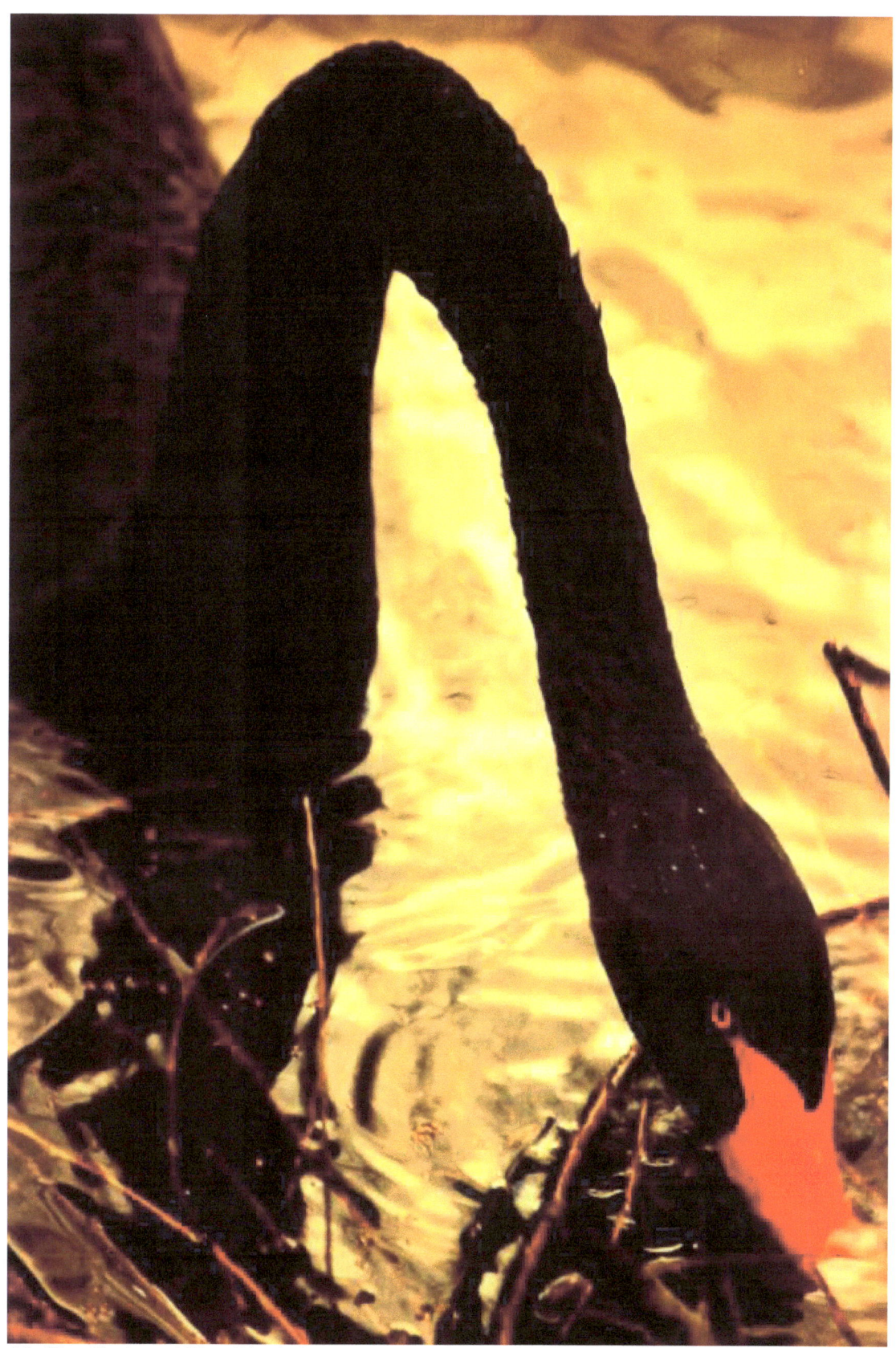
40. The Forlorn, Wise Black Swan

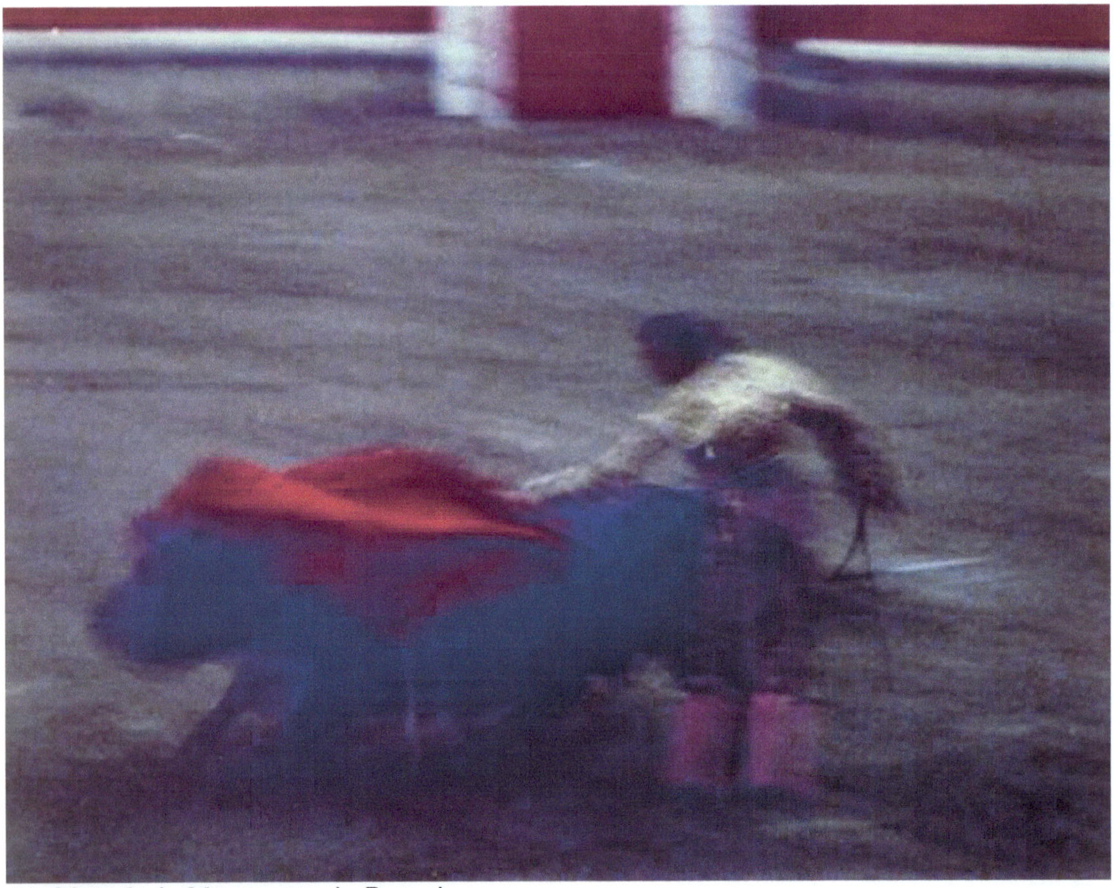

41. Matador's Manoeuvre in Barcelona

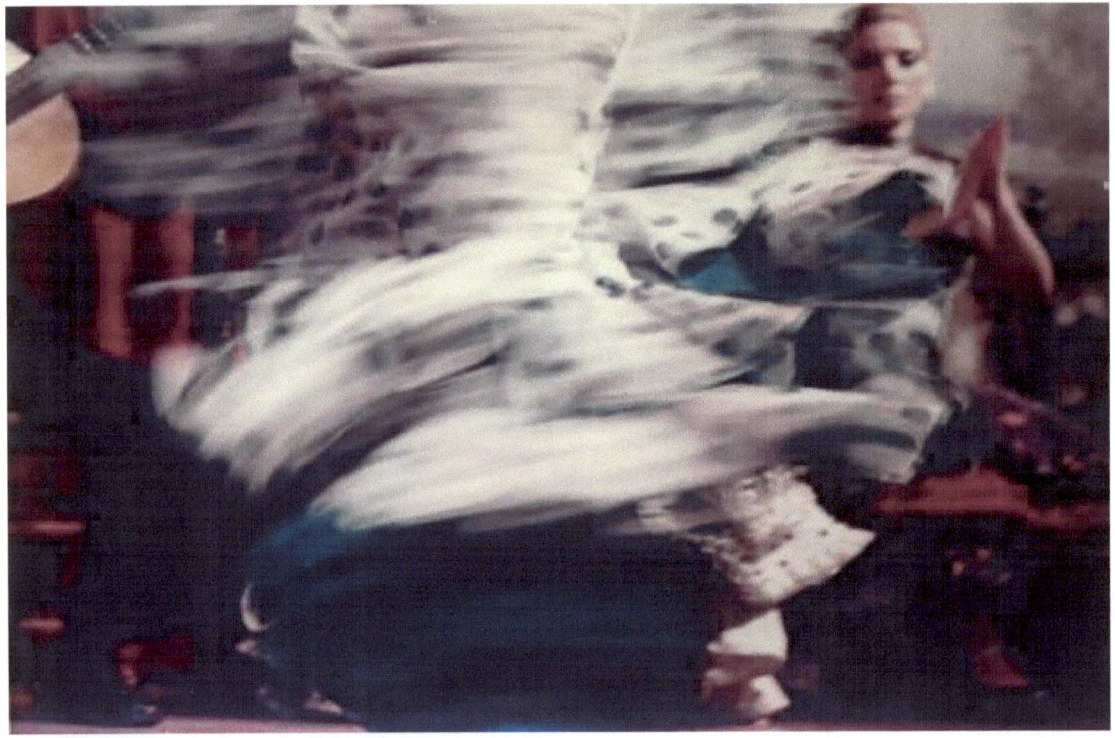
42. Flamingo Dancer in Barcelona

Creating a Semblance of Impressionism

I had tried to create a semblance of impressionism in some of my photographs just for fun and experimentation. These measured manipulations were accomplished mostly when taking the picture. I had already succeeded in capturing a notion of speed and motion in my photographs of the seagulls, matador, and flamingo dancer, as shown in images #32-36 and #41-42. Thus, trying to create impressionistic images had felt like a good next step. The results are shown in the following pictures:

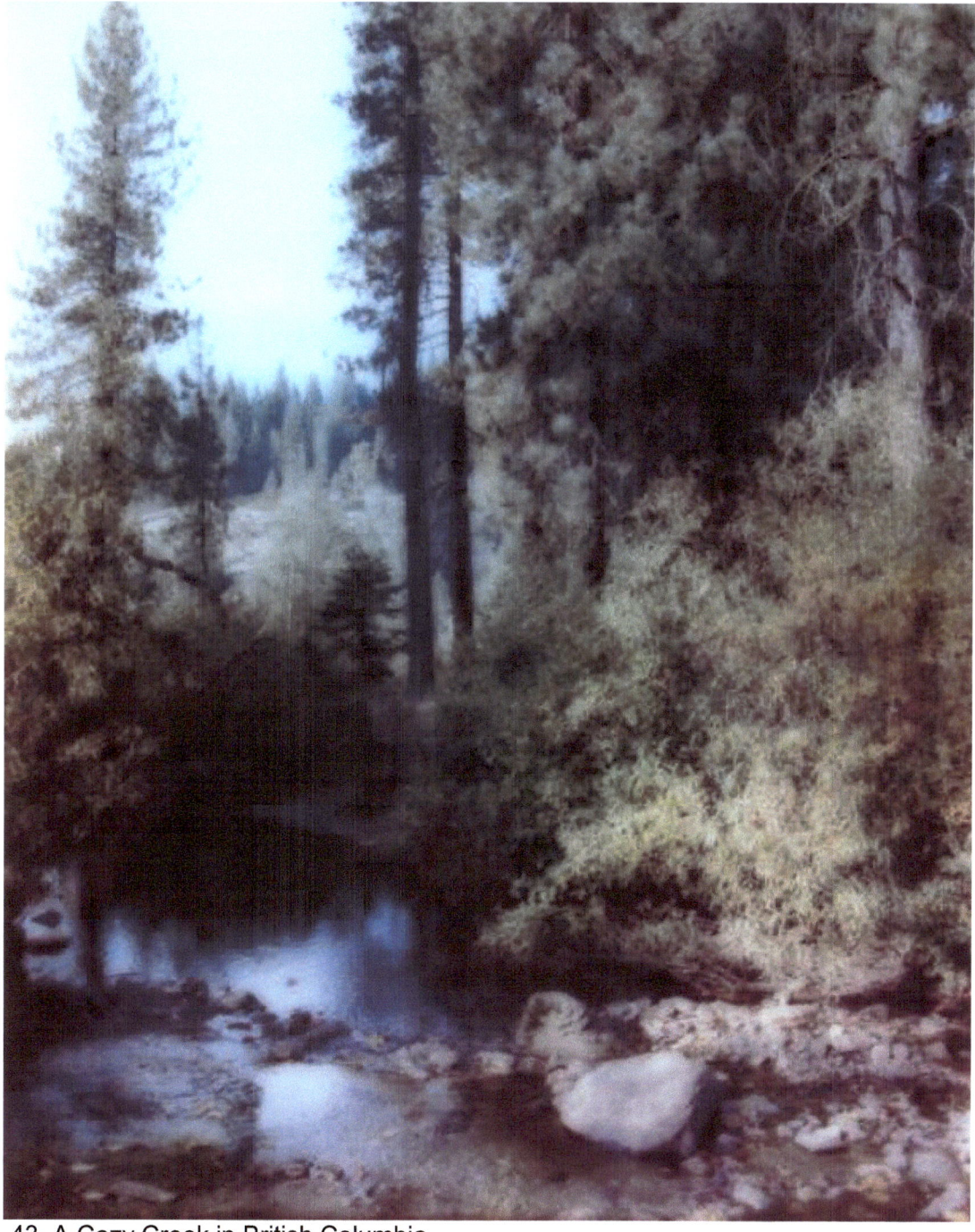

43. A Cozy Creek in British Columbia

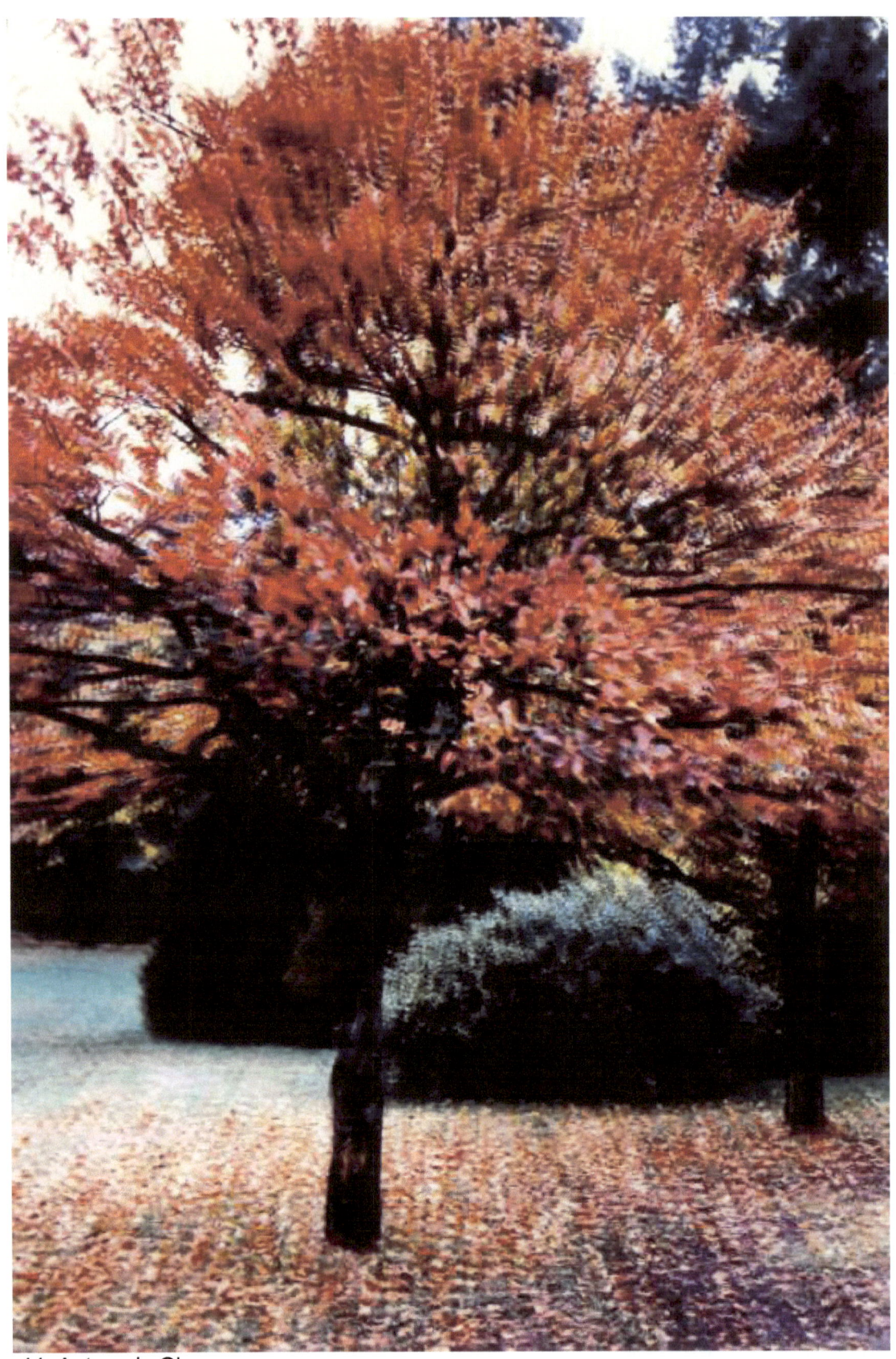
44. Autumn's Glory

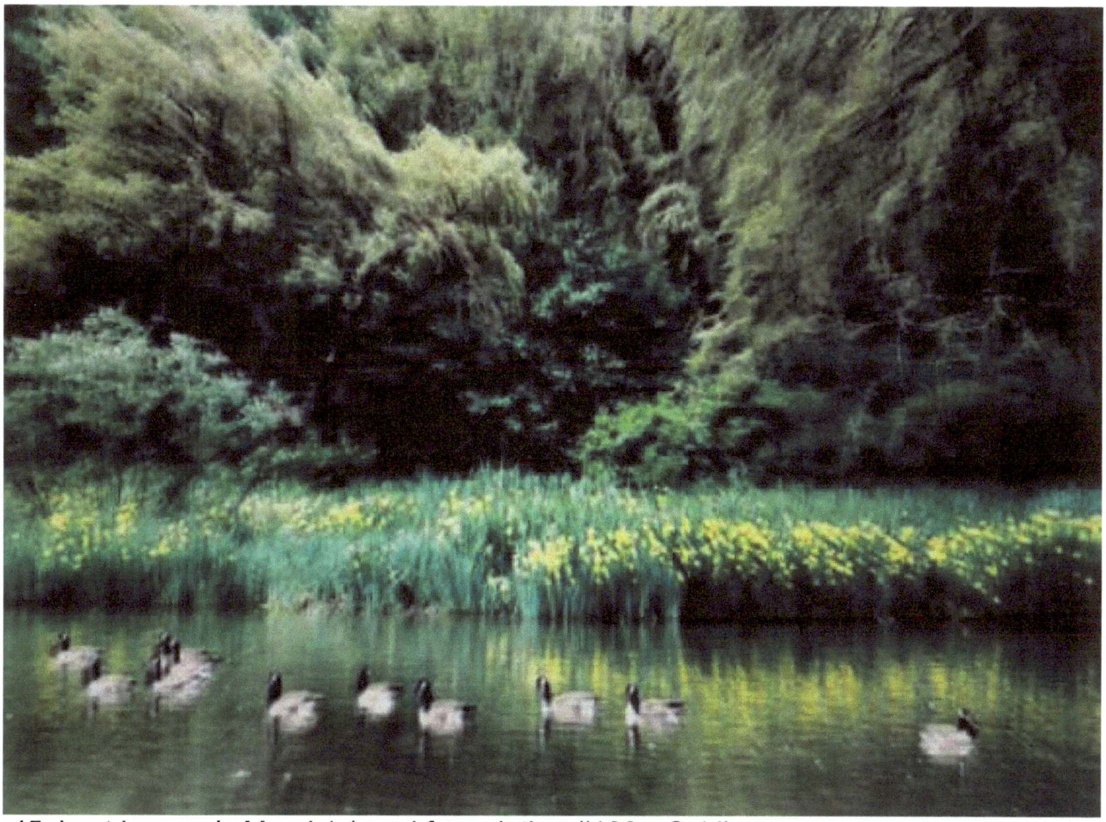

45. Lost Lagoon's Mood 1 (used for painting #120—Sold)

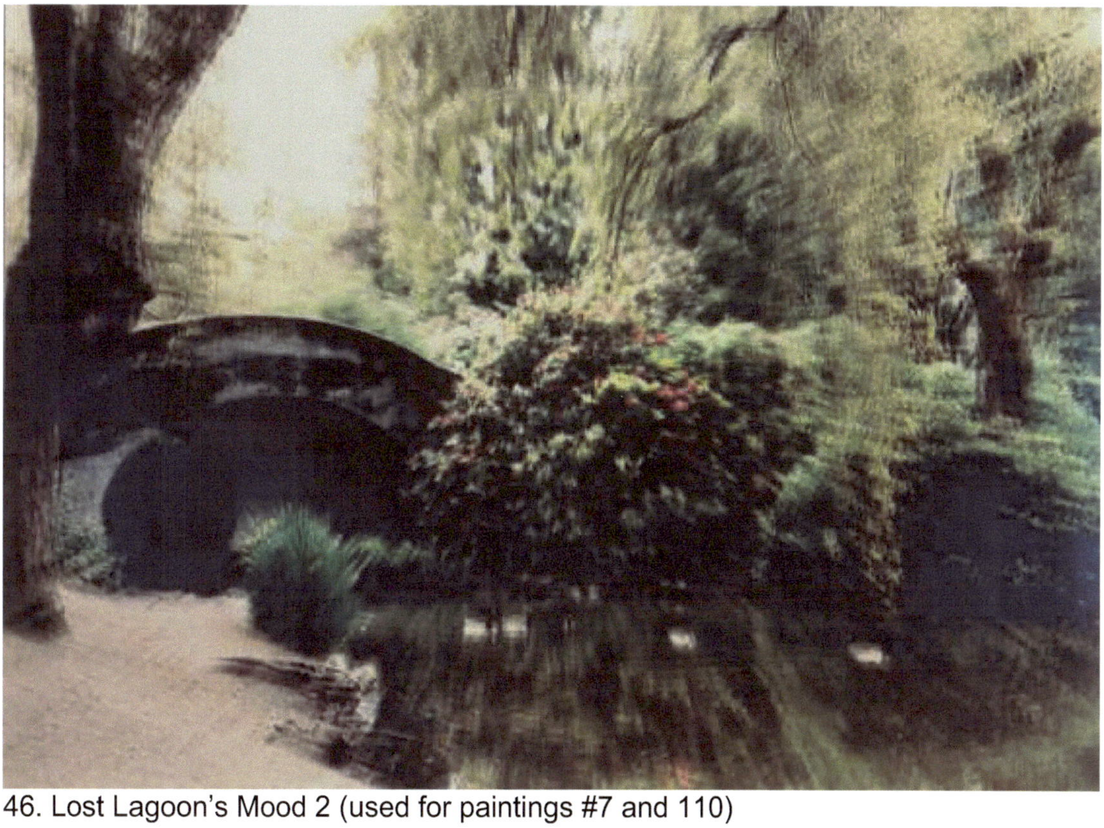

46. Lost Lagoon's Mood 2 (used for paintings #7 and 110)

Besides its likely mood-evoking capacity for others as well, the following picture is included mostly for my memories of this dim, secluded refuge for analysing my gloomy life during that pathetic, gloomy period of my life. My weird choice and attraction to this spooky spot feels crazy, while I also wonder now whether I had realized the chance of a wild animal smelling my stinking thoughts and coming around to teach me a lesson. Now, in my old age, I tremble even looking at the picture and recalling myself sitting there pensively until the last daylight and sometimes even in a spooky darkness.

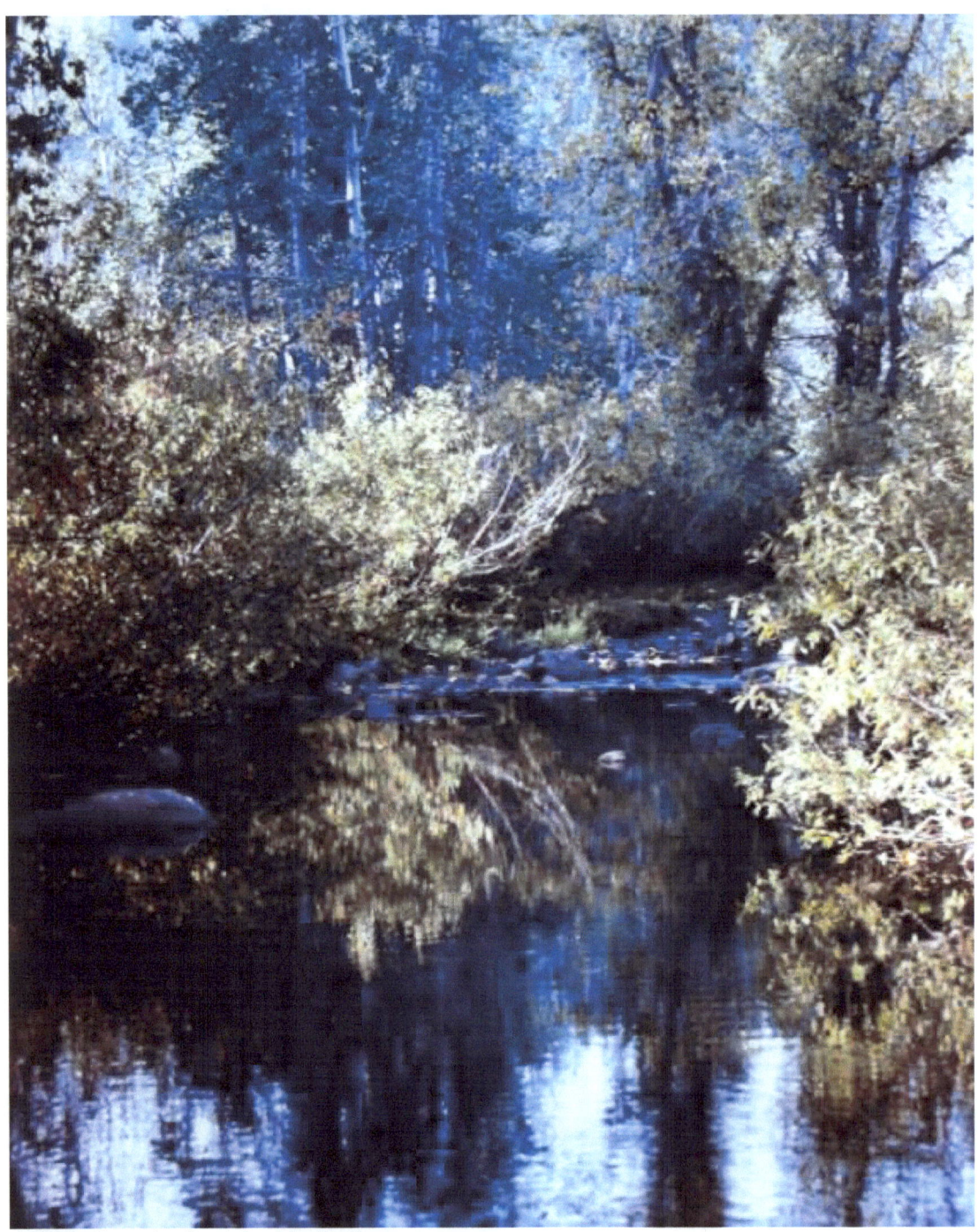

47. My Spooky Spot for Meditation

Lions Gate Bridge

Lions Gate Bridge crosses over Burrard Inlet to connect downtown Vancouver and Stanley Park to North Shore, which extends towards the Pacific Ocean and beyond. Living near the mountains in North Vancouver gave me an opportunity to take timely pictures of downtown and Lions Gate Bridge, thus a few of them are shown below. In particular, fog and clouds have always fascinated me during nature's frequent magical shows; although so much clouds most of the year depress us Vancouverites often. At the same time, at least so many of those clouds' unpredictable configurations render great opportunities for romantic photographs and paintings, thus curtail my resentment of their dominance over our beautiful city, while we crave sun too often. Many pictures of such occasions, i.e., cloud's peculiar configurations mixed with playful sunlight or the moon, are offered throughout the book.

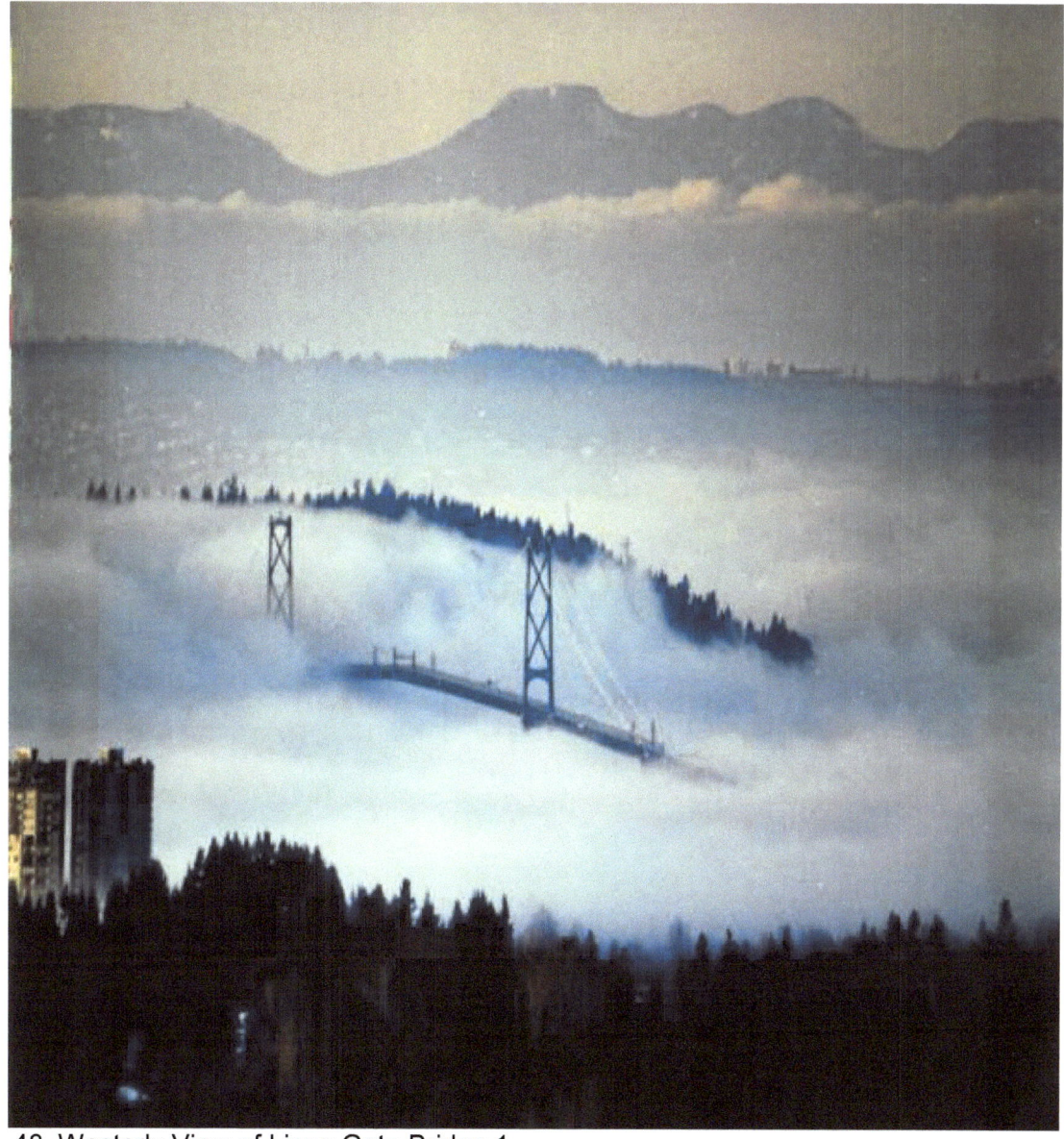

48. Westerly View of Lions Gate Bridge 1

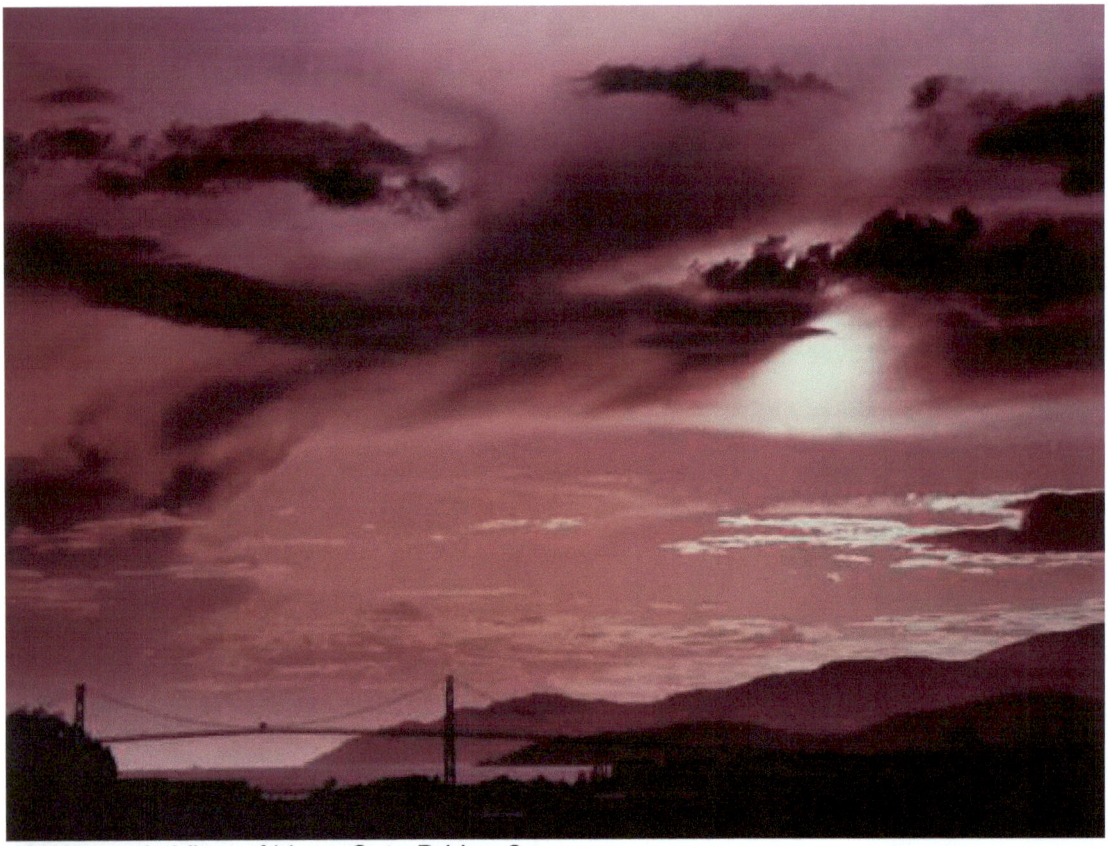

49. Westerly View of Lions Gate Bridge 2

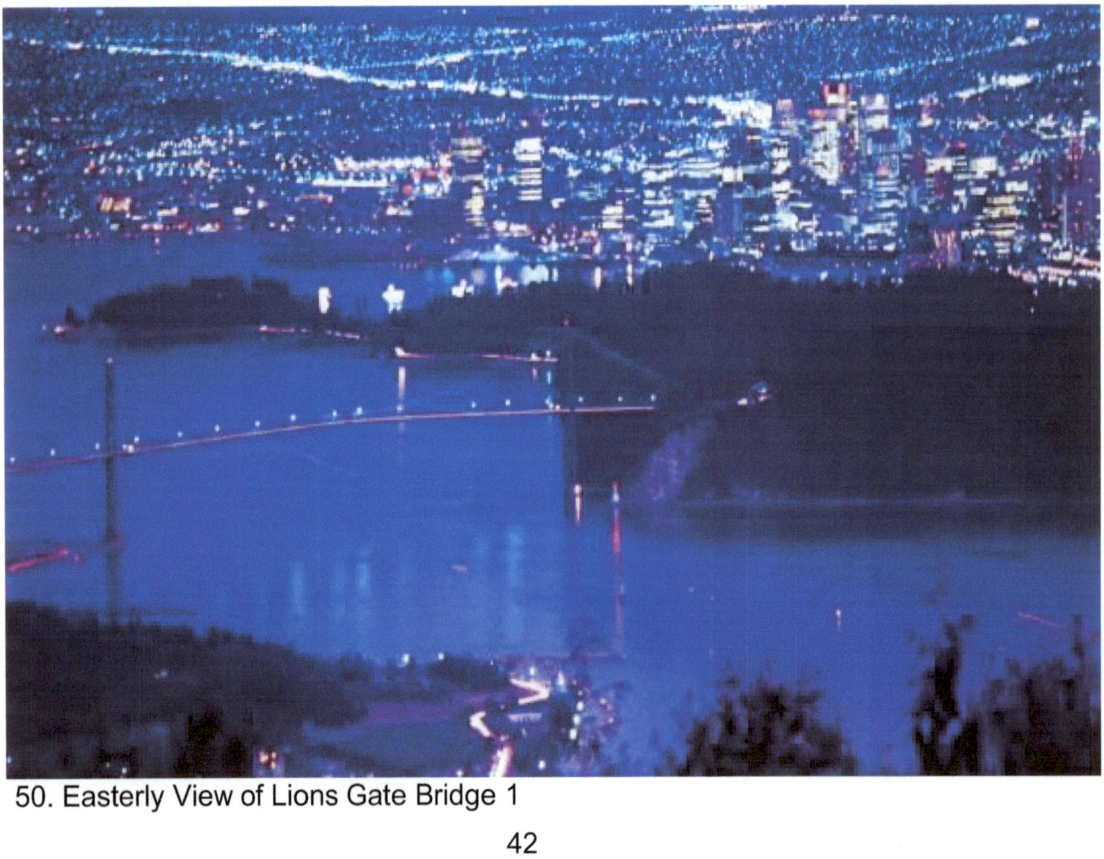

50. Easterly View of Lions Gate Bridge 1

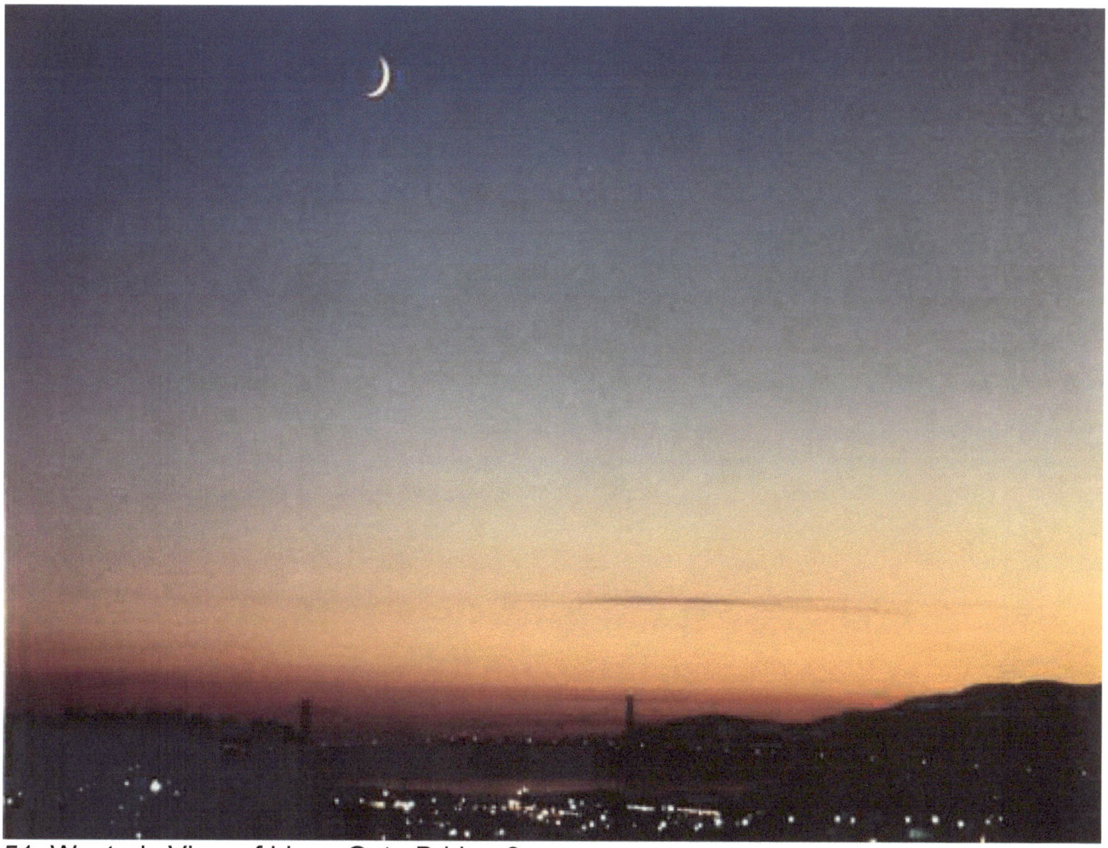

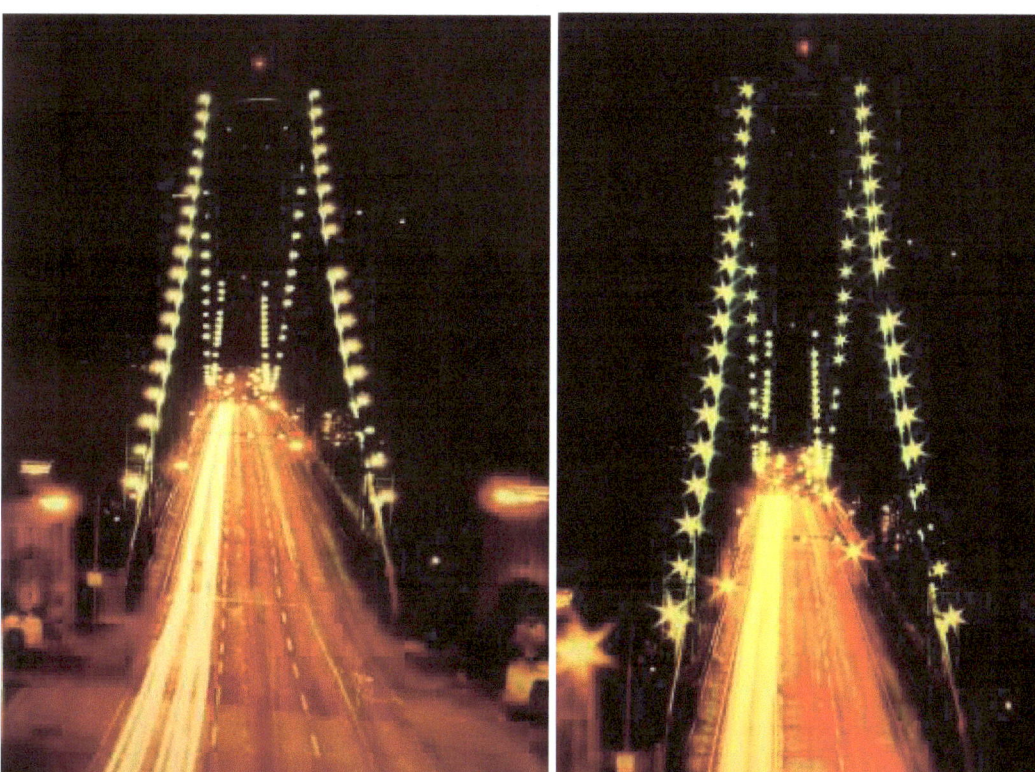

51. Westerly View of Lions Gate Bridge 3

52. On Lions Gate Bridge 1

53. On Lions Gate Bridge 2

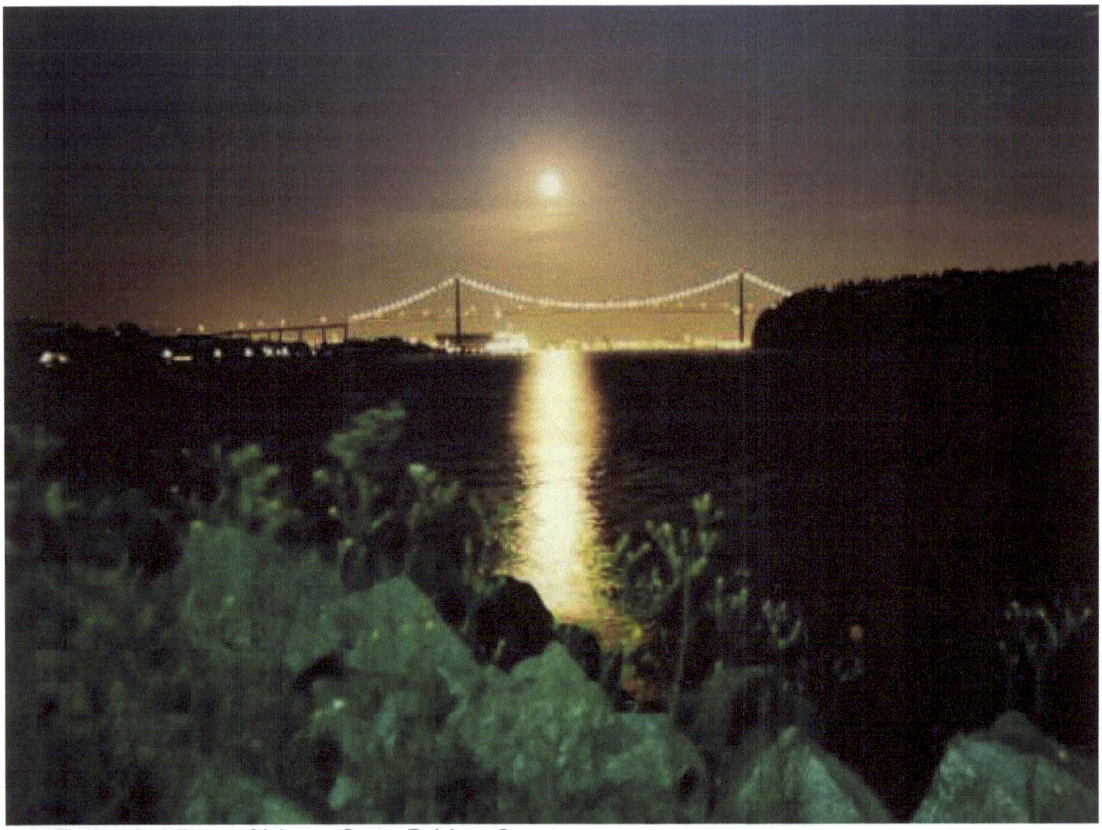

54. Easterly View of Lions Gate Bridge 2

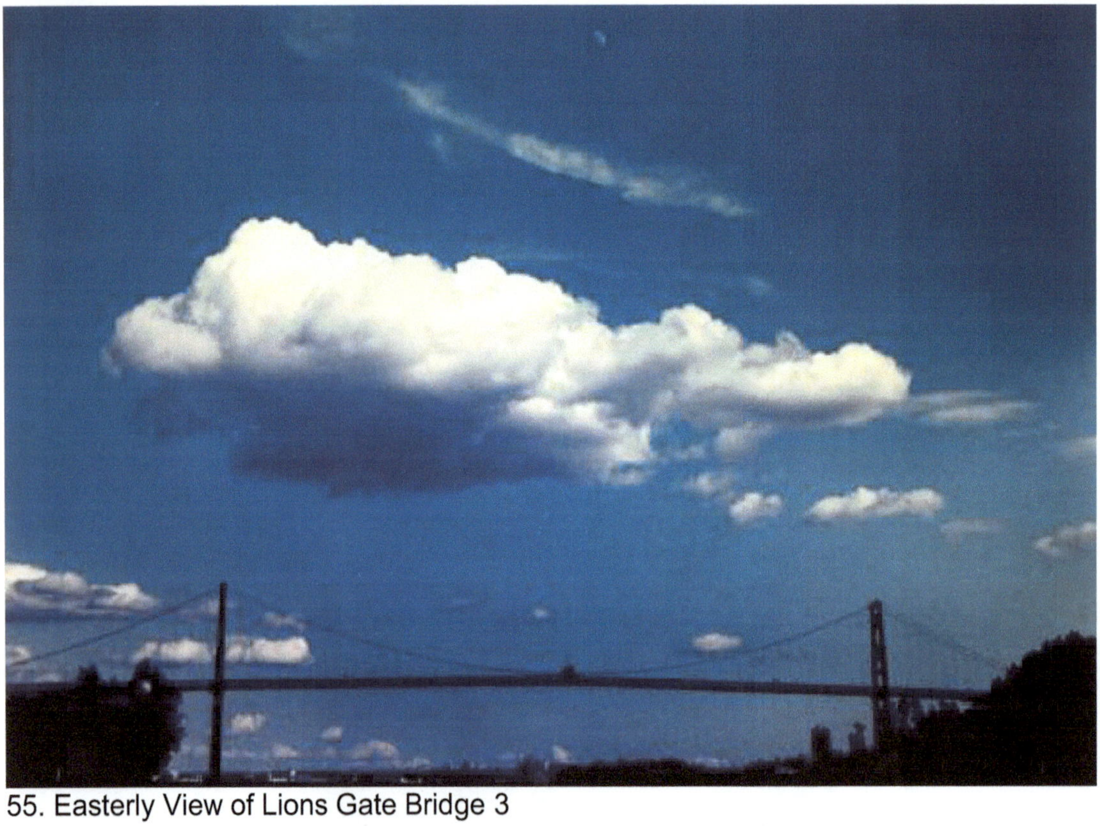

55. Easterly View of Lions Gate Bridge 3

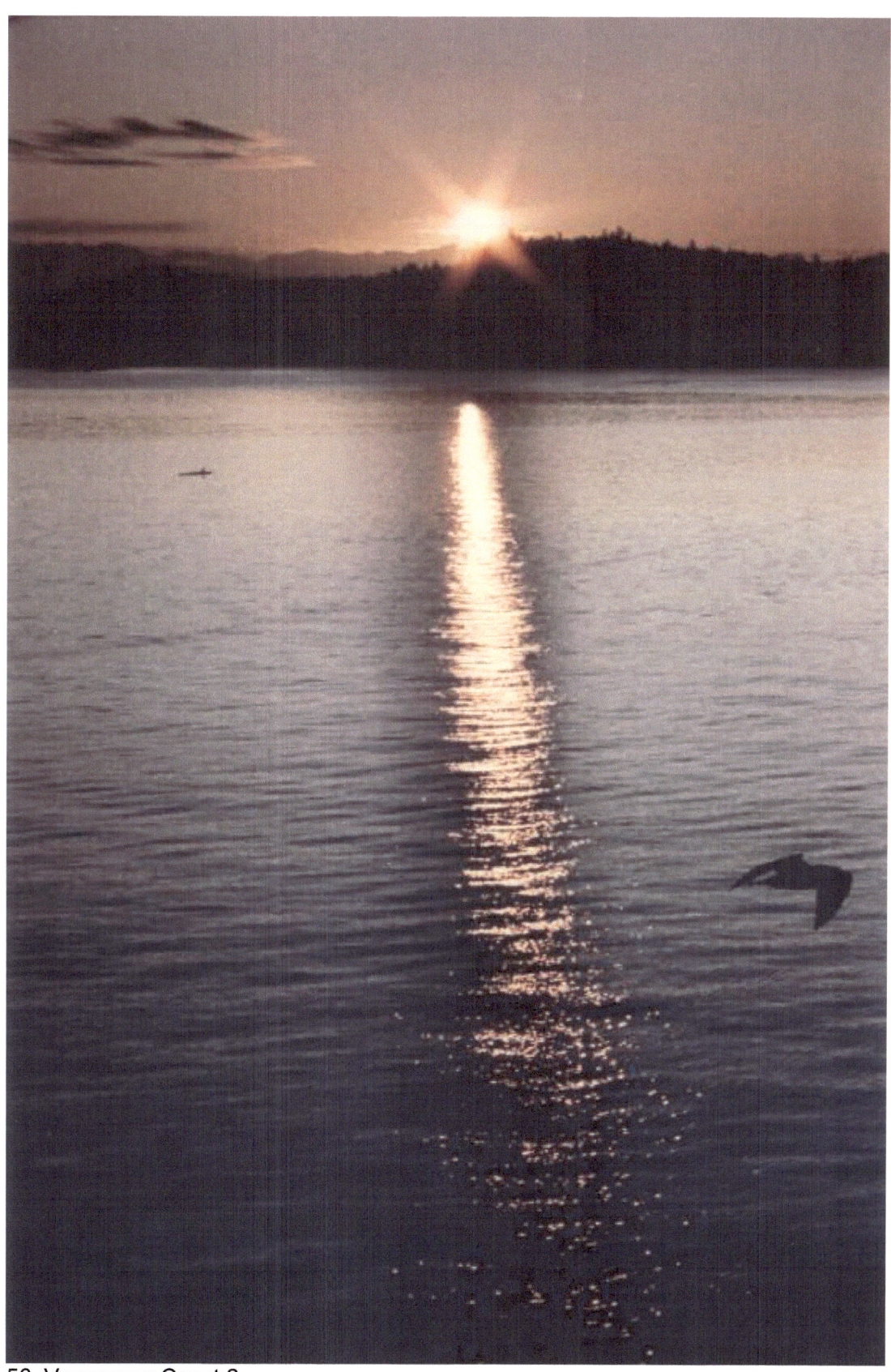
56. Vancouver Coast 2

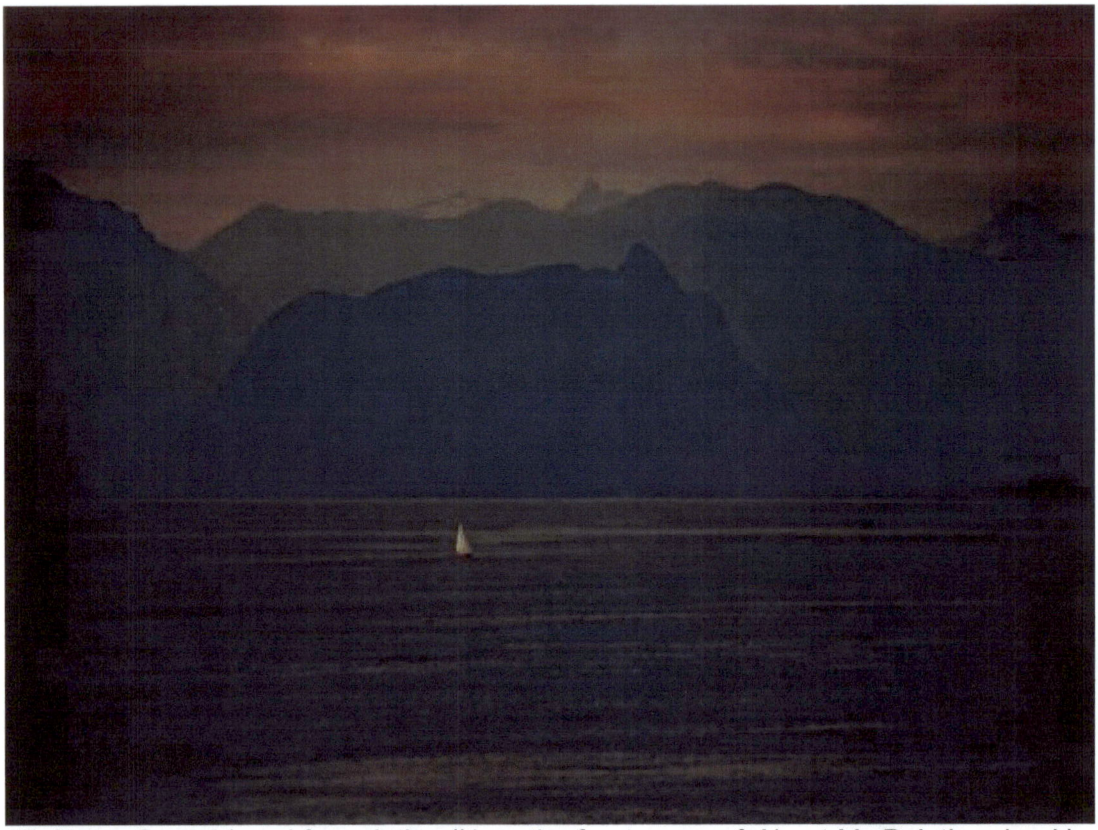

57. Howe Sound (used for painting #1 on the front cover of *About My Paintings* book)

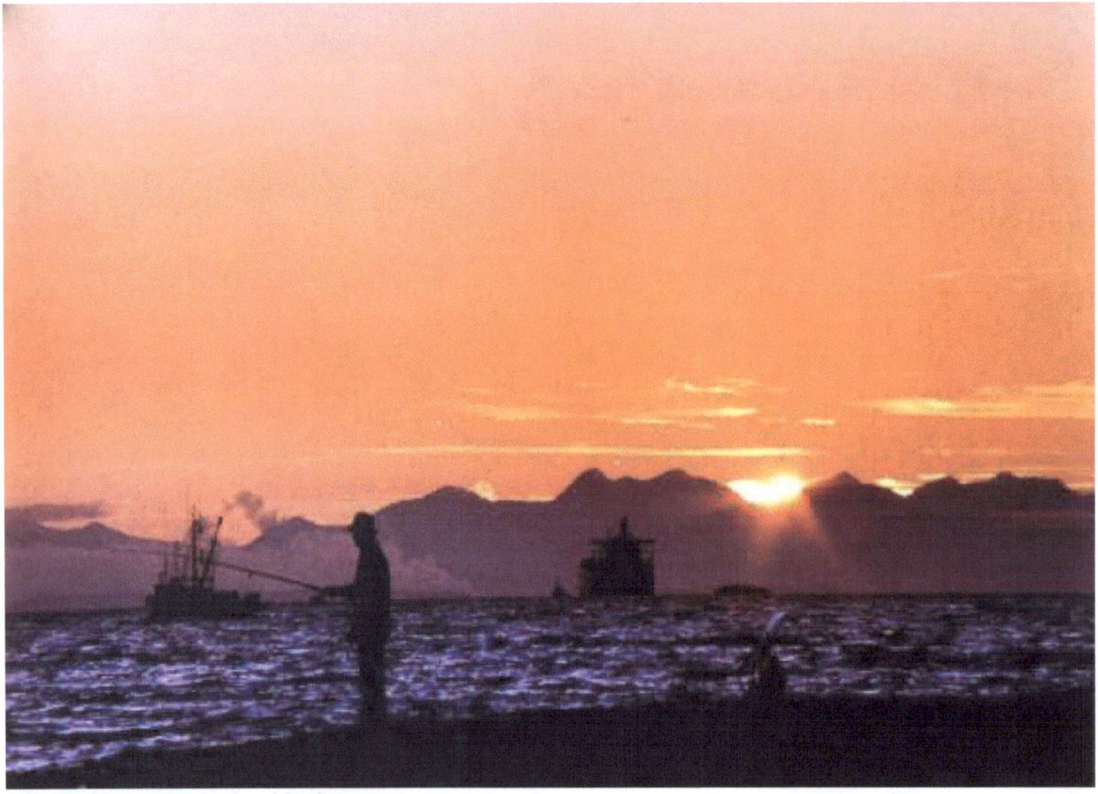

58. Fisherman at the Harbour

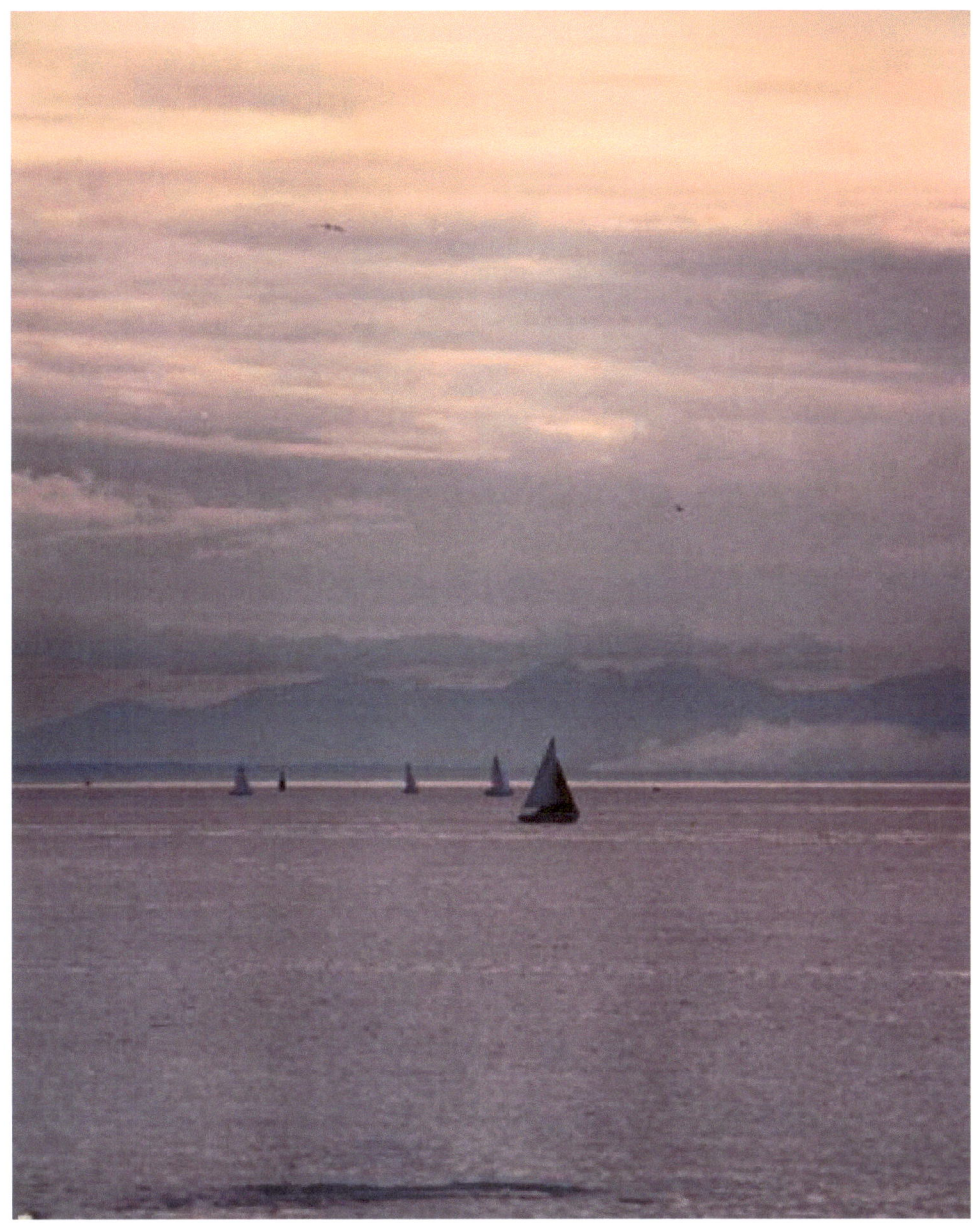
59. Vancouver Coast 4

Outskirts of Vancouver

As we cross the Lions Gate Bridge to North Shore, we can drive westerly towards Horseshoe Bay and then up to Whistler and beyond along the scenic west coast next to the Pacific Ocean. Traversing this route frequently and photographing nature had become a big leisure time for me during the first ten years of arriving and living in North Vancouver. A few trips to southern parts of British Columbia had availed its own opportunities for photographing fascinating landscapes. Accordingly, some pictures from Vancouver outskirts are depicted in the following pages.

In particular, the Howe Sound vista at Horseshoe Bay is absolutely breathtaking, especially in some particular atmospheric conditions, like the one I had captured in the photograph # 57 at dusk from a cliff in Whytecliff Park, which is itself an exotic place to visit in Horseshoe Bay. In fact, that majestical image of Howe Sound had triggered my urge to become a painter and then paint it many months later. That painting's image is printed on the front cover of *About My Paintings* book, which also offers an excerpt from my novel, *My Lousy Life Stories*, under the heading of *Howe Sound*. The full story in the novel, especially, reflects my dramatic mood that day.

60. Last Light on Pacific Ocean

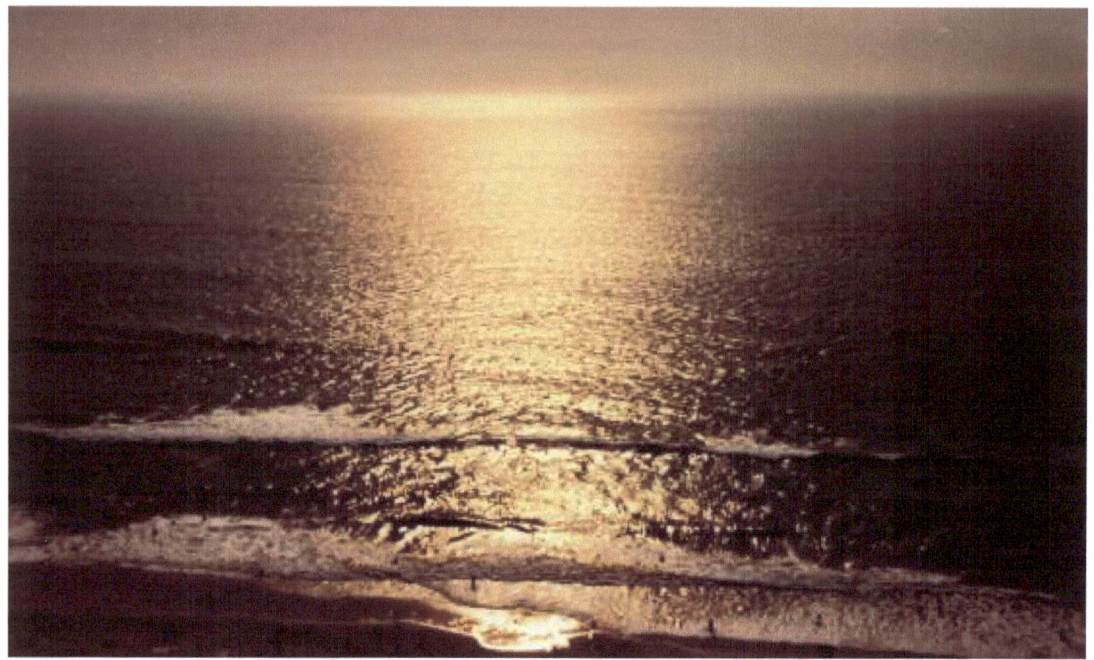

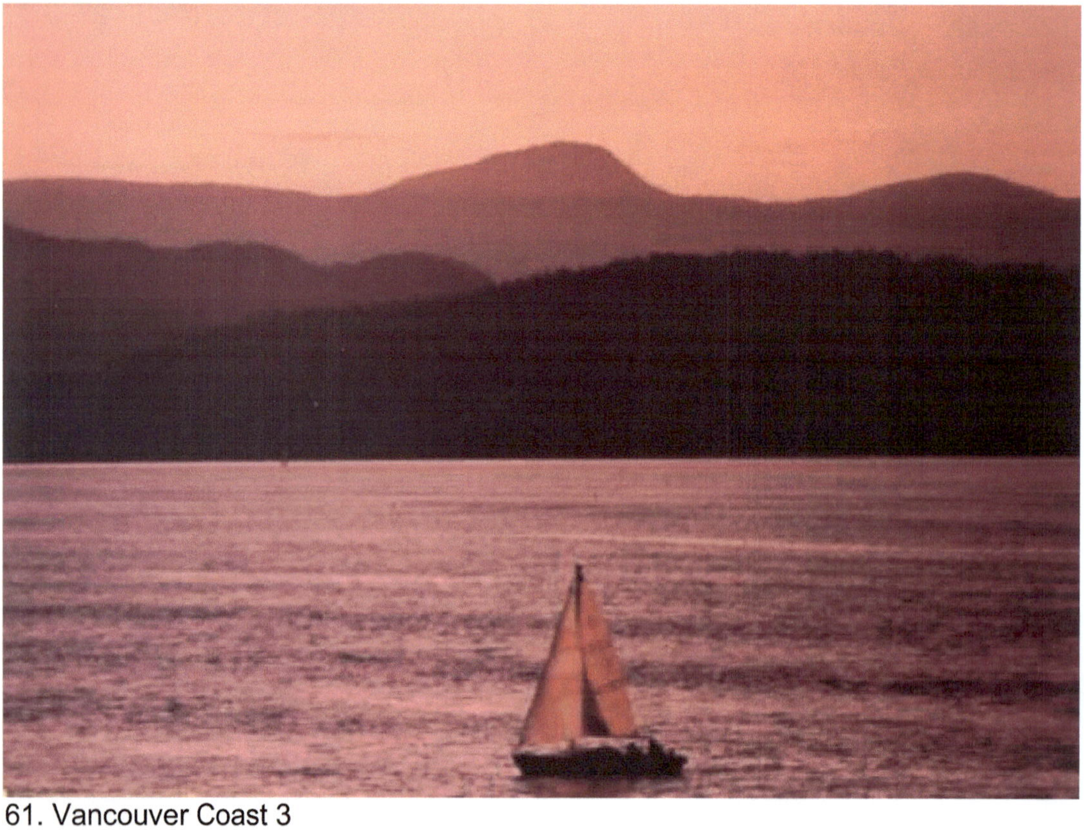

61. Vancouver Coast 3

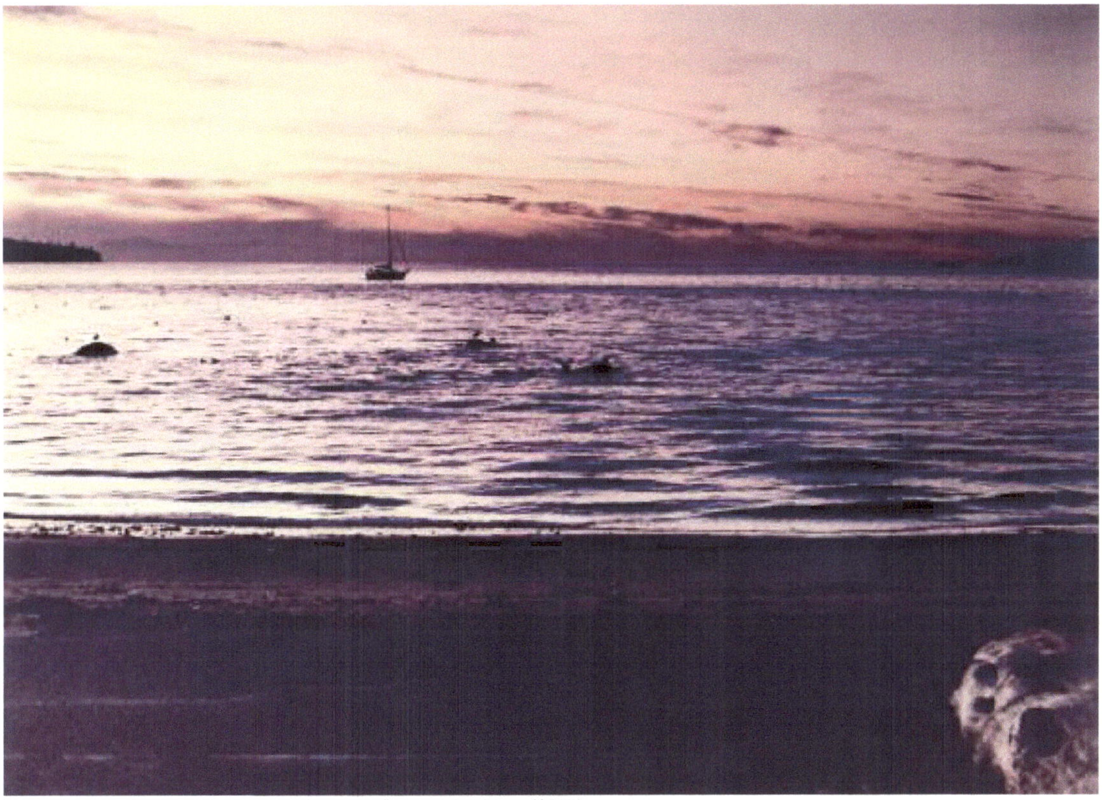

62. Vancouver Coast 4 (used for painting #87)

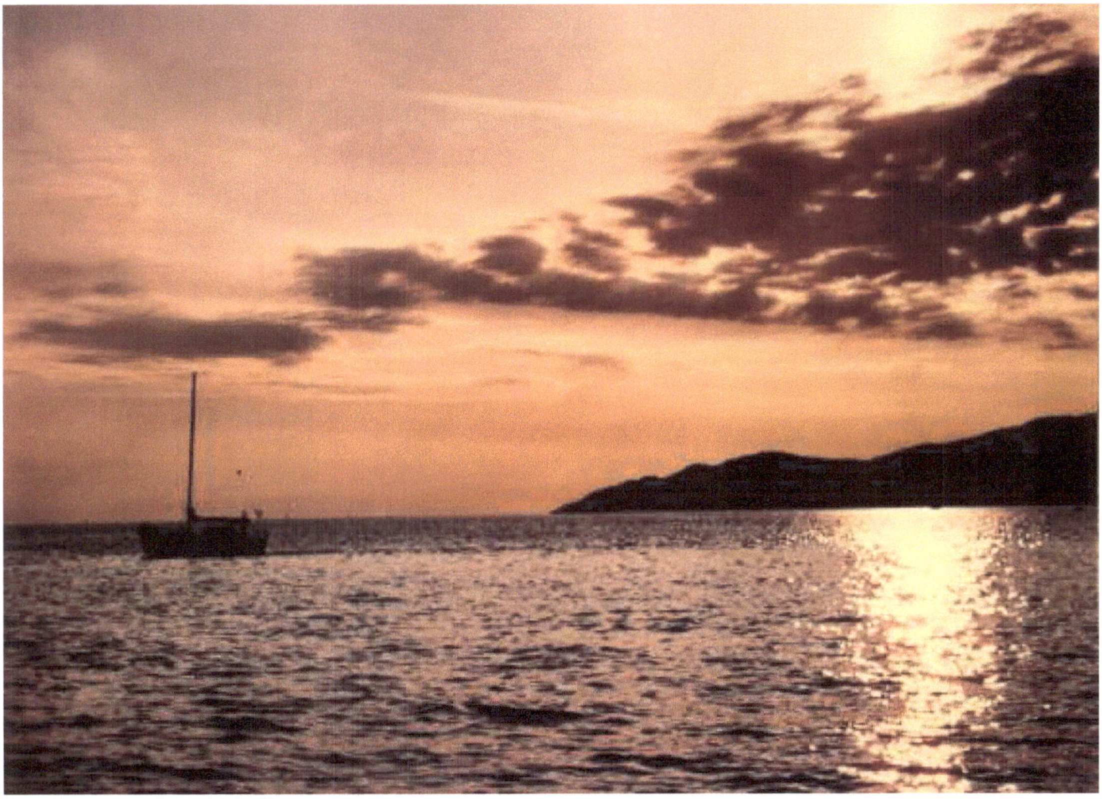

63. Calm at English Bay

Downtown Vancouver-Part II

The convenience of living in North Shore and limited travelling due to job obligations had resulted in many photographs of Burrard Inlet, neighbouring parks, and downtown Vancouver. Accordingly, a second set of cityscapes are included in this part before switching to personal and general photographs.

Photographs #64 and #8 were taken only 1-2 minutes apart from the same scene, so were #61 and #3. Still, the colour and mood differences in each scene are quite unique due to nature's constant wonderful plays; and that has been the reason to print these rather similar pictures in this book. You may compare and enjoy nature's fast changes deepening our sentiments and experiences.

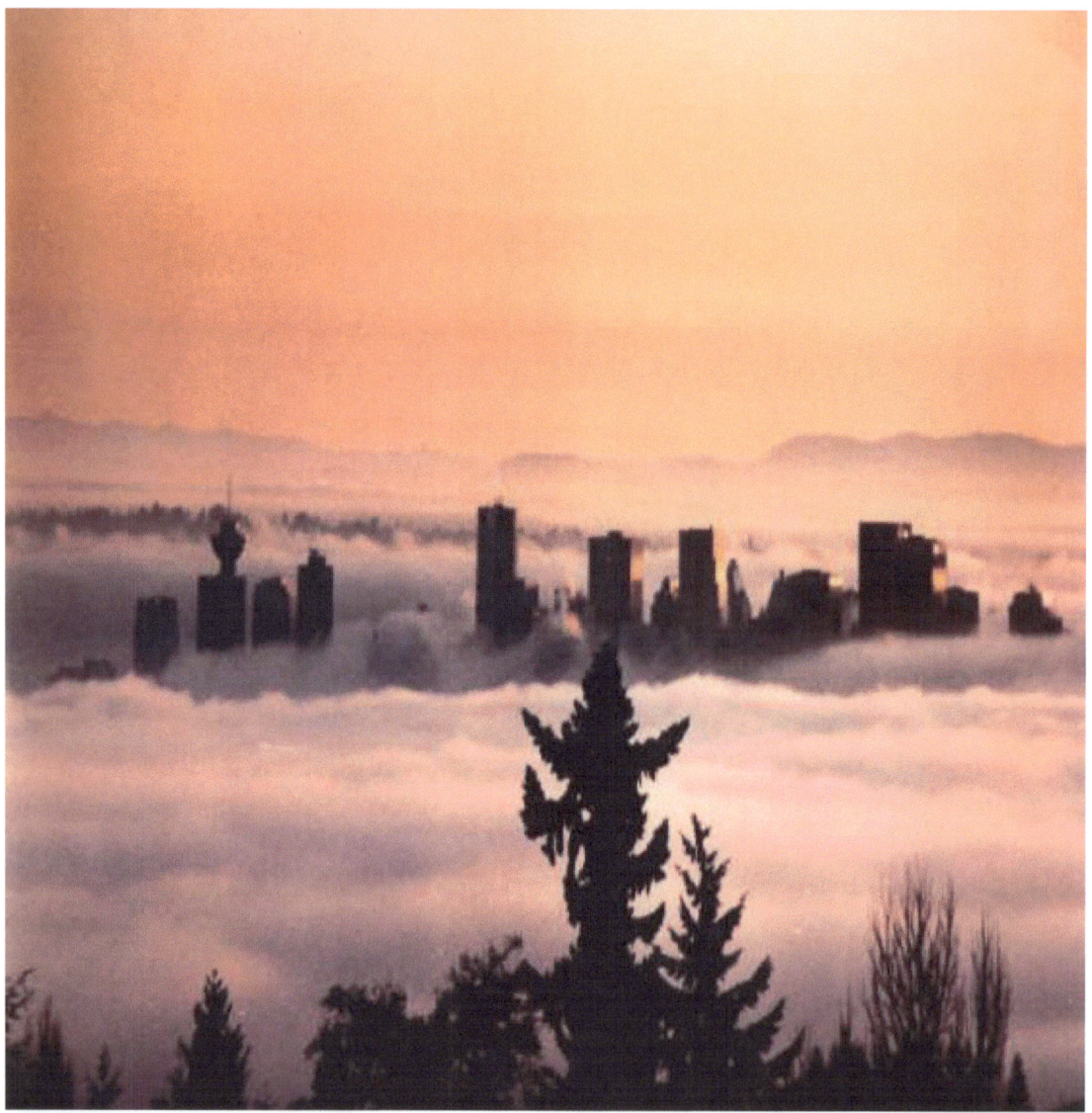

64. Downtown Vancouver 6

Picture # 65 in the next page shows a seemingly quiet night in Burrard Inlet, yet the time-lapsed image, #66, reveals the amount of activity in the Inlet even at the dead of night, as evident by the long lines drawn on the film by those vessels' lights. The intermittent light at the lower part of #66 might have been created by the Sea Bus.

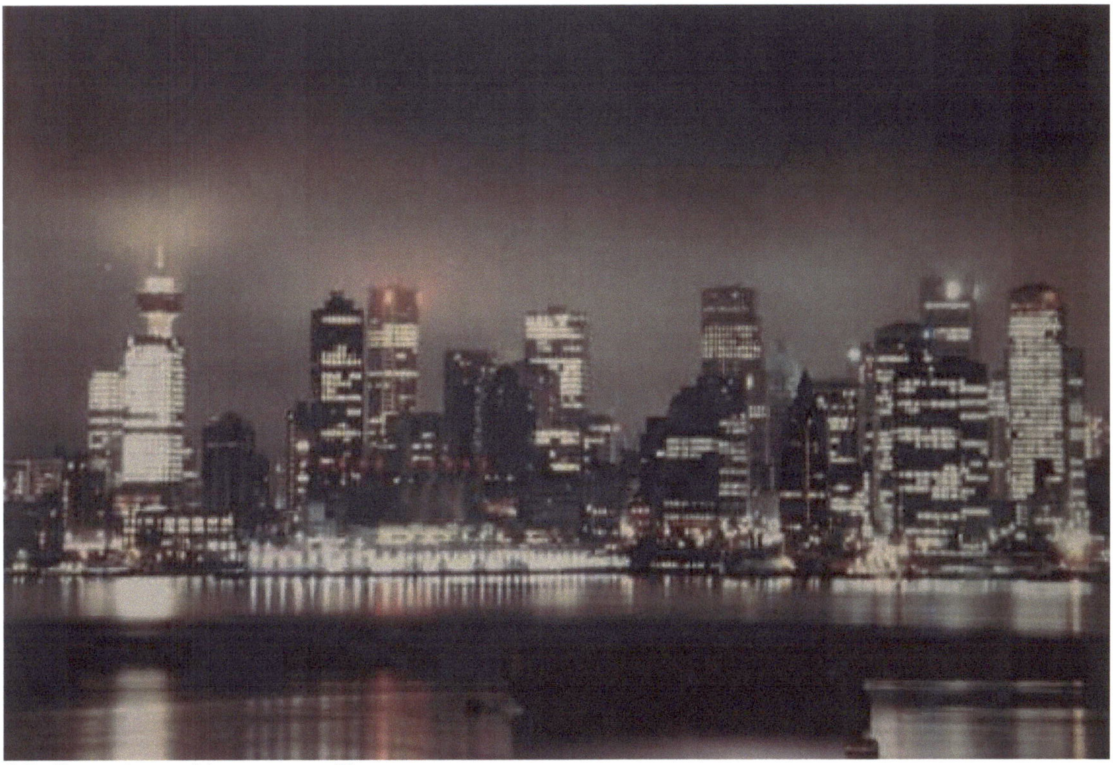

65. Downtown Vancouver 7

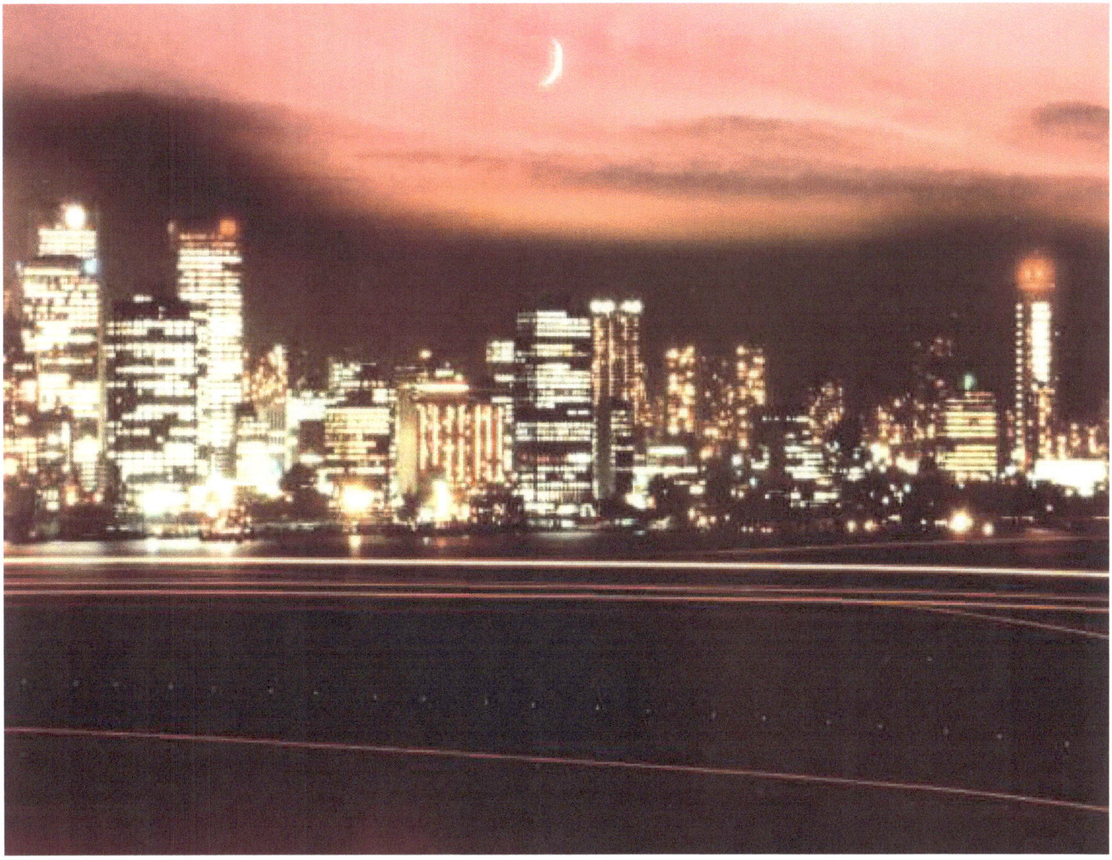

66. Traffic in Burrard Inlet

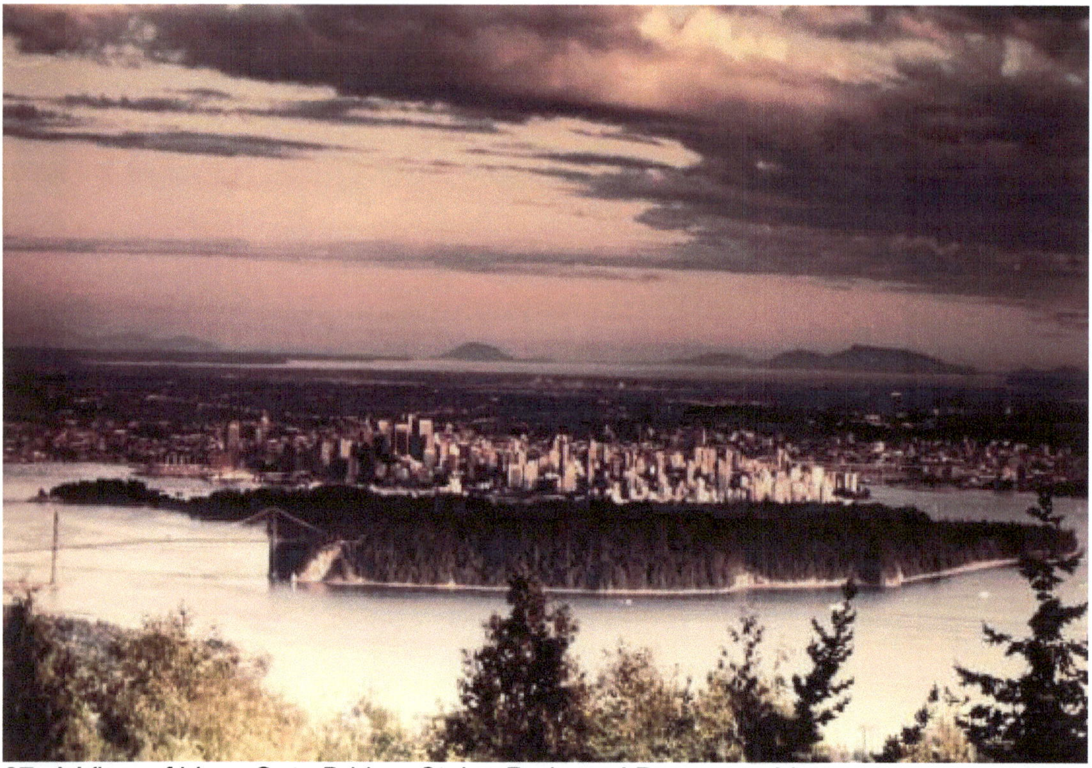

67. A View of Lions Gate Bridge, Staley Park, and Downtown Vancouver

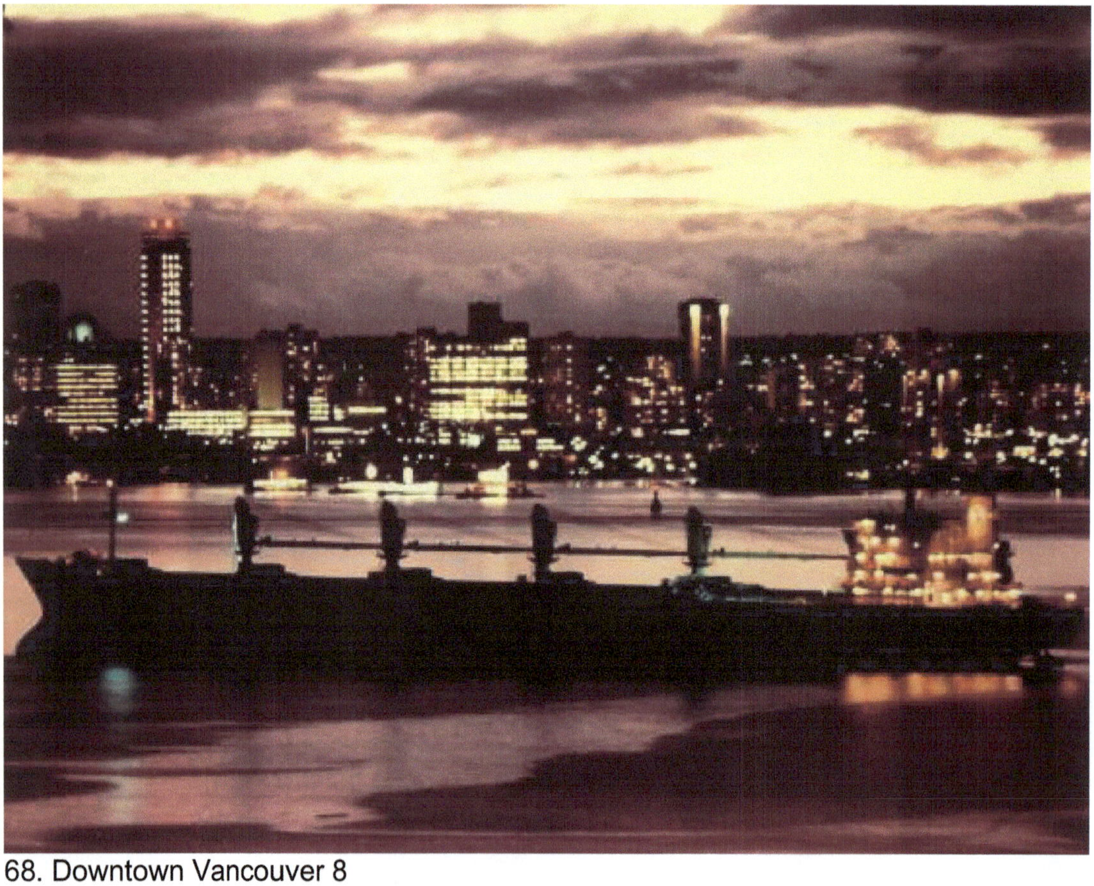

68. Downtown Vancouver 8

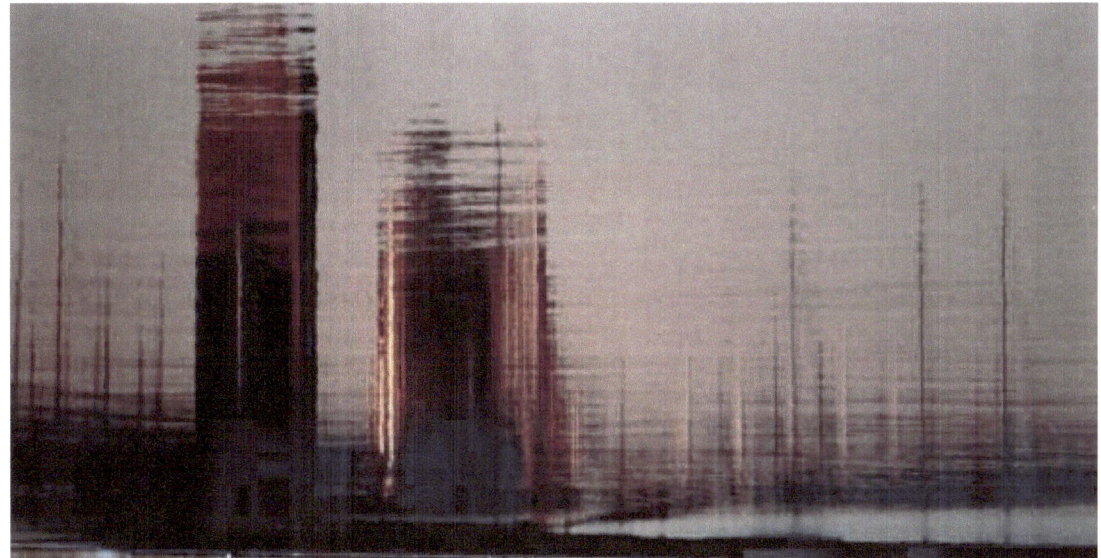
69. Sailboats Imagery in Burrard Inlet 2

Trees and Leaves

Discussing even the basic roles that plants play in humans' welfare, including their romantic, biological, and psychological importance for us, takes a few volumes and hundreds of pictures. Some of the photographs in this section might at least remind us of plants' romantic and psychological impacts on our spirits. The mere calm that some vistas, or even pictures, of nature exude soothes our burdened psyches tremendously.

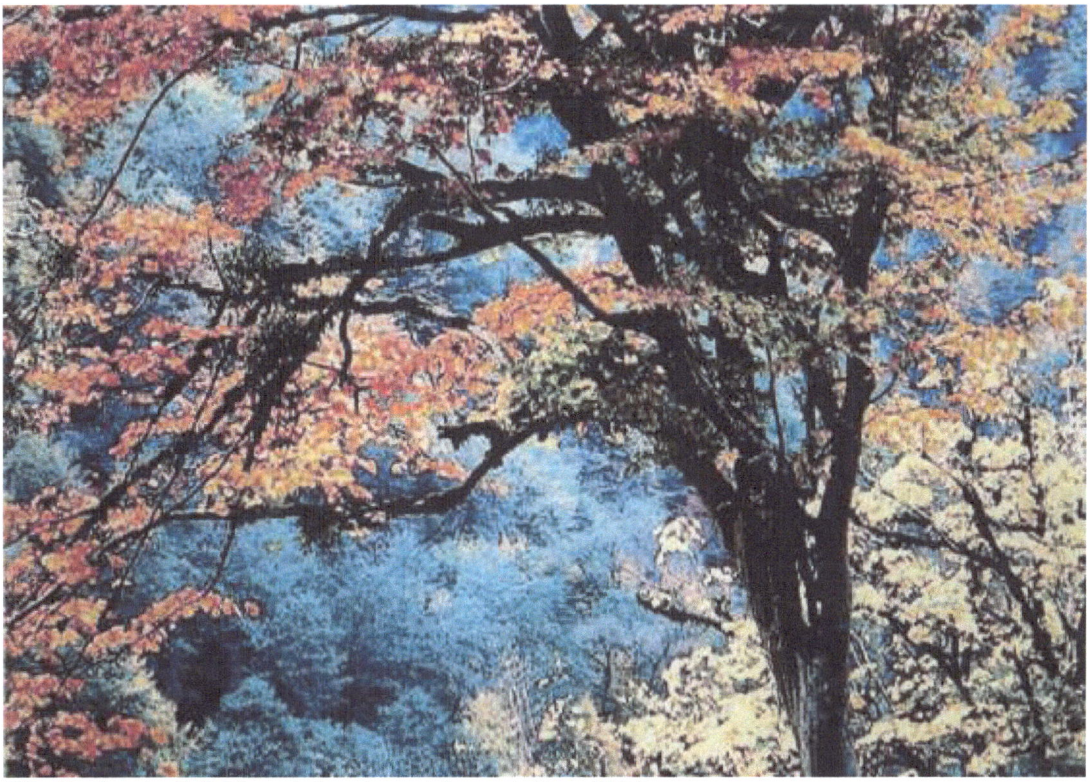

70. Spring in BC Mountains (used for painting #30)

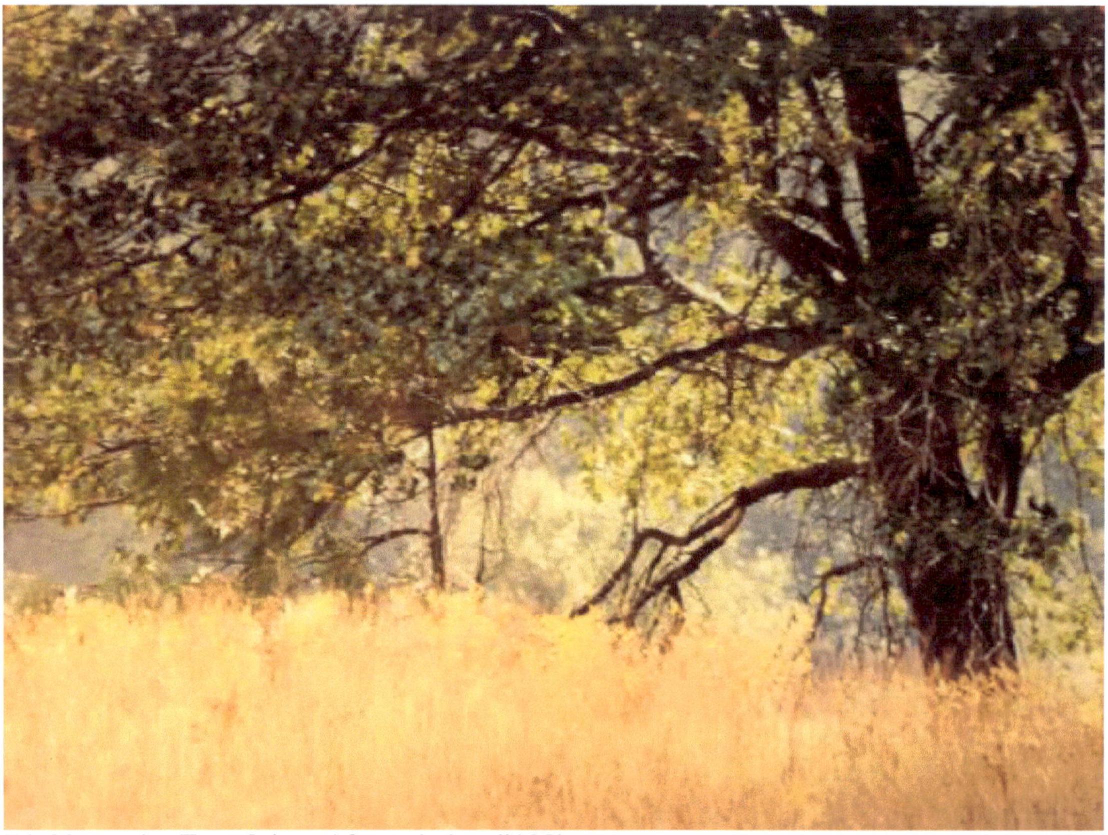

71. Yosemite Tree 2 (used for painting #108)

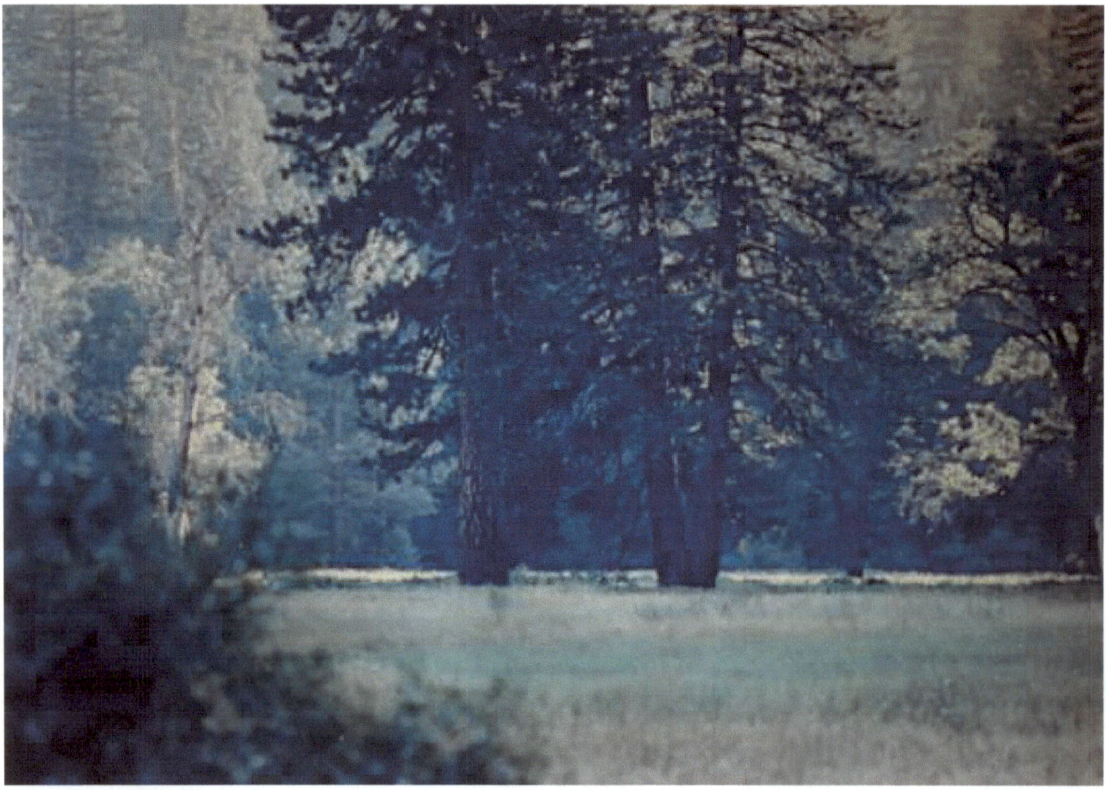

72. Yosemite Field 4

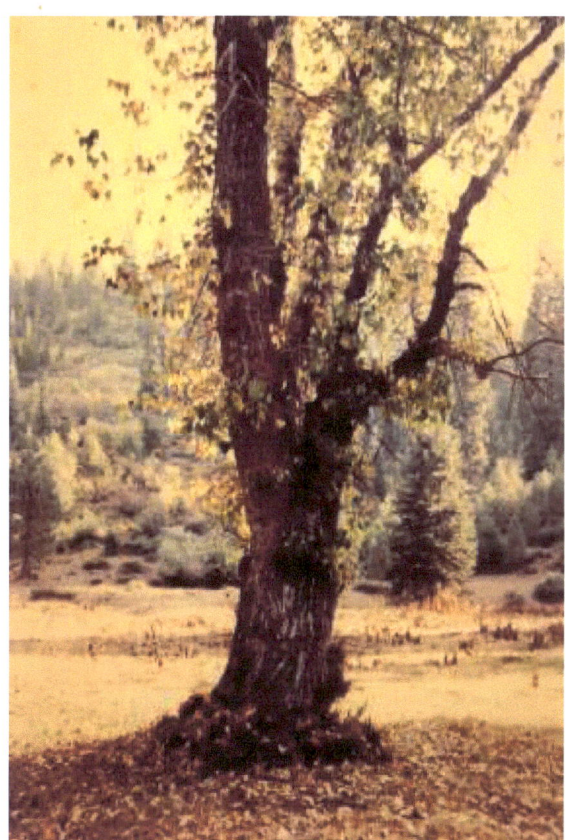
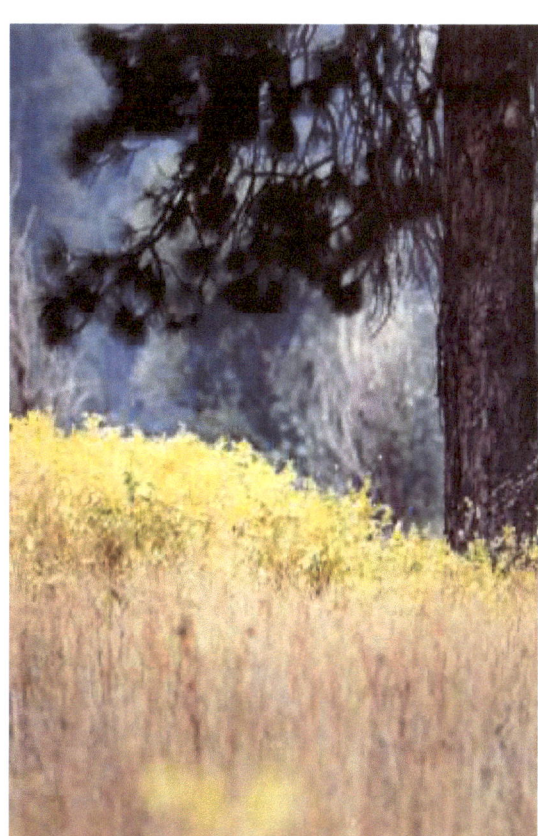

73. Yosemite Tree 3 (used for painting #25)   74. Yosemite Tree 4 (sold before taking its photo)

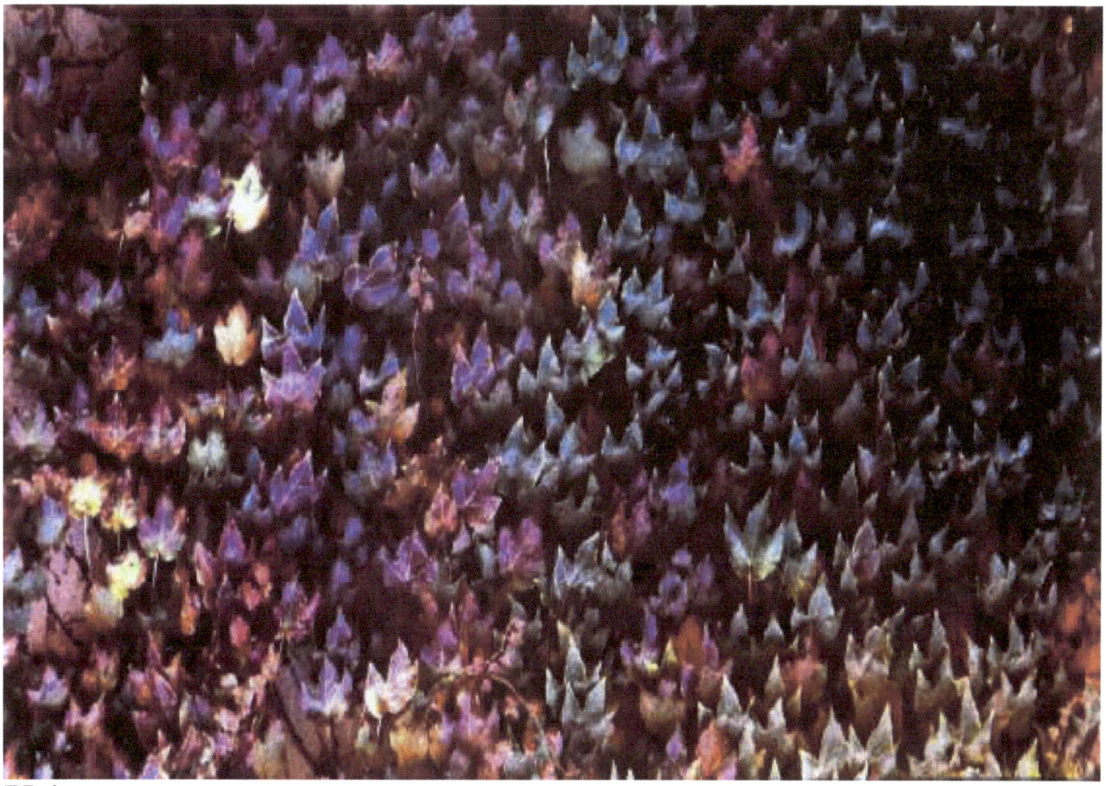

75. Ivey

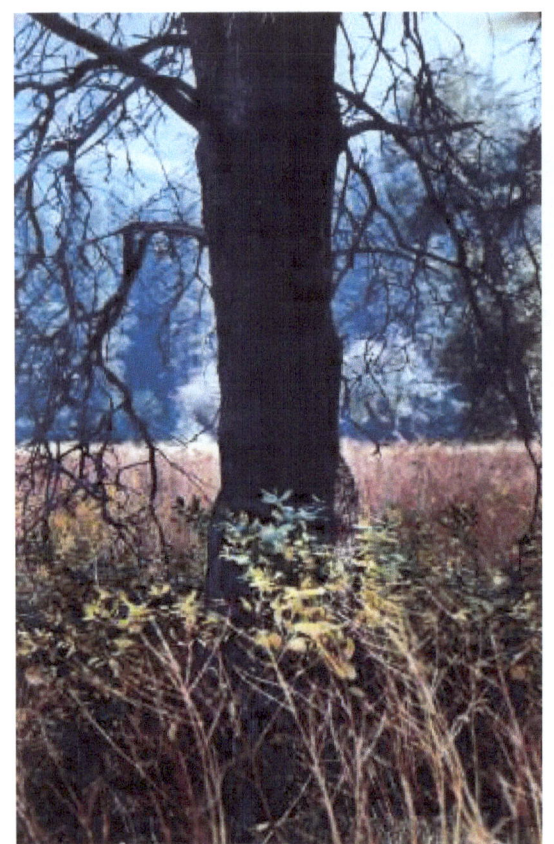
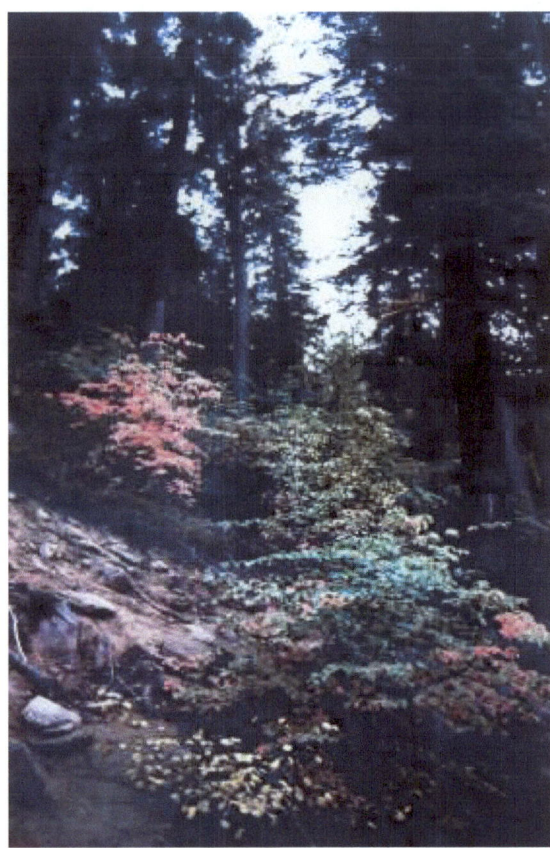

76. Lonesome Tree (used for painting #15)   77. Stanley Park Hills (used for painting #14)

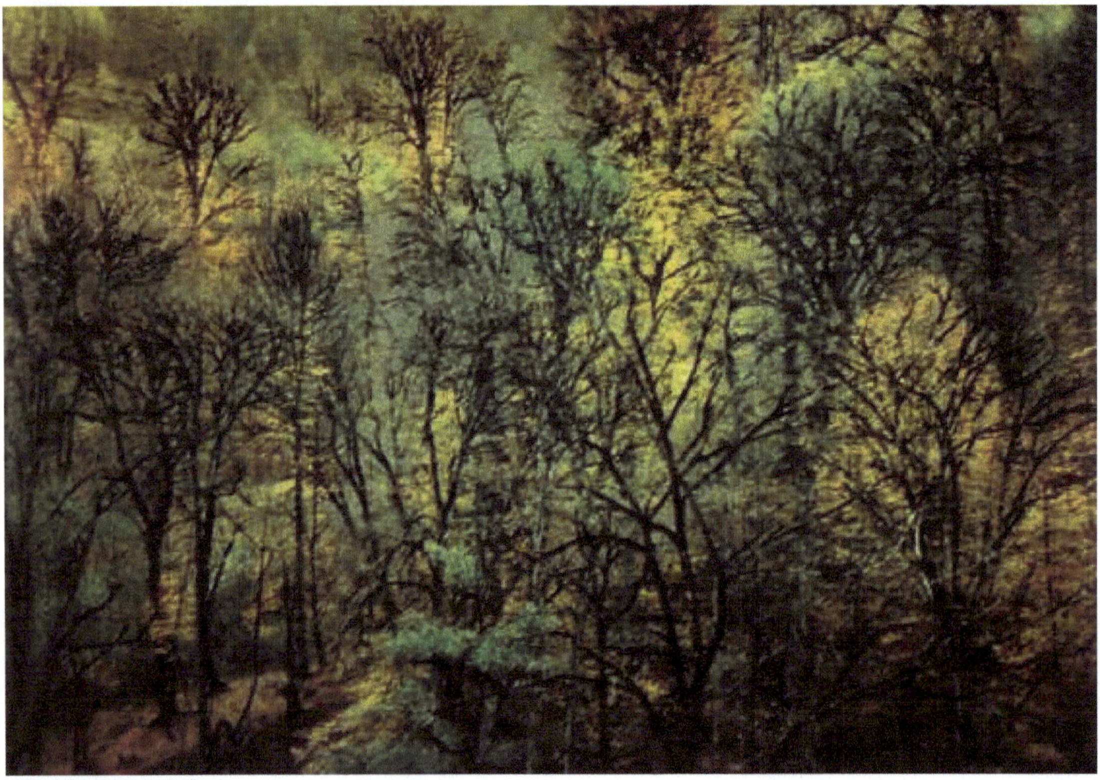

78. Lines and Colours

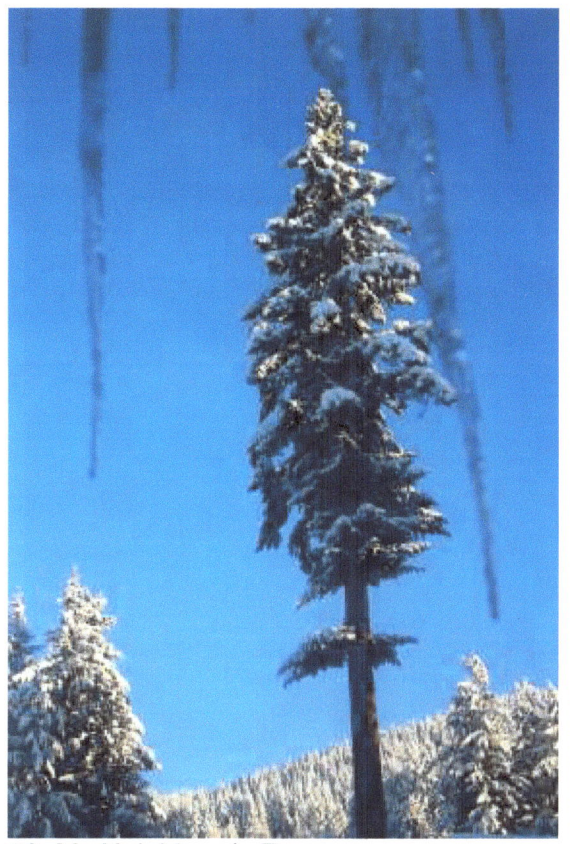
79. My Neighbour's Tree

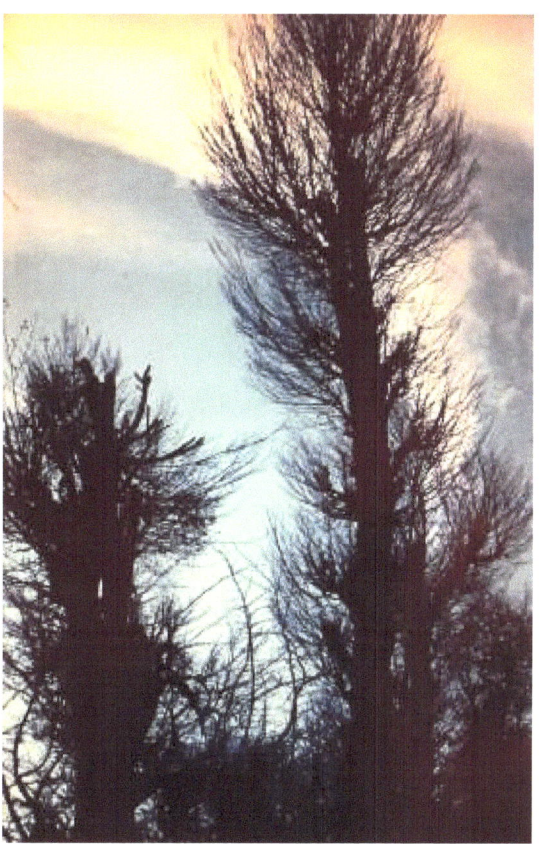
80. Silhouette (used for painting #29)

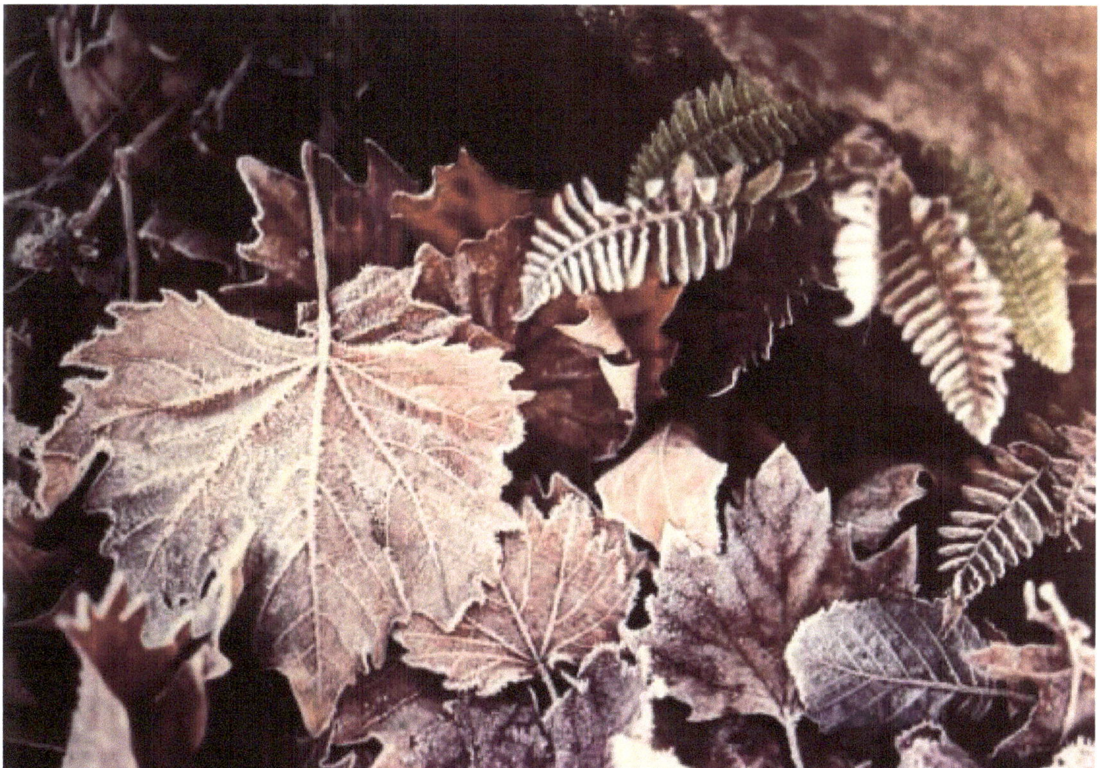

81. Frosty Leaves 1

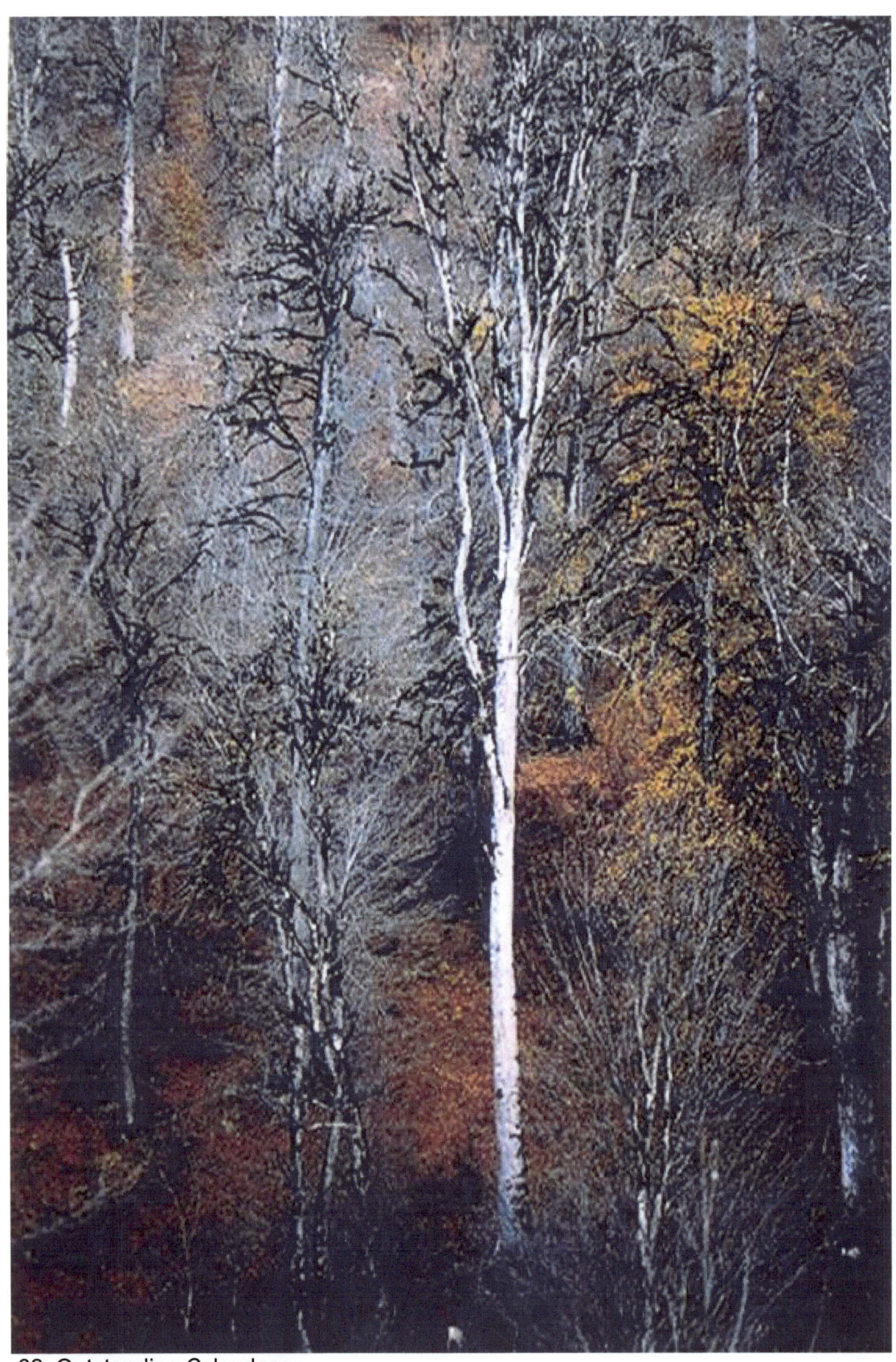

82. Outstanding Colourless

Flowers and Fruits

Even more than trees and leaves are the direct and precious roles of flowers and fruits in our wellbeing. Depicting them in our paintings and photographs in the form of still life has played a big role in art for their clear appeal to, and appreciation by, our psyches as well. Besides their aesthetic and nutritional contributions to my daily life, the mere opportunity of photographing or painting them has always given me a huge joy almost equal to the endless delight that birds have given me, as noted earlier.

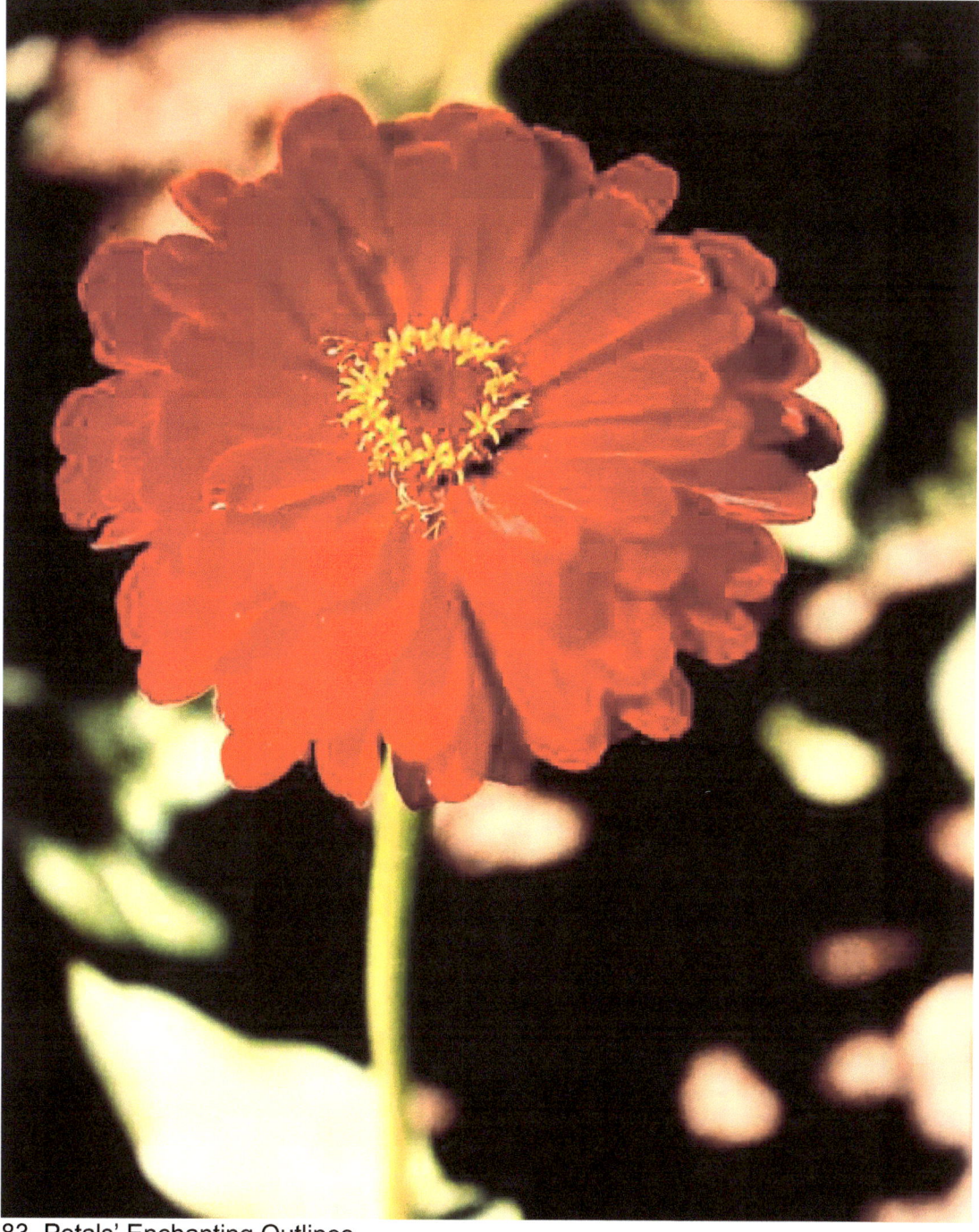

83. Petals' Enchanting Outlines

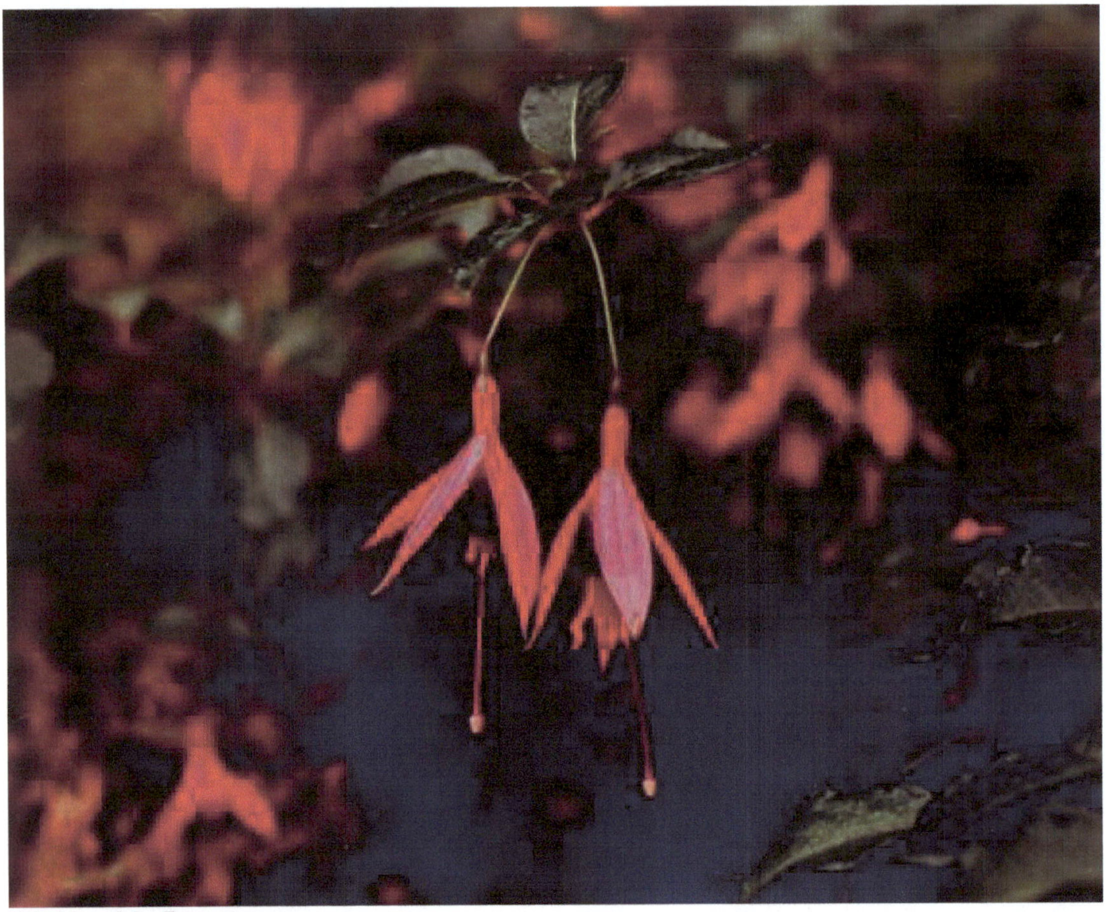

84. Humble Beauty

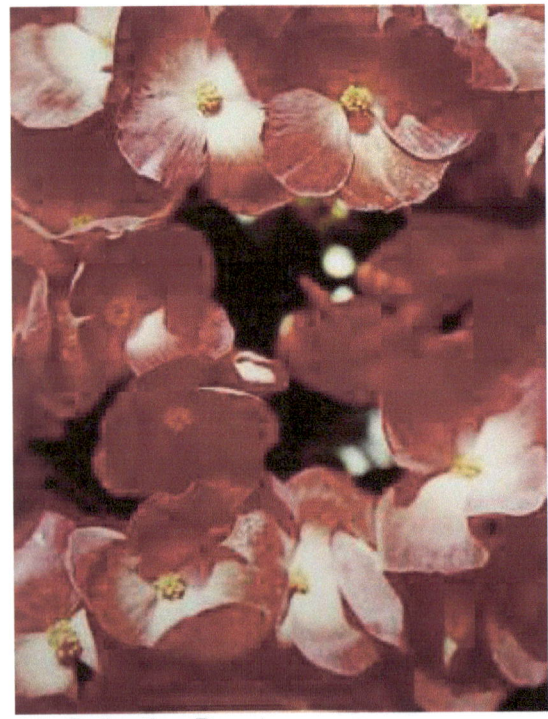
85. Collective Beauty

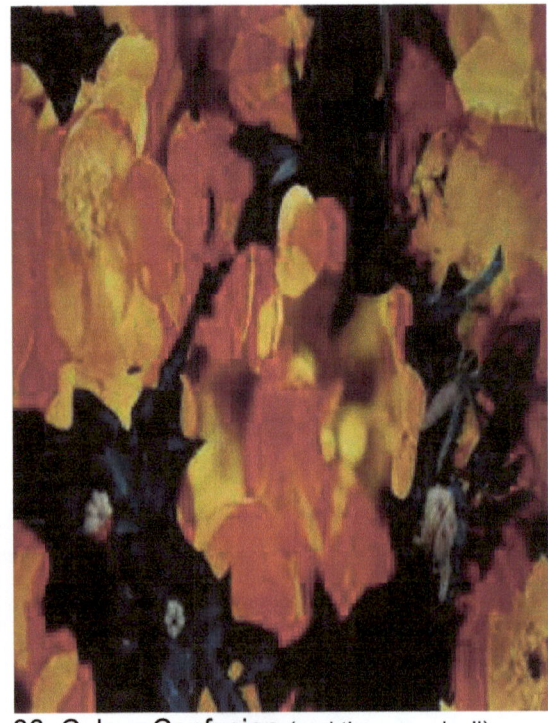
86. Colour Confusion (and the nosy devil)

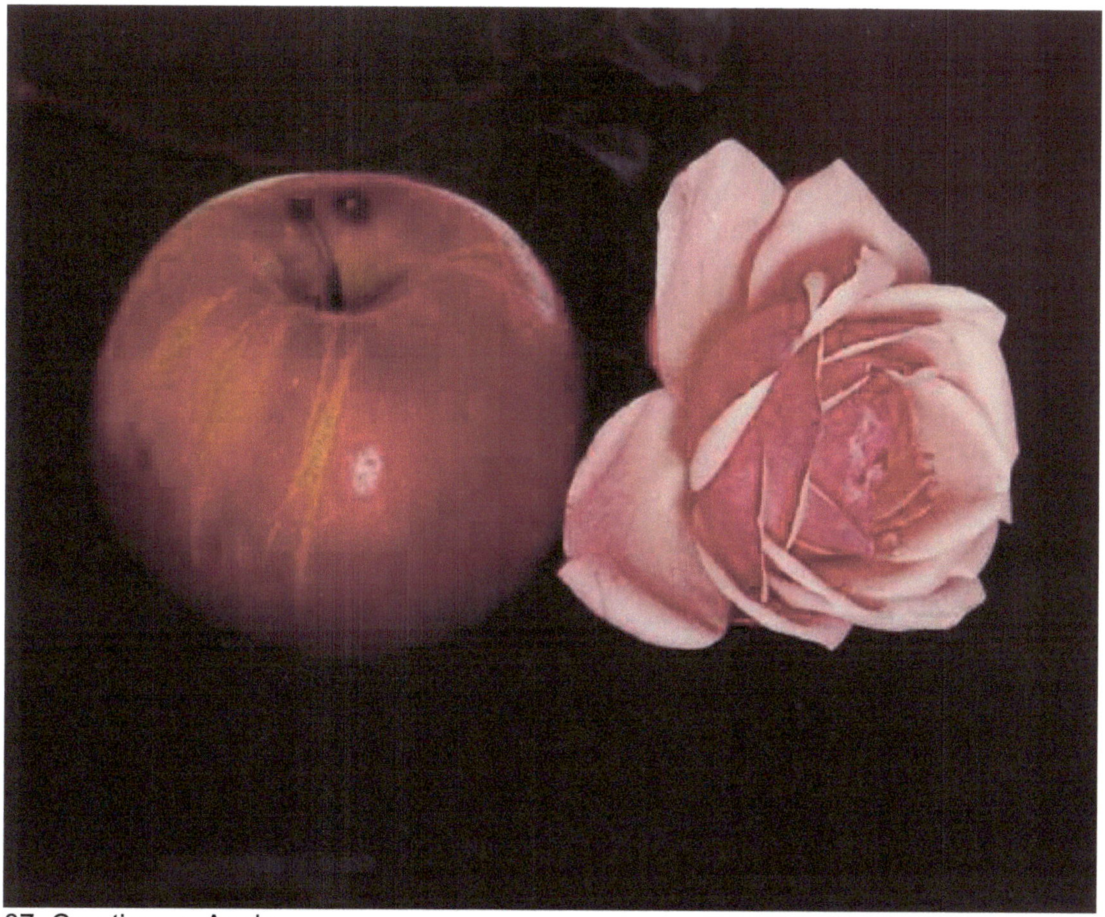

87. Courting an Apple

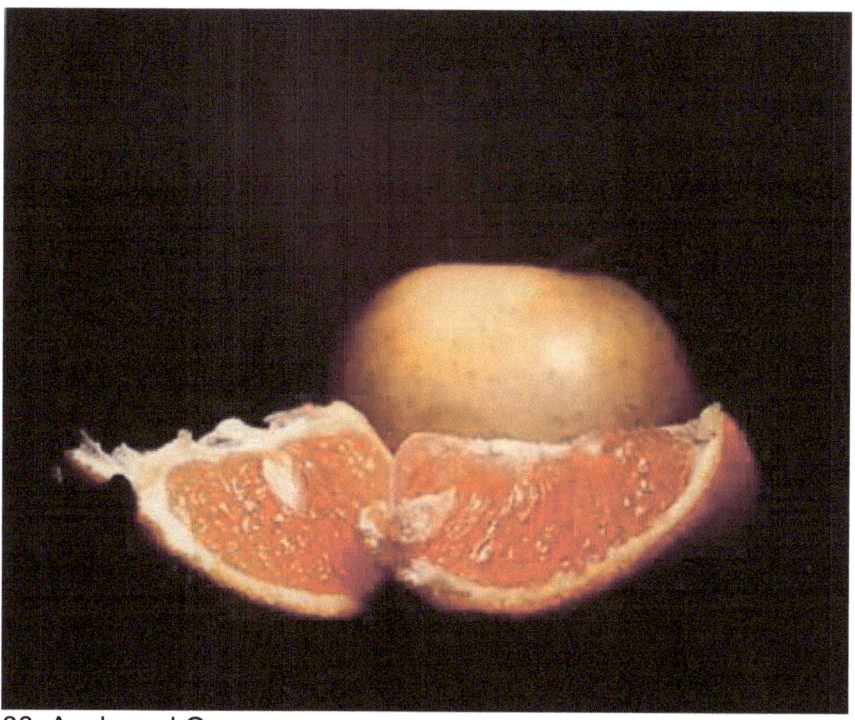
88. Apple and Orange

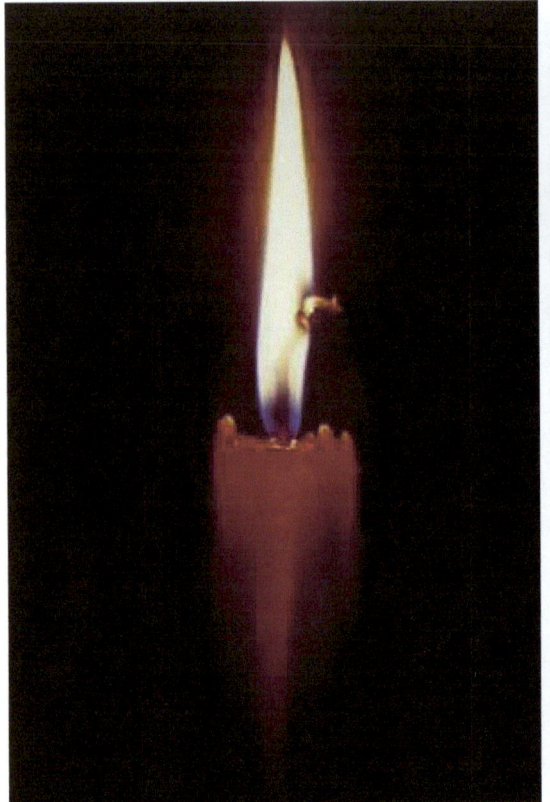
89. Subtle Lights of a Candle

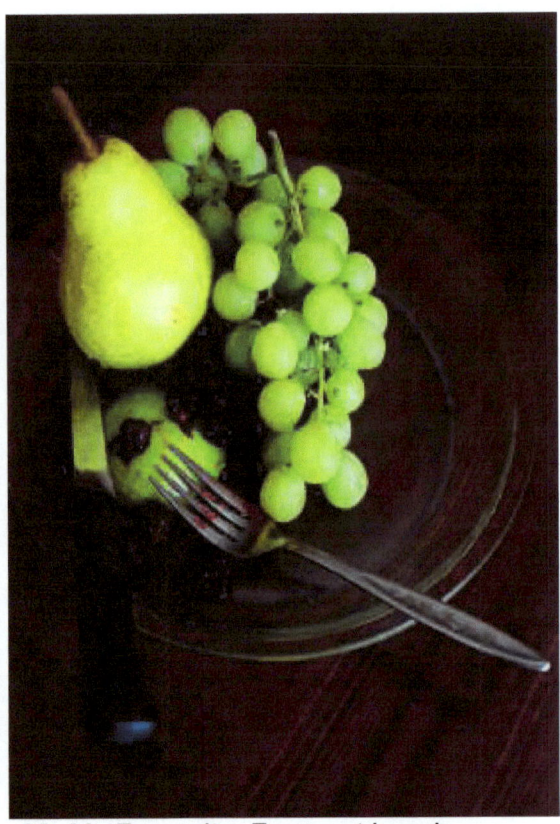
90. My Favourite, Frequent Lunch

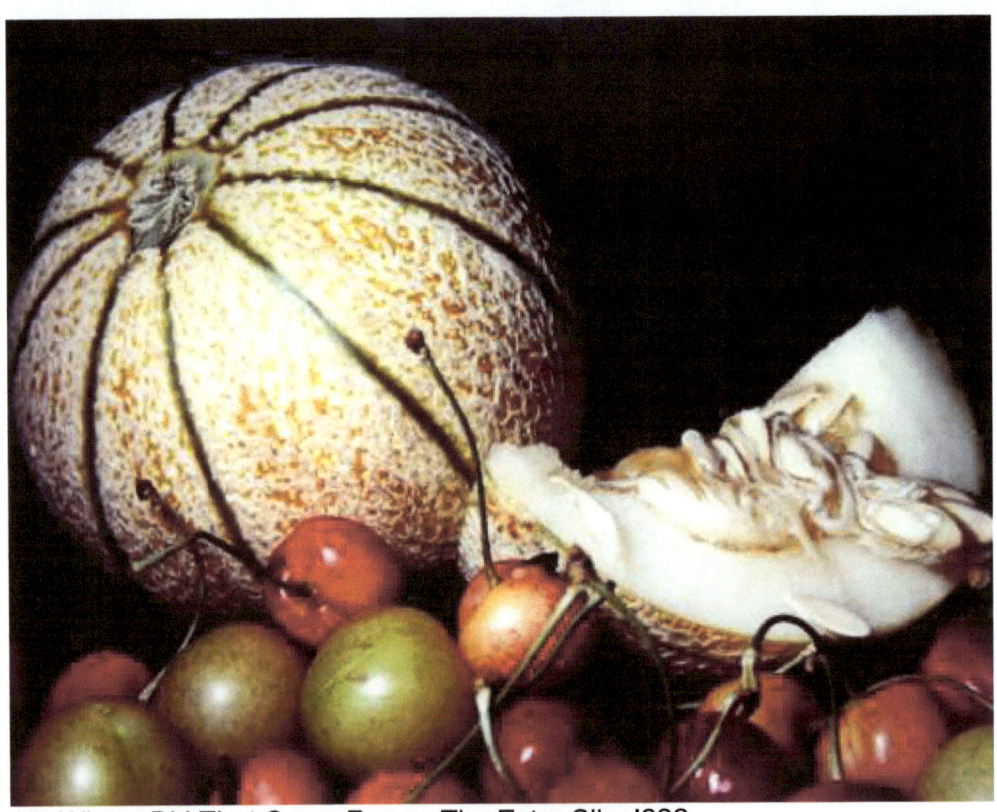
91. Where Did That Come From—The Extra Slice!???

Especially Water Lilies

Some plants, like orchids, roses, and tulips, have particularly become the symbols of romance and a source for relaxing our psyches. To me, water lilies stand at the top of the list of exotic plants that satiate our innate search for tranquility and beauty along with a subtle urge for self-exploration and identity. Then, when we find those beautiful, hardworking fish swimming around water lilies, our sentiments reach a new height, in my opinion, going by the rather large number of my photographs and paintings around this subject. Most likely Claude Monet had felt the same way about water lilies and possibly colourful fish in ponds.

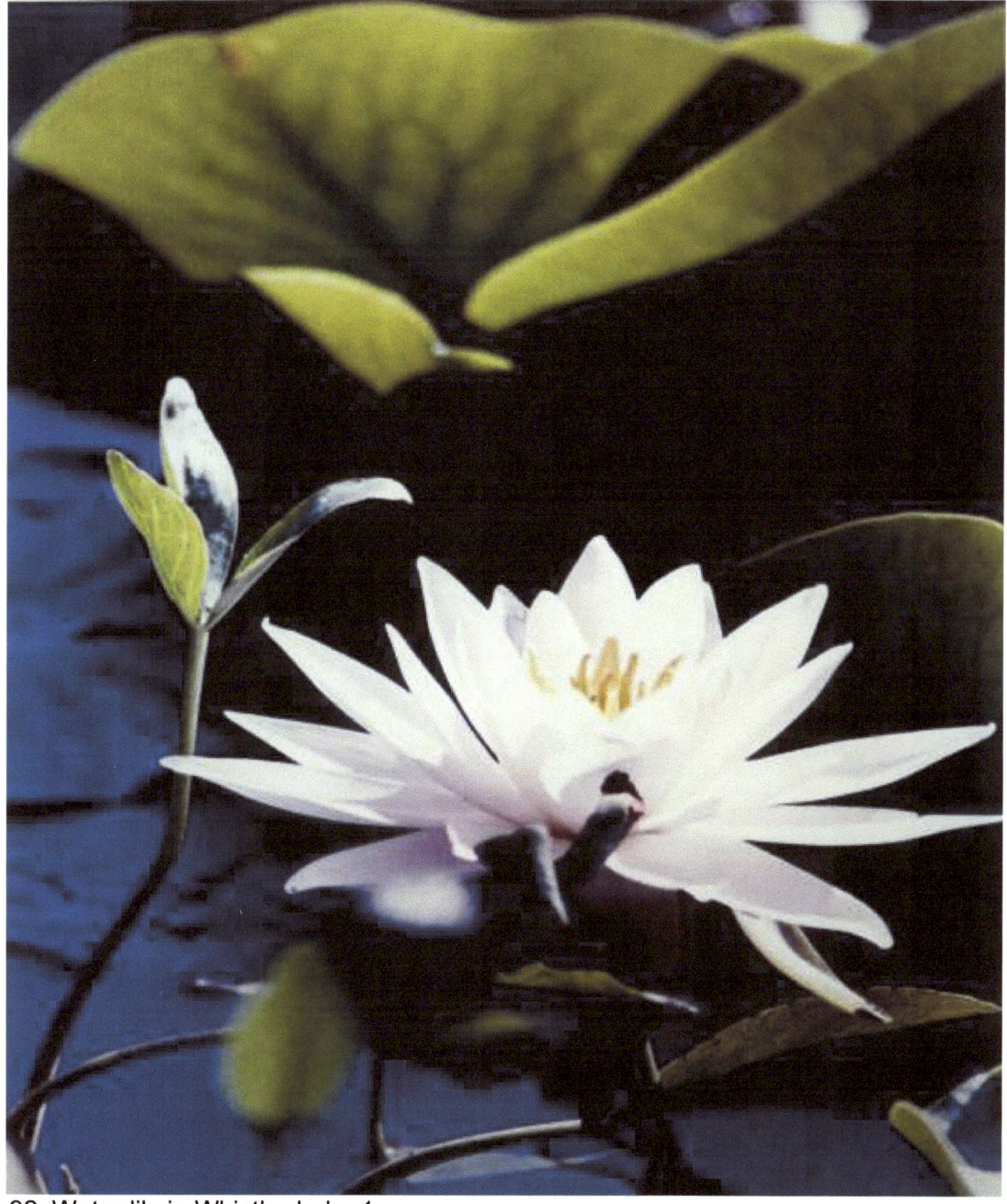

92. Water lily in Whistler Lake 1

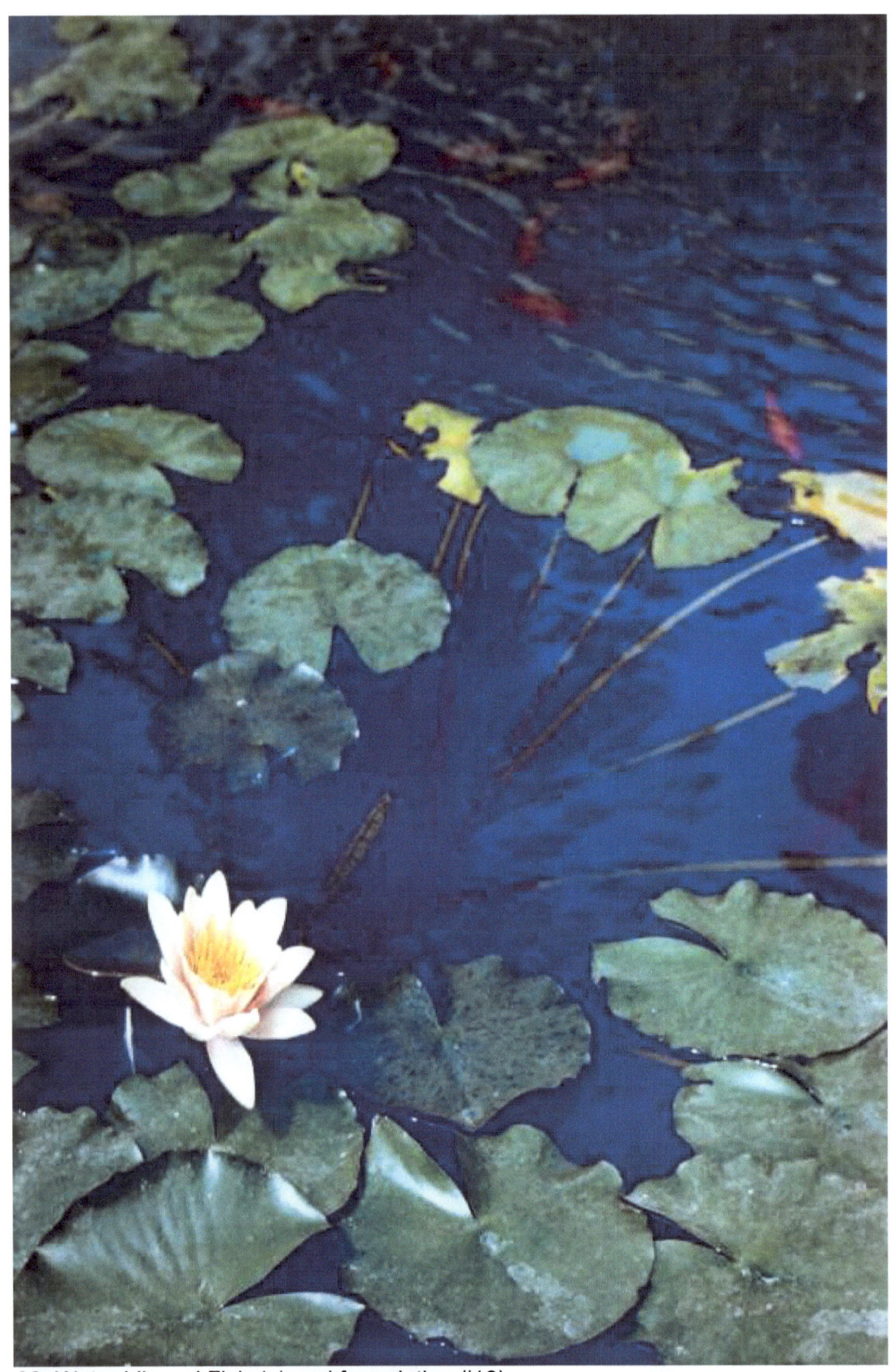

93. Water Lily and Fish 1 (used for painting #18)

94. Water Lily and Fish 3

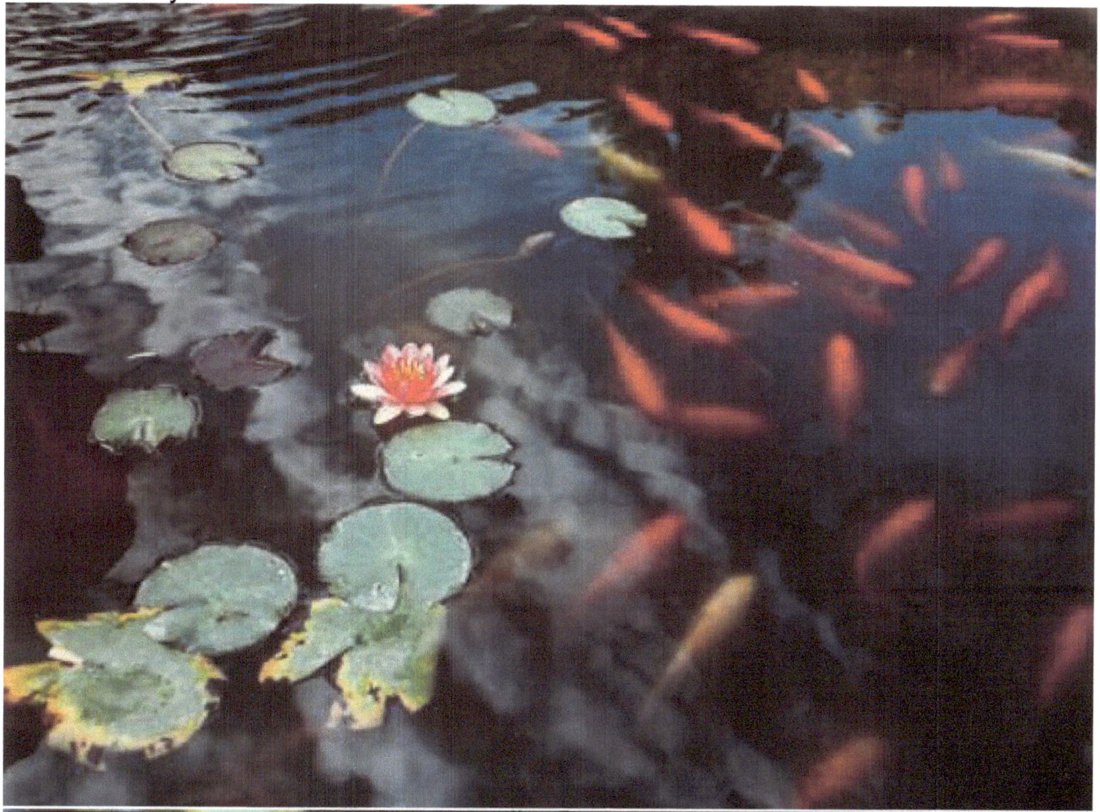

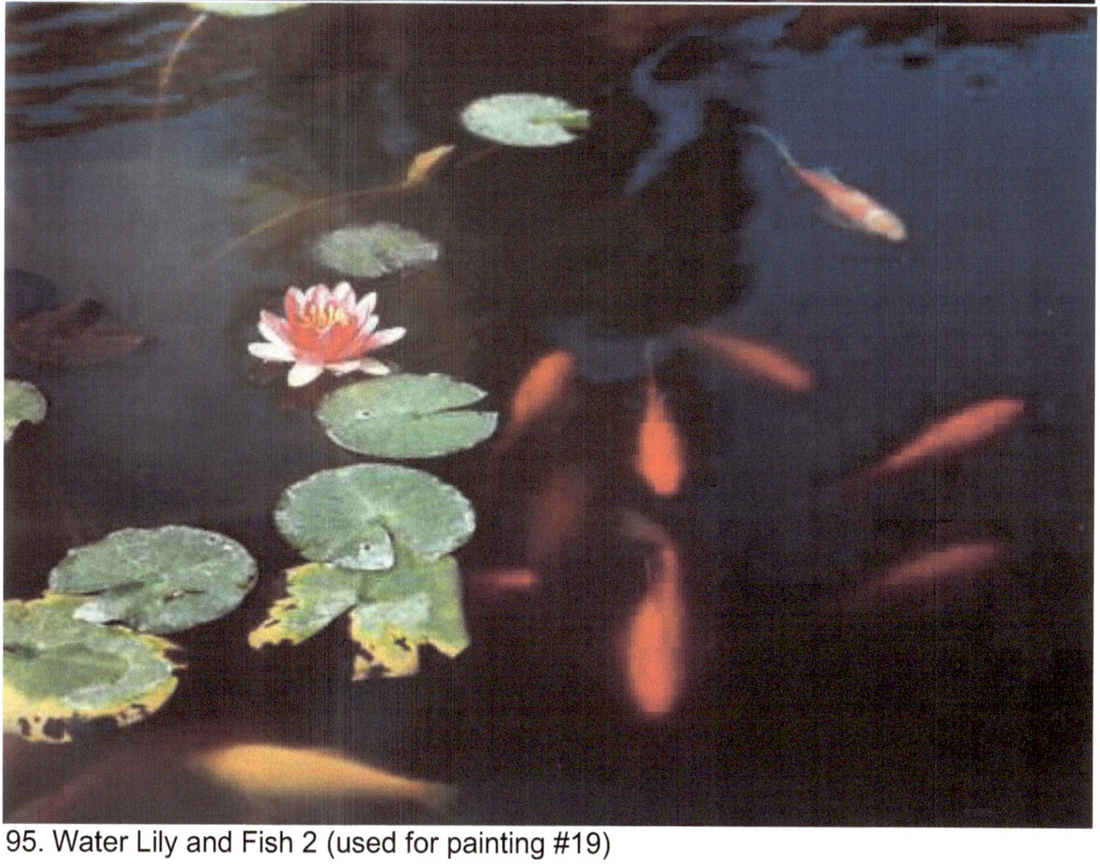

95. Water Lily and Fish 2 (used for painting #19)

96. Water lilies in Whistler Lake 2 (used for painting #109)

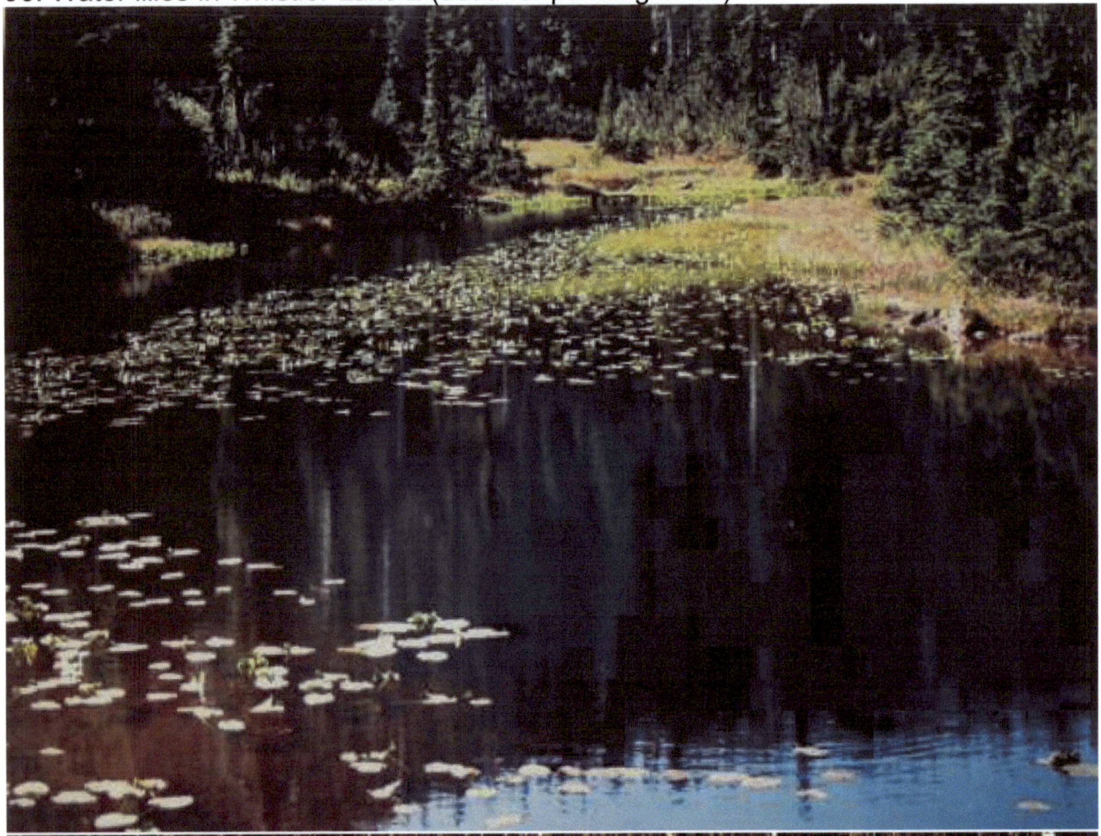

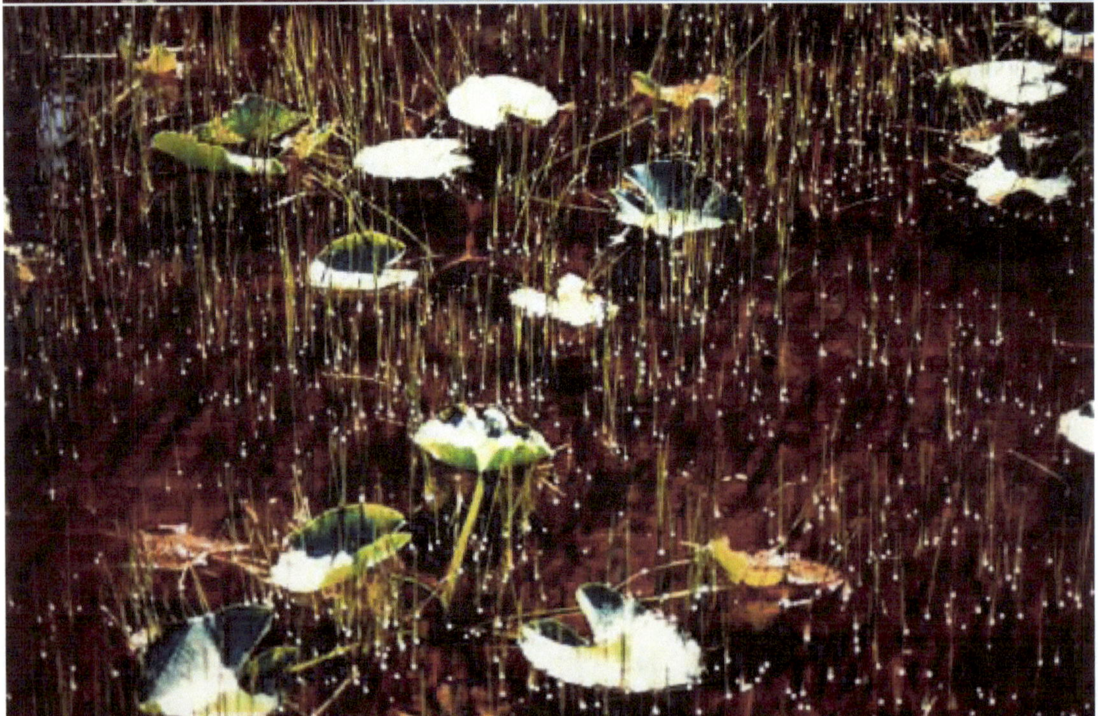

97. Water lilies in Whistler Lake 3

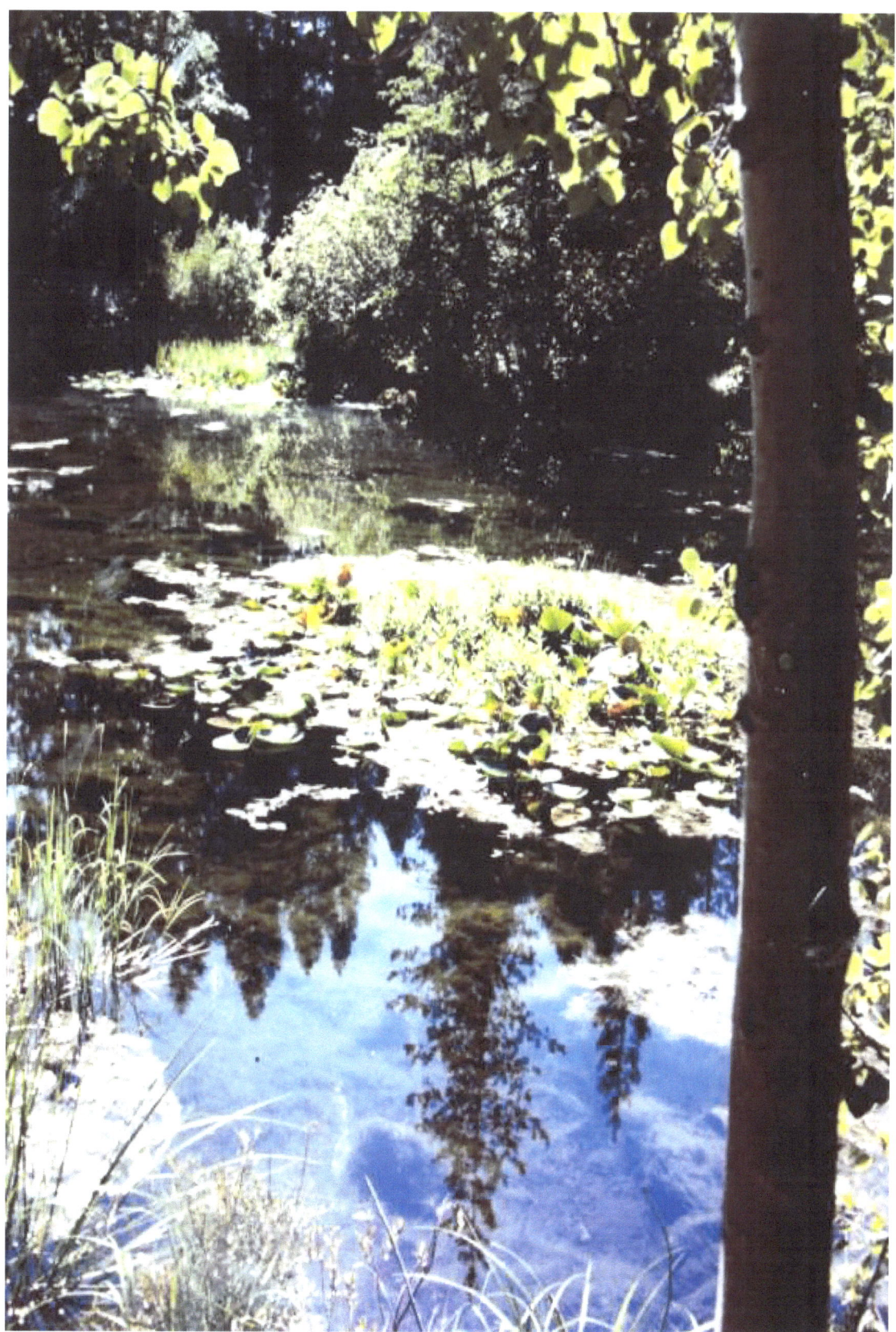
98. Water lilies at Whistler 4 (used for painting #21)

Arts' Value and Outlook

The purpose and value of art, including mere artistic writing, are becoming less defensible as humanity is rushing towards annihilation and people must just strive to survive mentally and physically. Propagating or expecting a wide acknowledgment of this harsh idea among people is surely naive. Worse, this outlook about art applies to many other social pastimes that we are addicted to these days, including senseless movies and shows, sports, etc. At the same time, reversing humans' looming destiny is impossible without a universal acceptance of these sad facts and without everybody's commitment to rebuild new social mechanisms often at the cost of undermining their personal selfish desires, including artistic expressions—*such a wishful thinking!*

In *About My Paintings* book, I have quoted some philosophical points by Emil Zola and Sergei Rachmaninov regarding the value and purpose of art. Accordingly, another quote by Celen Sabbarin* in 1886 about Monet's paintings under the heading of *Science and Philosophy in Art* seems suitable for this book as well in line with our artistic efforts and perceptions.

"'Poppies at Giverny' is an expression of hopelessness, of the unattainableness of absolute truth, and a confirmation of science's teachings, in the ultimate uselessness of human efforts. To the appreciative such a picture would be unbearable as a constant companion; though it is the crowing effort of Monet's genius, and proclaims him the philosopher of the impressionist school.

The mathematical principles are fully expressed in this picture, and vivify the thought that geometry is soulless, and that natural forces are relentless and pitiless… Monet does not offer any solution to the result to which his pictures lead. He is occupied in giving expression to the most serious truths of our life. He is recording the chronicles of modern thought." *Monet, A Retrospective,* Edited by Charles F. Stuckey; Published by Hugh Lauter Levin Associates, 1985, page 127.

To me, Helen's words, especially the first sentence, are succinct, although made fourteen decades ago when the situation with humans' mentalities and welfare had not been as catastrophic and hopeless as it is now. I also wonder if her rather short life, in spite of her major triumphs, had somewhat related to her state of mind! How sad she would be if she lived today and how she would find the right words to express her utter disappointment with humans' uncultivated mentality?

Would she choose to live among us even with a new pseudonym?!

Most likely my pessimism about both humans' chance of salvation and the value of art is much higher than Helen's, as evident in my writings and analyses of facts regarding our immature social priorities and ideologies, such as freedom, democracy, and capitalism. In fact, judging the way humans have historically behaved against their long-term welfare in favour of their immediate interests and pleasure, they will most likely become only less cognizant of their priorities as humanity dwindles. Instead, they will cherish art, sports, movies, and all other unessential activities even more to amuse themselves in their showy societies and lifestyles, while becoming even less capable or interested in realizing humans' true needs and the harsh facts of life.

Still, grasping photography's few unique values feels warranted and has goaded this book, too, as explained on page 10 in *Magic of a Click* section. For one thing, photographing objects, people, and ourselves simply gives us the chance to eternalize

---

* Celen Sabbarin is the pseudonym for **Helen Abbott** (1857-1904), an American who studied piano in Paris from 1878-1881 and later became a biochemist and doctor.

or recall some special moments in our lives. In particular, the power of rejuvenating a special moment or satiating our souls with memories that some photographs trigger in us, such as my dad's portrait (#100) or birds pictures for me, is authentic and hardly possible by a painting, despite the beauty and feeling that some paintings emanate as well. The exact effects of lights, colours, and delight that some photos of nature and humans erupt cannot be captured in a painting truthfully and convincingly for our ultra sensitive psyches that always seek authenticity and spontaneity.

This *personal* merit of photography is stressed here, since rarely our photos find public appeal as artistic products as well—so unlike other art forms where a person's mere knack to offer a novel effect makes him/her a kind of artist, even if it sounds or looks odd. *Gosh, how bizarre and useless our modern arts and music are becoming!!*

The above general observation was mainly for making a few points. **First,** this book's intended title was Stories, Meanings, and Memories behind My Paintings. The crucial words 'Meanings and Memories' were dropped for brevity and eluding possible redundancy. **Second,** a few simple photos, such as #57 (Howe Sound) and #100 (my dad), had required ample remarks about my special mood and memory when I had taken them and now, especially since I often speak with my dad's spirit through his portrait about our ironically similar fates. This point is elaborated in the next section. **Third,** to stress on the value of some pictures that awaken these types of profound personal sentiments, enrich our psyches, and stir our urge for self-exploration. **Fourth,** these words might justify my motive for including a few personal stories in the next few sections, as well as three particularly sentimental pictures in Appendix B.

A Splendid Memory

As much as my self-portrait at the age of 17 (on the back cover) tickles me with an amusing embarrassment about my mindset at the time, I have always cherished my sudden urge to photograph my father when I visited him in Los Angeles in 1982. The significance of my abrupt courage, finally at the age of 37, to ask my dad's permission to take his picture and his initial shock, followed by a delight relief perhaps, triggered a superb moment for me and possibly him, too, as I believed he had felt my deep love and respect for him, despite our historical controversies and convoluted relation for so long. Surely, these words, especially the ones underlined, sound weird in this day and age, but they reflect the precious basic family values that had enriched our mindsets in the past, which are now sadly replaced with vain symbols of civilization and ruined our cultures and kids.

Many incidents had damaged the senses of trust and passion between the father and son, including a highly emotional event that is elaborated in my novel *Midnight Gate-opener*, plus the incident that caused his outburst about my grandma's pictures explained on pages 74-6 of this book. Until that historical day in Los Angeles in 1982, I had never had an urge to take my father's picture, although I had been photographing many people, including my grandma. The idea had never occurred to me, maybe due to the reserved role that fathers played in families those days, especially in nations with traditional family structures. Maybe I had only respected that barrier or never felt a desire to take his picture due to our tainted relationship. However, I had felt both brave and delighted that special day in LA to use the opportunity of taking his portrait next to his beloved tape-recorder. Then, we had sat and talked serenely for hours after so long. He was 62 years old at the time, but his portrait shows how much younger and more charismatic he had looked compared to me at the same age in 2006 going by my self-portrait painting on the back cover of *About My paintings*.

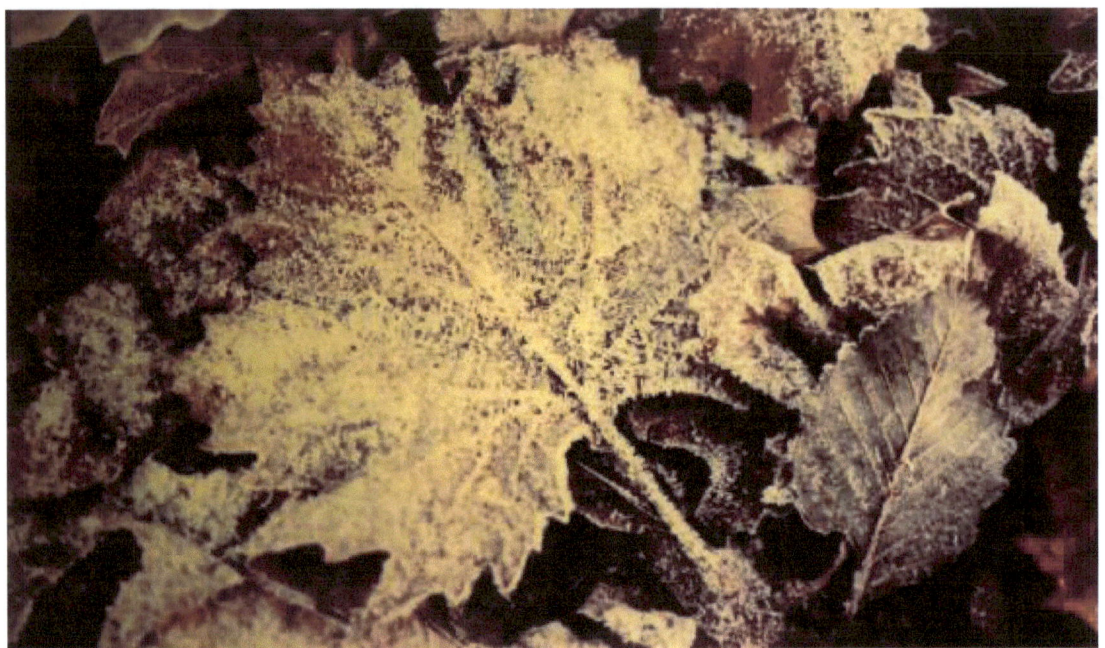

99. Frosted Leaves 2

My sudden desire to photograph my dad for the first time had been heartfelt after our lifetime bizarre, confusing relationship—*something like frosted leaves of a tree!*

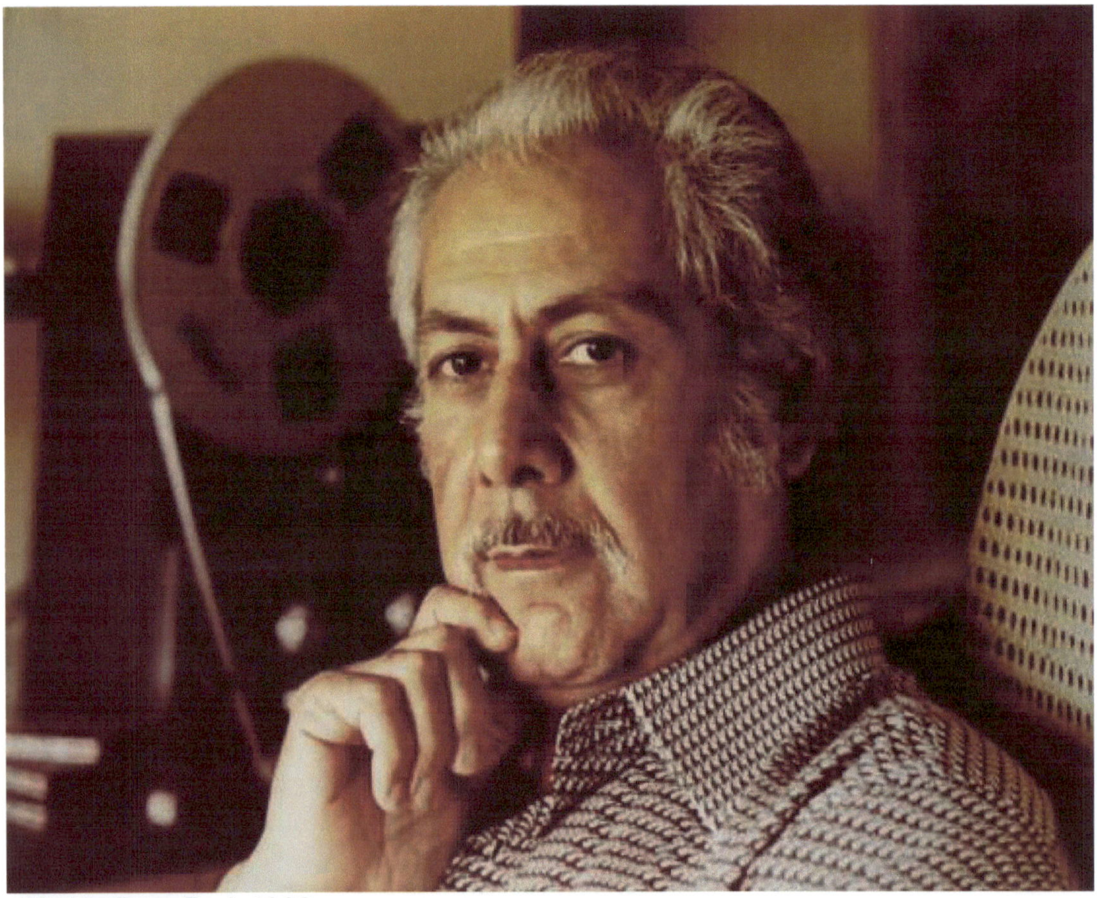

100. My Dear Dad, 1982.

The simple, unique property of photos to eternalize our memories of people and events was stressed before. Sometimes, however, this subtle power of photography becomes ultra precious when it stirs very special moments and enriches our souls forever. A few of my photographs trigger this unique sentiment in me, especially my father's portrait shown above by making that particular moment and my dad eternal for me. Including that portrait in this book seemed useful also for giving readers a chance to associate my words about him with a face—a common urge to satiate our inquisitive psyches, which photography fulfils best. *Many unique merits of photography are being unravelled, eh?!* Moreover, I wished to begin on a good note by expressing my sincere gratitude to my dear dad before mentioning some of his weaknesses and my rather convoluted feelings about him in the next two sections.

Sadly, my dad had apparently failed to fulfil his dream of fathoming a sensible path for a meaningful existence that he had seemed eager to discover. In spite of his active professional and emotional life, including many mistresses and love affairs, he lived lonely rather desolately after probably realizing that no amount of self-gratification could calm his need for self-exploration and artistic expressions. He and I, and possibly my son as well, seem to have been inflicted by the same type and level of curiosities with most likely similar sad endings for us as well. He was meticulous in dressing up and keeping a pleasant appearance, including a precise trimming of his mustache and sideburns almost daily after every shave.

After living in Los Angles for a decade and getting fed up with life and women in that environment as well, my father returned to Iran and I never saw him again after my immigration to Canada in 1982, except for his visit to Vancouver in hopes of at least seeing his grandchildren. Unfortunately, my ex-wife's chronic disrespect and apathy persuaded him to go stay in a hotel for a week before returning to Iran. I met him a few times, but never got the insight to apologize for our bad behaviour and his lost opportunity to learn even a little about his grandchildren. My brothers living in California had shown similar apathy to him, however he succeeded in keeping his cool and staying clear of his unfeeling family with some admirable patience and integrity. He stuck to his pride and lived alone for the rest of his life, while we (his ungrateful children) remained distracted with our own immediate obligations with no opportunity to explore the meaning of compassion. Sorry dad.

The temptation to paint my dad's picture haunted me a long time during 1990s, but I decided that no matter how good the outcome, it could never portray the sincerity and spontaneity of the above picture, which has been hung in my study and giving me a lot of energy daily to endure life. Instead, I painted two portraits of Luciano Pavarotti whose voice my dad never stopped admiring and listening to. Luciano's portraits are printed in *About My Painting* book. *This story also explains my particular reason for painting Pavarotti out of many other people who have also deserved my artistic rendition of them or whose characters I have admired!! My dad and I sharing lots of interests and admirations for certain celebrities has been curious in itself.*

The Father and Son: Subtle Rivalries and Affections

Confessing to my mushy feelings for my father in the last section surely revealed a lot about my current mindset and psyche, but it also felt useful for commemorating him as a rather artistic and passionate person, in spite of his shortfalls as a parent. Especially, I am grateful to him for inadvertently making me ponder life's realities more closely later in my life, instead of following vain social norms and teachings that ruin people's minds and sense of humility. Introducing me to photography had been useful for developing my passions for painting, writing, and academic research in social issues, too. At the same time, including a few comical or historical tales in this section about his wild life and our subtle confrontations is mainly for demonstrating the daunting effects of the so-called modern lifestyles and demands on family and social health, which lead to torturous, confusing lives for most parents and children in depressing environments.

As noted briefly in the Introduction, my dad suddenly gave me his beloved Zeiss Ikon camera when he returned to Iran from his 3-months tour of Europe with a fancy Canon camera and Mercedes. He also thought me the main principles of photography. Maybe he simply did not have any use for his old camera or was only hoping to make up for his neglect of his family for so long rather selfishly. All summer, my depressed, vengeful mother had cried in private and cursed him in public any chance she had found, especially around her so-called friends who had teased her for enduring a womanizing, carefree husband. Her outstanding talent to exaggerate his atrocities and badmouth him had just killed the last grains of hope that my siblings and I could have mustered about the possibility of ever tasting the meaning of family.

Many traumas during childhood had already tainted my brothers' and my lives, as we could not fathom the complexities of life, marital conundrums, and humans' idiocies in general. My novel, *Midnight Gate-opener,* reveals more details about that dire period with my dad being the second antagonist after me. It is mostly a comical tribute to my parents around the story of a curious boy hoping to make sense of life, while his fragile psyche is strained by a weird family daily. The main event causing a subtle encounter and hostility between the father and son for years before we made up in a soothing manner is explained in the novel. *Those comical, melodramatic incidents might prove illuminating for some curious readers!* Yet, quoting a few funny stories from that novel about small rivalries between the father and son seems suitable here just for fun.

I always believed my dad was a nice gentleman overall when compared with other people, especially men, who are usually so full of themselves for no reason at all other than their inherent arrogance built around their ignorance or possibly their wealth. My dad was at least cultured and kind in some respects and had many artistic talents that he had nurtured passionately, especially in music. He was a rather good violinist and performed in community orchestras voluntarily just as a hobby, while he pursued a serious career in government. He liked gardening and had archived a large collection of classical music and operas that he enjoyed regularly, usually alone; or he went to classical performances in Tehran and Los Angeles after divorcing my mom and going to live in the US—most likely with big hopes about the chance of rebuilding some form of relationship with his sons who lived in California. He often had a female companion when going to operas and symphonies, yet lived and died lonely in a gloomy manner —the same destiny I appear to be pursuing hopelessly as well. He was a charismatic, bemused man that women exploited for relieving their own loneliness and martial issues, sometime despite their seemingly intimate friendships with my mom or maybe even out of spite for her on a few occasions. It was all a big mess to endure in the end, I tell you, especially when I was drawn into one of those romantic episodes. I learned so much about adults, especially women, during adolescence and lost my innocence early on. The way women competed amongst themselves to lure my dad for various reasons was amazing and amusing for me as a naïve, curious lad. Especially, married women in their thirties and forties behaving so vulgarly singed my heart during teens, in spite of the female attention I was also enjoying. Then again, humans have never stopped teaching me new lessons all along. It has simply been too disheartening and amazing to witness people's accelerating urge for more vanity and arrogance the more modern they claim to become, which has then turned me into such a cynical individual.

My dad looked bewildered in the end after trying so much to manage his life and cope with a dysfunctional marriage for thirty years until my mom finally asked him for a divorce. He looked gloomy despite all his fun, sins, and solo excursions for decades, most likely as his desperate way of coping with marital issues. Sometime, his subtle love for his children was obvious, while also suffering his helplessness to express his feelings for them or guide them due to family structure per se—especially my mom's crooked way of seeing life, badmouthing habit, and ignoring the purpose of marriage. Obviously, both my parents had played their roles in pushing each other into deeper desperation and retaliations in their own crooked ways at the cost of ruining our family.

My novel, *Midnight Gate-opener,* offer many details about those elucidating times, including my father's convoluted feelings for his kids. They reveal plenty of secrets and atrocities related to those vulgar adults, too, yet I do not think they mind my openness now that they must have all joined the eternity if they have at least respected 'hundred' as the maximum human life expectancy. Honestly, the manner they sinned so proudly, they probably would not have minded if their secrets had come out even then, as most of them had turned into public gossips, anyway. Ironically, their kids' tortures about the same things I saw and felt singed my heart, too, while trying to read their minds behind their petrified looks about their vulgar mothers' flirtation, and possible affairs, with my dad so casually, while their fathers looked so sad and helpless! Then, sometimes, I felt ashamed and guilty, too, for being the son of a man who had been an instrument for, if not the main root of, their parents' misery. Often, I wished I was allowed to bring my camera to those regular parties to take pictures, especially of those kids' frightened, perplexed faces. All those gross lessons about humans' characters and sexuality, along with a sense of narcissism women were instilling in me, had probably goaded me to take that silly self-portrait on the back cover, too!

Another related incident is included in the following section mostly as my sincere tribute to my late grandma and dad, but also for fun. It outlines a conflicting, comical incident between the father and son after I took a bunch of pictures of my religious grandma (his mom). Sadly, I do not have those great pictures to include in this book. Luckily, at least my dad's portrait, #100, still hangs in my study and we chat about old times occasionally. Ironically, the portrait I had painted of my son also hangs next to my dad's picture, but we do not chat much due to my son's zeal to keep me out of his mind or even humiliate me. Now, all those memories also give me a certain level of appreciation for the Islamic revolution forcing Iranians out of their immature craving for immoralities of the Western societies that were spreading so fast during the Shah's regime and contaminating our culture.

It feels appropriate to thank my dad also for making me a classical music/operas fanatic inadvertently, like photography, just by playing them regularly any free time he had found inside the house. He did it despite my mom's ongoing nagging about all that atrocious noise according to her. He just kept doing his own things and played those kinds of music loudly with no attention to her complaints. My frustrated mother's wild screams over the sopranos' high notes in operas still ring in my brain when I recall those times. Now, I wonder how my dad had himself become obsessed with classical music in Iran while growing up in a family who at best played only Persian music.

In all, my dad's eternal effect on me, especially about photography and classical music, has engraved my sincere affection for him, while I have always focused on his qualities, subtle affection for his children, and our funny rivalries in taking memorable photos. Particularly admirable had been his gentle character that had allowed our final reconciliation before we had lost touch for good due to life's dreadful demands on me in a narrow-minded, spiteful family of my own.

My Gorgeous Grandma's Lost (Confiscated) Portraits

One of my simpler, sad encounters with my dad is explained by the following scattered excerpt from pages 318-322 of *Midnight Gate-opener* novel. It depicts the humour of existence that has become funnier and sadder these days in our abysmal societies.

The problem had begun as I had felt out of touch with my friends and adolescence life after my father had built a big house in the outskirts of Tehran. It had made public transportation, especially at night and winters, cumbersome for a lad with no personal car. Thus, I begged my parents, and they agreed at last with grievance, to let me stay in my grandparents' house most night after my late ventures in the city with my friends. In return, this new system had caused many inconveniences for many people and me for varied reasons, including my artistic endeavours through photography.

*****

When I moved to grandma's house, I realized her potential as a marvellous model for my new artistic expressions (as a photographer). She was very attractive, even for a 66-year-old woman. Her subtle smile and penetrating black eyes gave her such an appealing character and looks… I took a few pictures of her with her Islamic hijab. Taking picture in an informal pose for any unofficial purpose is by itself against the Islamic rules. Yet, she was quite thrilled to model for me with a subtle alluring grin. She looked into the camera with a charm you might expect only from professional models.

I kept abusing my discovery of Grandma more every day. I felt the same kind of pride and ownership over my model that any professional fashion photographer does, nowadays. I asked her to remove her hijab and let me take pictures showing her hair. She obliged with great enthusiasm. Her hair was bundled into a bun behind her head with a hairpin. I asked her to remove the hairpin. She did. I was surprised by the lustrous, long hair she'd been hiding all those years under the hijab. She ran and fetched her comb to straighten the thick, grey hair. She let it slither over her shoulders. I took some thirty or so pictures in that session alone with all kinds of poses and moods. I asked her whether she ever used lipsticks and she said sometimes. So I took a few more pictures with the lipsticks on.

Feeling beautiful and charming are inherent needs of all women at some degree, I reckoned. Even age doesn't change this powerful urge in women. This is true even if you restrict them under the harshest Islamic hijab and rules all their lives. Past their initial shyness, they most likely won't refuse showing off their charm if the opportunity arrives. Grandma proved she wasn't an exception. At 66, she surely imagined it was her last chance to leave behind a trace of her allure and beauty. I was her last hope to immortalize herself. (So she was abusing me, too, in fact!) Of course, finding such hidden talents in Grandma was rather shocking for me at the beginning. Yet, I didn't stop to ponder my deed's morality. And now I feel guilty for all that callousness, too.

She was really enjoying herself, though, for being properly photographed ever in her life. Meanwhile, I was quite thrilled for my discovery of such an untapped source exposing my artistic genius. I was so excited with the outcome I even had many of those pictures enlarged. I showed them to some guests in a party at our house. Father noticed the pictures and gathered them quickly with incredible anger and disgust. I'd never seen him so frustrated and disappointed in me. He shouted at me in front of the crowd, including Mina, "You should be ashamed of yourself for doing such a sinful thing. How could you force your grandma to do this? How could you make such a religious person agree to show off her hair like this? Or wear lipstick? You bastard!"

I fled to my room scared stiff. I was shocked also because he'd never spoken to me that way. At the same time, I was amazed, because Father had never seemed religious and he was always running after women himself. This was the first time he was showing any kind of religious sensitivity or whatever the heck it was. When I thought about his attitude deeper later, his religious beliefs felt extremely vague and funny. For one thing, he seemed religious enough only for his own mother's benefit, whom I had now sullied with my bad influence! On the other hand, if he had even the slightest faith in Islam, he did not give a damn about his lovers going straight to hell for their lack of hijab and basic Islamic morals, not to mention his role in seducing and sullying those poor souls and spreading so much sin around him wherever he went…

I hid from Father in my bedroom for a few days. Maybe I shouldn't have abused Grandma despite her own enthusiasm and role. But I wished I could tell everybody she was guiltier about this matter than I was. I wanted to explain how she'd encouraged me subtly beyond my belief. I could tell on her but I didn't. I guess this showed a little bit of my decency, after all. I just kept my mouth shut and accepted all the blames. Father was mad at me for one week before trying to make up for his outburst by asking me to go to the movies together—the two of us only. Never again he mentioned the photos, which he'd confiscated. Sometimes, I thought that maybe his harsh reaction had been only a sign of jealousy after he had seen the artistry I'd shown in those colourful pictures. Maybe he wished he'd thought about this subject and taken the pictures himself. Grandma was his mother, after all, not mine! Perhaps he wished he'd immortalized his mom himself, especially now that he'd realized his mom's hidden wishes and proclivity. Maybe he could've even rescued his mom from the religious grip that had ruined her entire life! I don't know! In the end, I couldn't figure out which interpretation matched Father's mind and personality best: Artistic jealousy, a crude Islamic prejudice, or any other complex motive, including his guilt for his own sins.

I felt sorry for Grandma for exposing her feminine tendencies to the whole world, which at the same time revealed her shaky religious beliefs, too. I also felt sorry for all other stuff that Jamal (my uncle) and I had done to her… By the way, Jamal somehow found out about the pictures I'd taken from Grandma, too… He got angry with me even more than Father had. I didn't understand these two atheists, reacting so passionately to such a small matter. Why were these two womanizers so prejudiced and sensitive only about Grandma's hair or wearing lipsticks? What did they have against the art of photography? What had I done wrong? Deep down, however, I felt their sentiments without being quite able to explain it. I knew I'd been wrong. Then again, she'd herself only encouraged me by showing great enthusiasm to participate in my schemes that proved to be crooked only later.

I wondered, when Grandma glared at me those days (when preparing for my grade-twelve exams), if she abhorred me, amongst many other valid reasons, for the fact that my artistry had brought her an everlasting disrepute. She might've felt deeply ashamed after hearing about his sons' overt reactions to the photos. She'd probably been even more surprised about this matter than I had been. Her ultra religious sister and other children had surely scorned her directly, too. Anyway, the bottomline was that I was a bad grandson for so many reasons, especially tainting her image as a devout Muslim. For six years, I'd kept giving her more reasons every day to resent me. And now I feel guilty for not recognizing Grandma's hurt feelings at the time and for not getting a chance to ask for her forgiveness. This is another big curse cast over me forever. Sorry Grandma.

*****

Despite my dire disappointment for not having my grandma's portraits, it has probably also been a blessing for eluding my temptation to include them in this book, plus the big possibility of my dad's continued disapproval even now if I did. It is hard to say how he feels about this matter these days in the heaven, though he probably believes even more now that all religions are simply irrational and God has never been behind the atrocities caused by them. I also prefer to keep my relation with my dad's portrait in my study in its present peaceful, joyous state. *Now, I wonder if this incident with Grandma should be considered another advantage of photography or its likely evil!!*

I also wonder what my dad had done with the grandma's confiscated photos and films, *and why I hadn't lured grandma to take new photos all over secretly this time!*

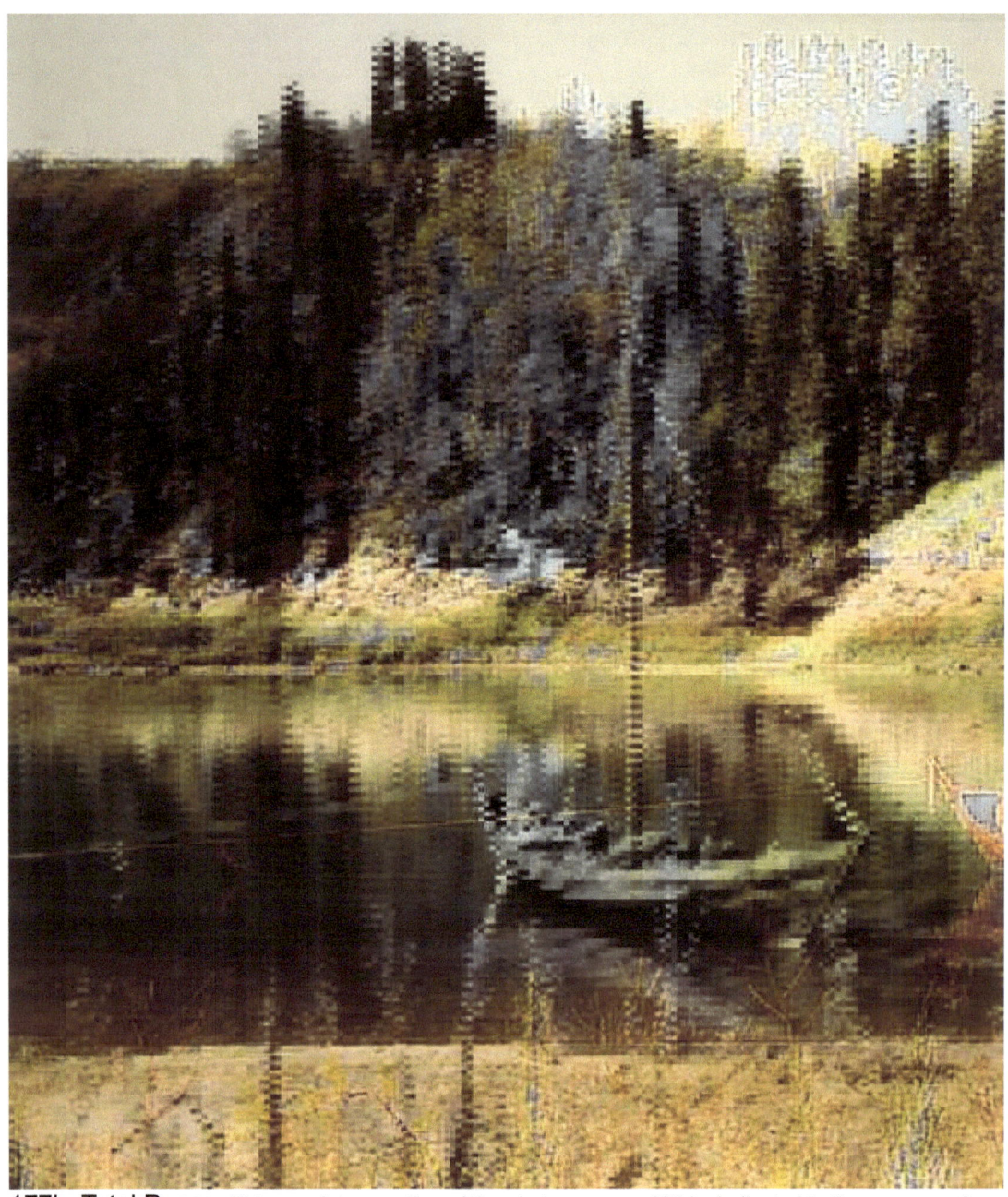

177b. Total Peace: This special recreation of the photo on page 127 is dedicated to the memory of my confused grandma along with my another big apology… **Sorry again Grandma!**

Portraits' Purposes

My sentiments about photographing my father and grandma's faces and painting some portraits, including my son's and my own, have been precious, as elaborated in the last two sections. The tale of painting my self-portrait in 2006 is told in my *About My Paintings* book along with my reason for including its image on that book's back cover. But, mainly, it had been for testing my knack for painting portraits, as a higher level of expertise beyond landscapes. It might have also been for satiating my curious mind's lasting thirst to explore my existence and mental growth thru that self-portrait perhaps! Perhaps I had also meant to eternalize myself in a self-portrait the way many artists do in their older ages, including my idols Monet and Van Gogh!

However, in spite of my big curiosity and embarrassment, I cannot fathom or recall what had made me take that idiotic self-portrait on this book's back cover with so much pride at the age of 17 in the mirror of my mom's dressing table? Is the excuse offered on page 72 plausible?[*] Had it been just for flaunting my emerging manly pride and popularity, especially by insisting to hold a cigarette in my mouth like an idiot adult? I had then printed that black and white film in a large format in my friend's darkroom and hung it in my room for years proudly. Perhaps I had also been testing my artistic knack or possibly even challenging my parents' dislike and nagging about my smoking habit. I had just kept smoking even in my room stealthily with mixed hopes about nobody raising the issue—as had been the case for a year or so. Maybe I had meant to push them to be less tactful and confront me directly at last, instead of bothering me with their annoying hints about their displeasure only in disguise!

It seems that even when our parents happen to be discreet and sympathetic, we sneaky kids like to provoke them whenever we can! Then, we perfect this devious art as adults to hurt one another eternally!!

Surely, a variety of psychological urges motivate us, especially the youths, these days to take thousands of selfies every year—god knows for what use, other than possibly posting them on line and forwarding them to one another to fill our stressful, boring lives. Still, some saner urges also motivate us to photograph or paint our own or somebody else's face. Luckily, delving into these epidemic psychological issues is too complex for me and beyond this book's scope. Still, my cynicism keeps growing about *The Purpose of Portraits*, in particular about the psychology behind so much selfies that people, mainly the youths, are indulging themselves with.

West Vancouver Hills and Mountains

A long stretch of mountains in North and West Vancouver extends to Horseshoe Bay and then up along the Pacific Ocean. Accordingly, it seems I have spent lots of time in the good old days to hike some of those mountain paths and take plenty of pictures that depict nature's infinite moods in various atmospheric conditions, especially at high altitudes. The persistent clouds in Vancouver had apparently also goaded me to go higher and higher on those mountains to increase my chances of taking good pictures, or any photograph at all, above all those dense clouds and fog! The photographs in this section also supplement the images about San Francisco Hills and Horseshoe Bay in the following two sections respectively.

---

[*] All those gross lessons about humans' characters and sexuality, along with a sense of narcissism that women were instilling in me, had probably goaded me to take that silly self-portrait on the back cover of this book, too!

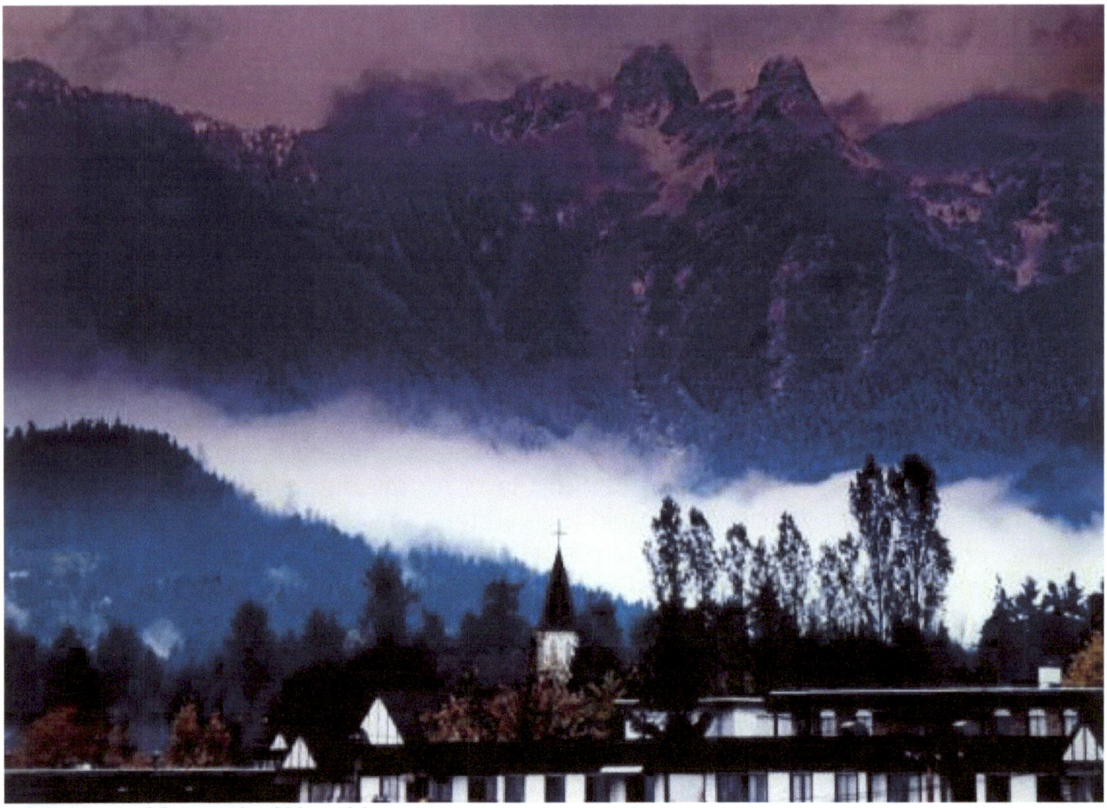

101. Lions Mountain, West Vancouver

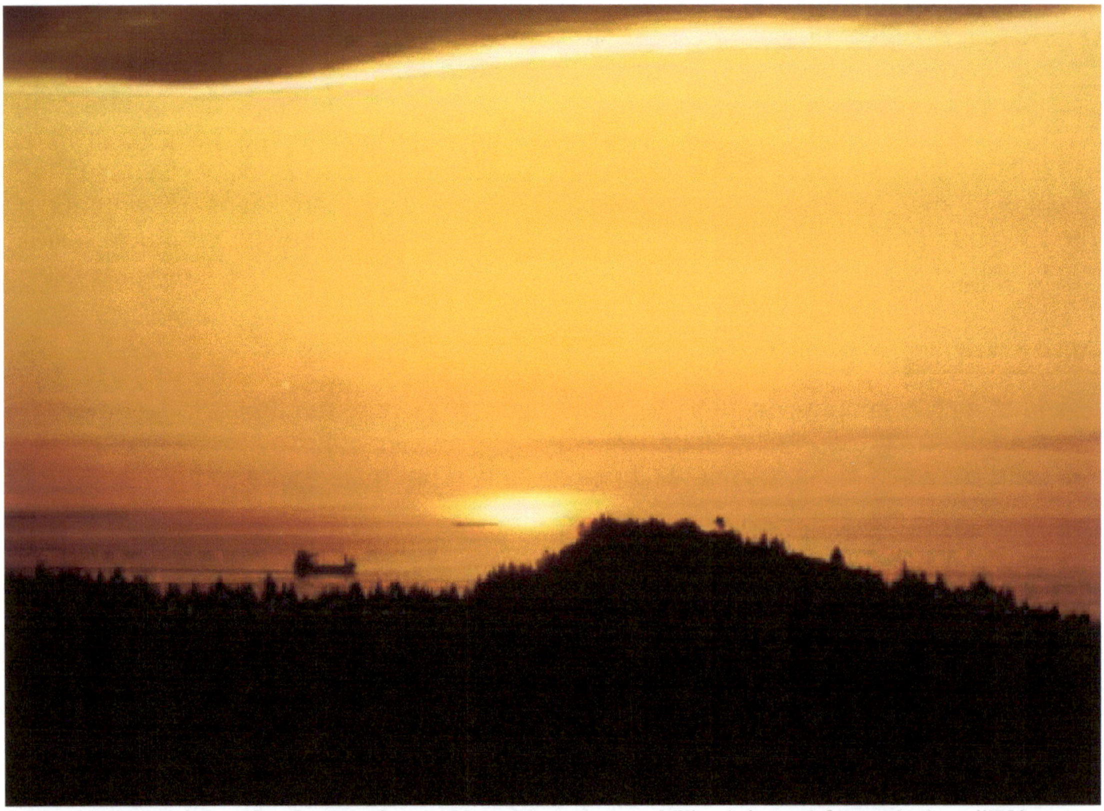

102. A View of Pacific Ocean from West Vancouver Hills 1 (used for painting #78)

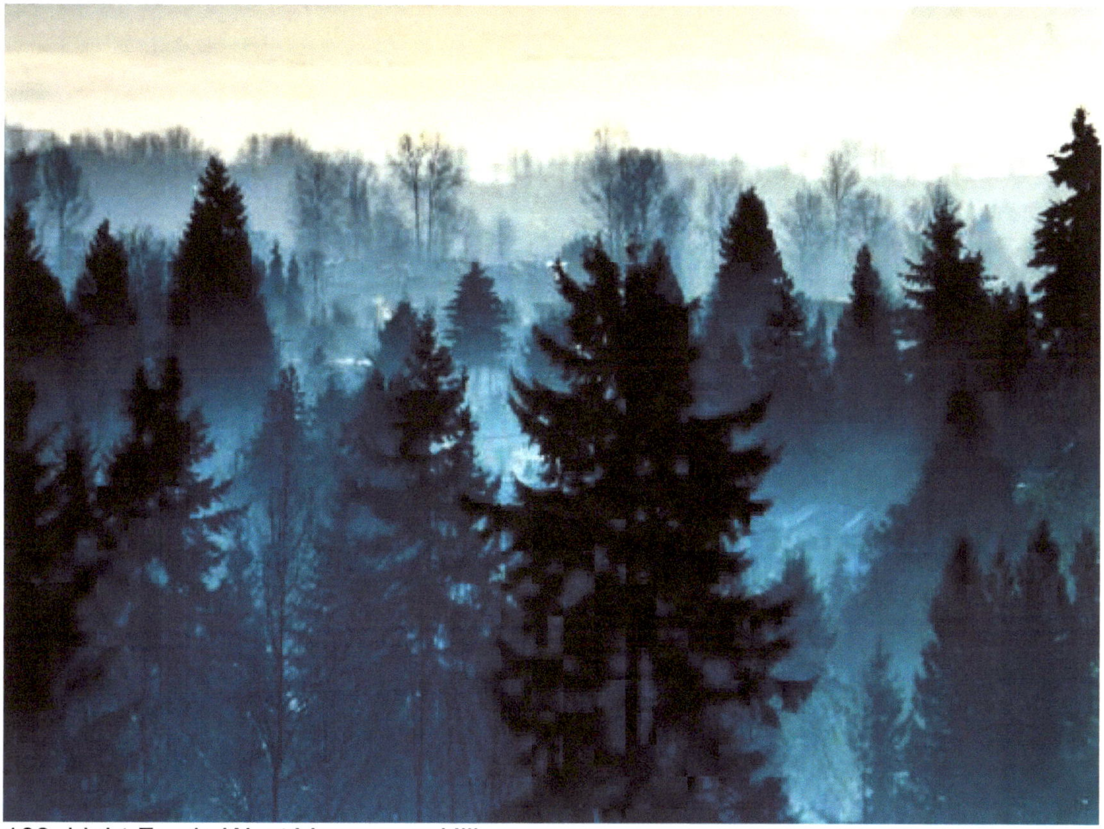

103. Light Fog in West Vancouver Hills

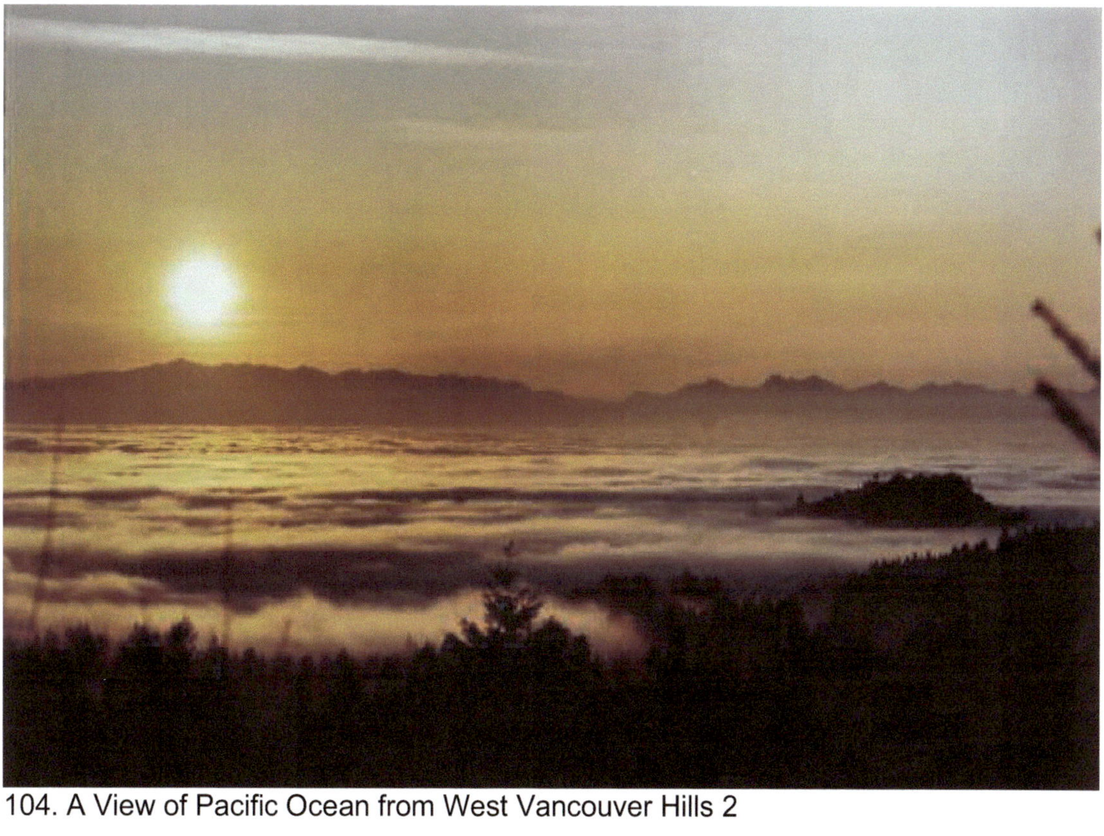

104. A View of Pacific Ocean from West Vancouver Hills 2

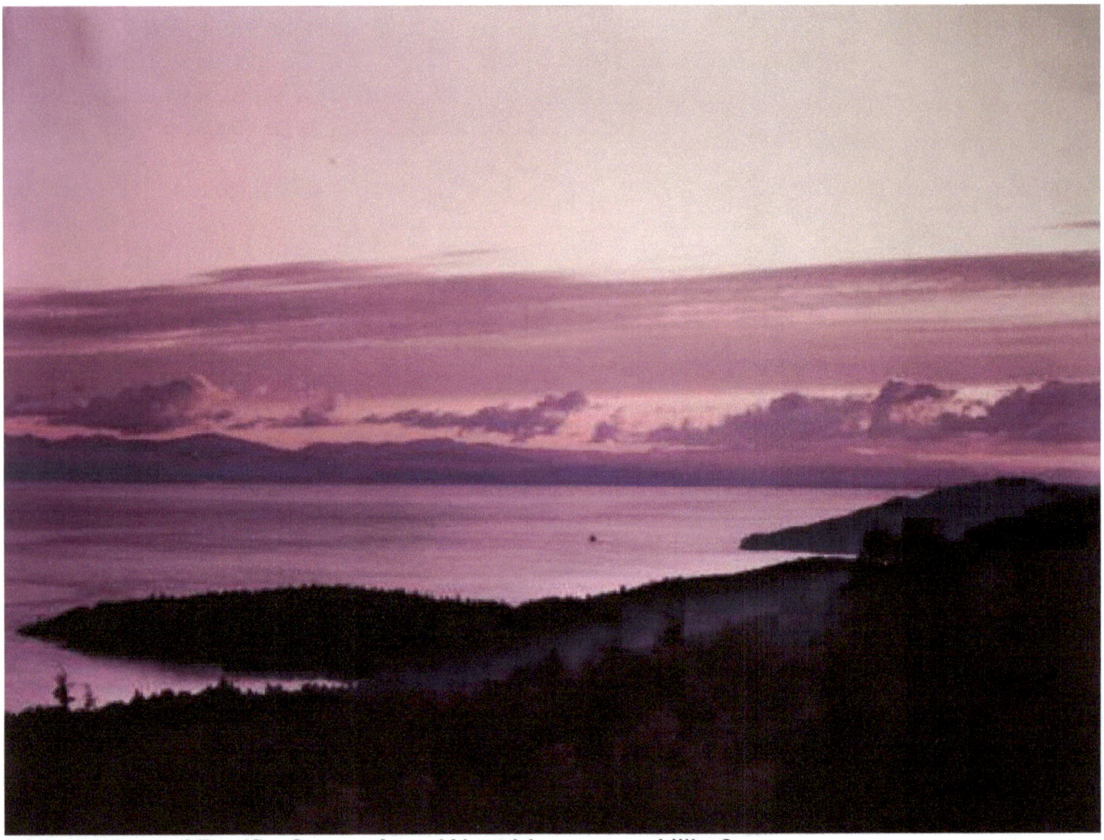

105. A View of Pacific Ocean from West Vancouver Hills 3

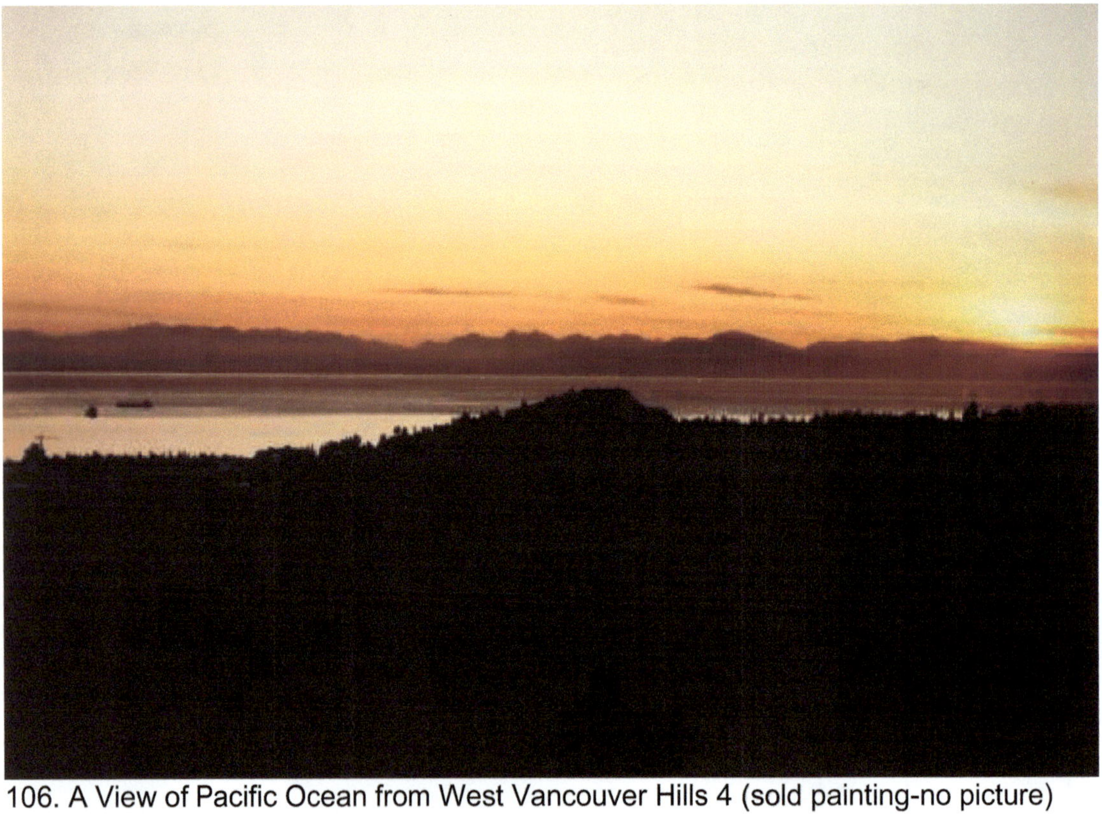

106. A View of Pacific Ocean from West Vancouver Hills 4 (sold painting-no picture)

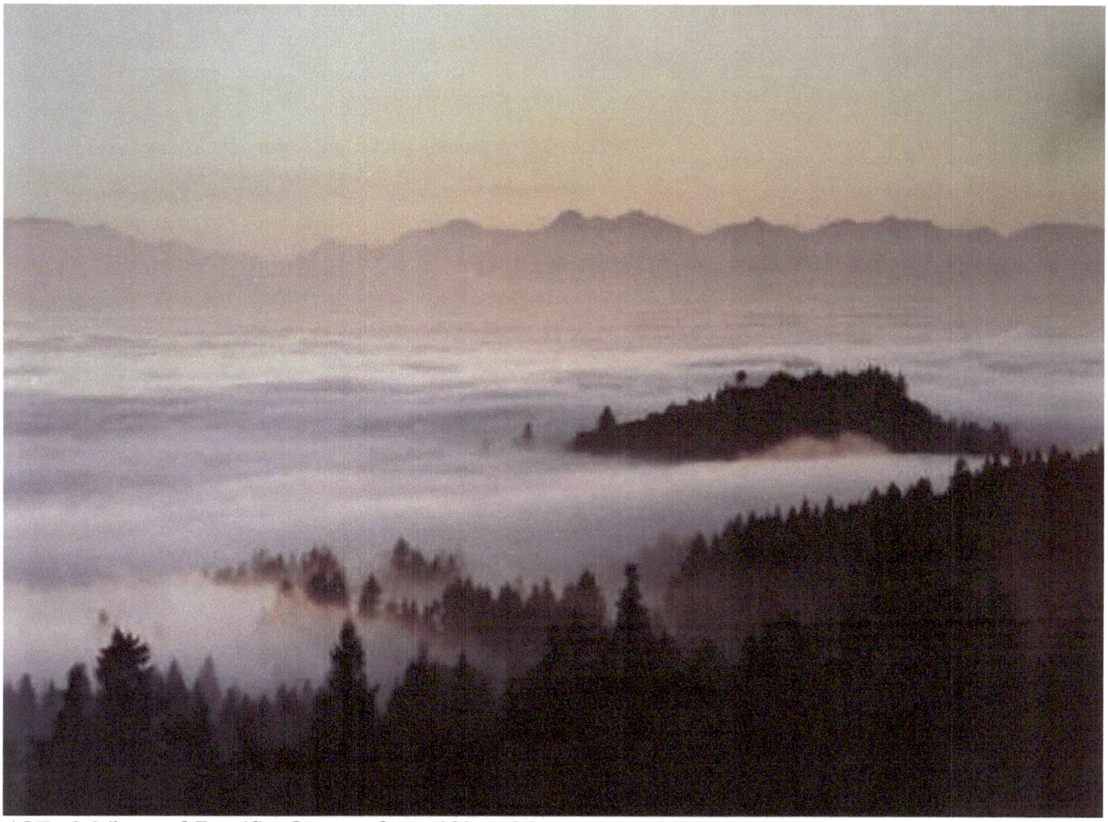

107. A View of Pacific Ocean from West Vancouver Hills 5

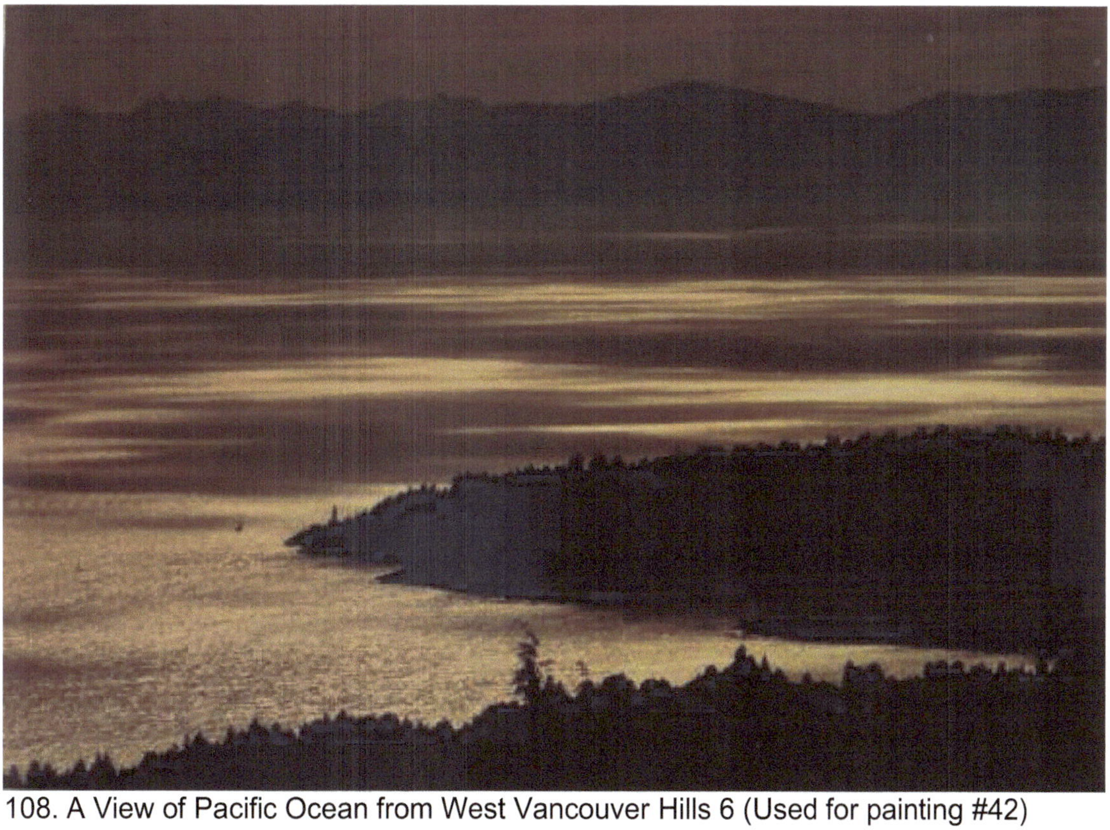

108. A View of Pacific Ocean from West Vancouver Hills 6 (Used for painting #42)

San Francisco Hills

My zeal to explore mountain paths and possibly capture some special ambiences of nature had apparently been quite active in all my travels going by the large number of pictures I had taken in San Francisco hills alone, some of which are included below to complement the ones shown in the previous section.

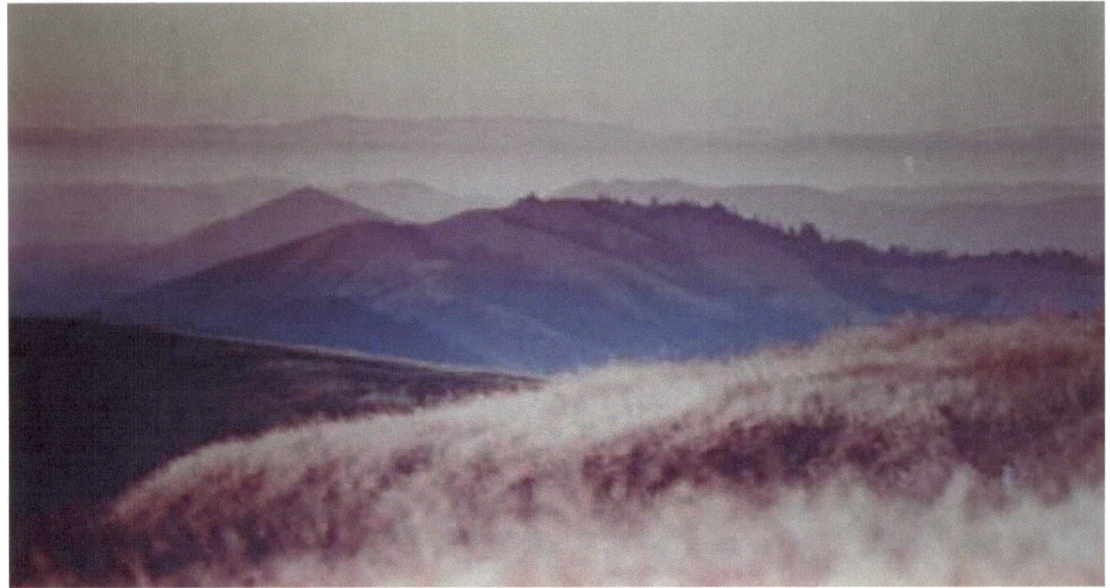

109. San Francisco Hills 2

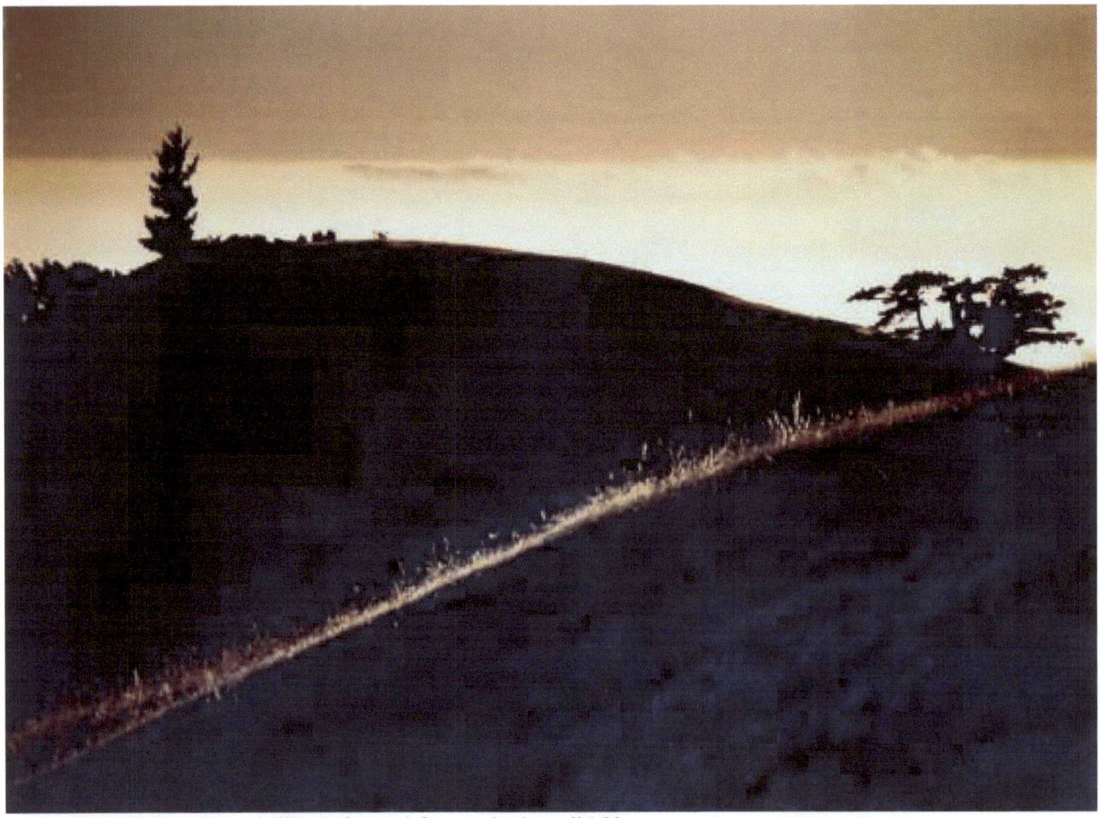

110. San Francisco Hills 1 (used for painting #12)

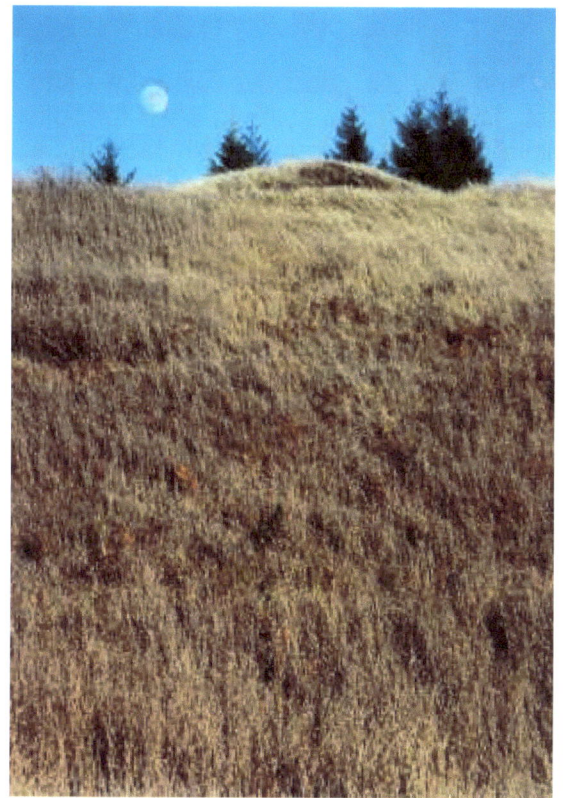
111. San Francisco Hills 3

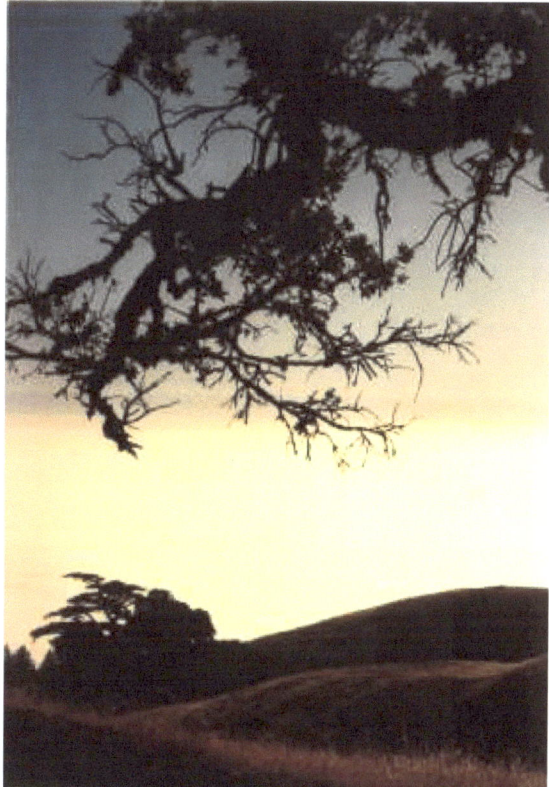
112. San Francisco Hills 4

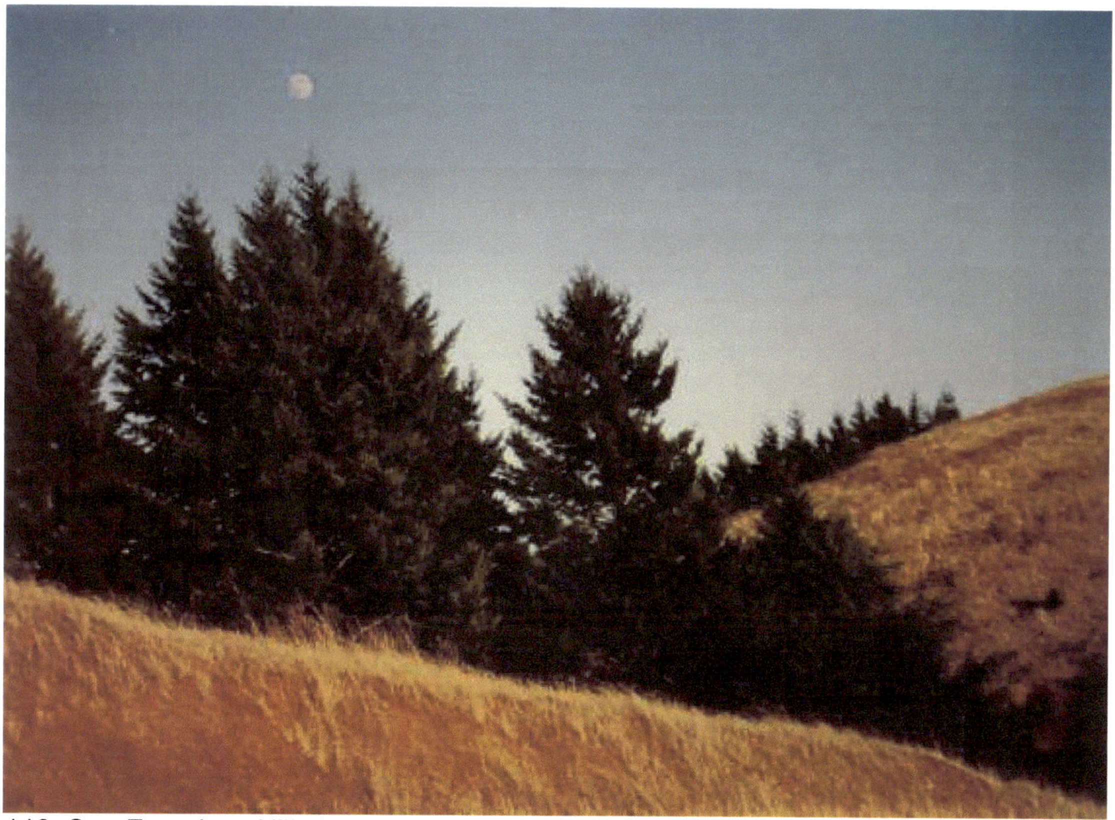

113. San Francisco Hills 5

Horseshoe Bay and Beyond

The cosy city of Horseshoe Bay stands at the end of West Vancouver where we can turn north to explore the Pacific Ocean's coast. The city has drawn me often for both photographic jaunts and deep reflections within the exotic ambience of Whytecliff Park and Howe Sound's breathtaking views. The tale of a sacred revelation at Howe Sound stirring my urge to become a painter is narrated in my novel, *My Lousy Life Stories*, and quoted in *About My Paintings* book, too. Photo #57, page 46, shows that scenery. More photographs from Horseshoe Bay and beyond up to Whistler are offered below.

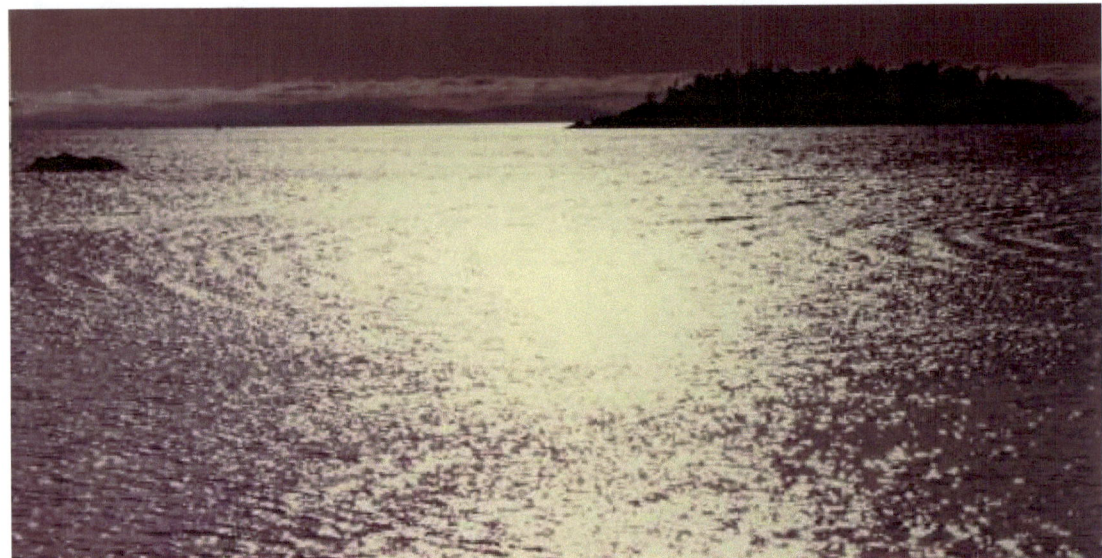

114. Sunset at Horseshoe Bay

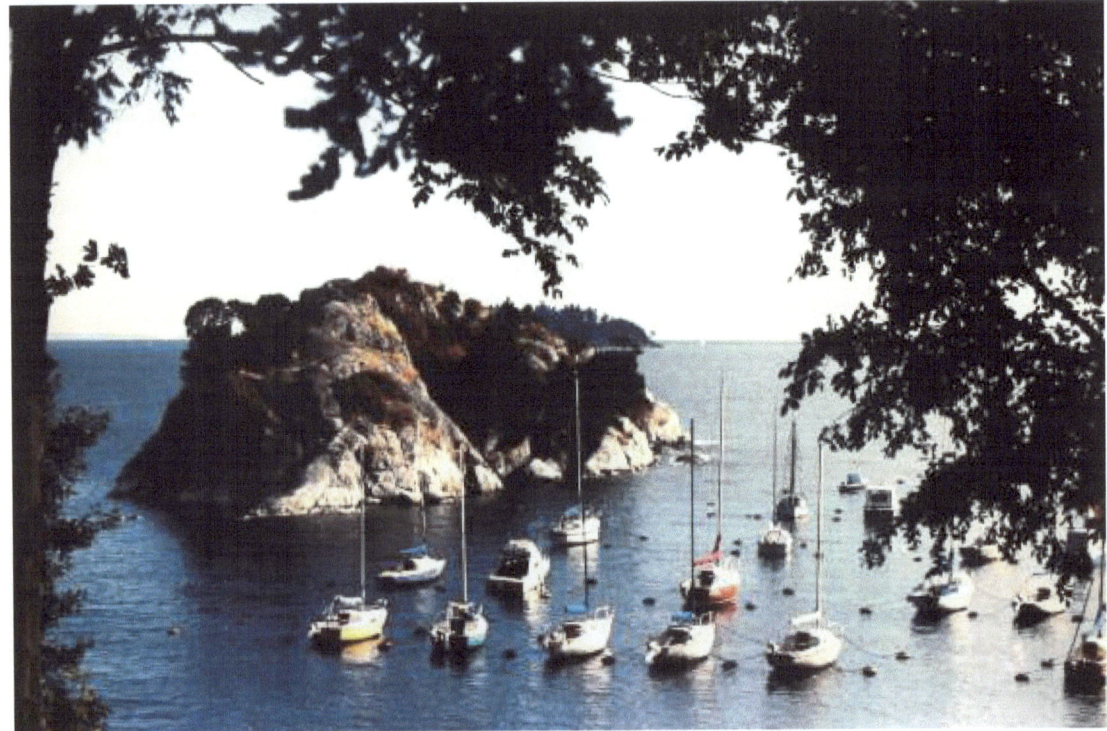

115. Boats Depot at Horseshoe Bay 1

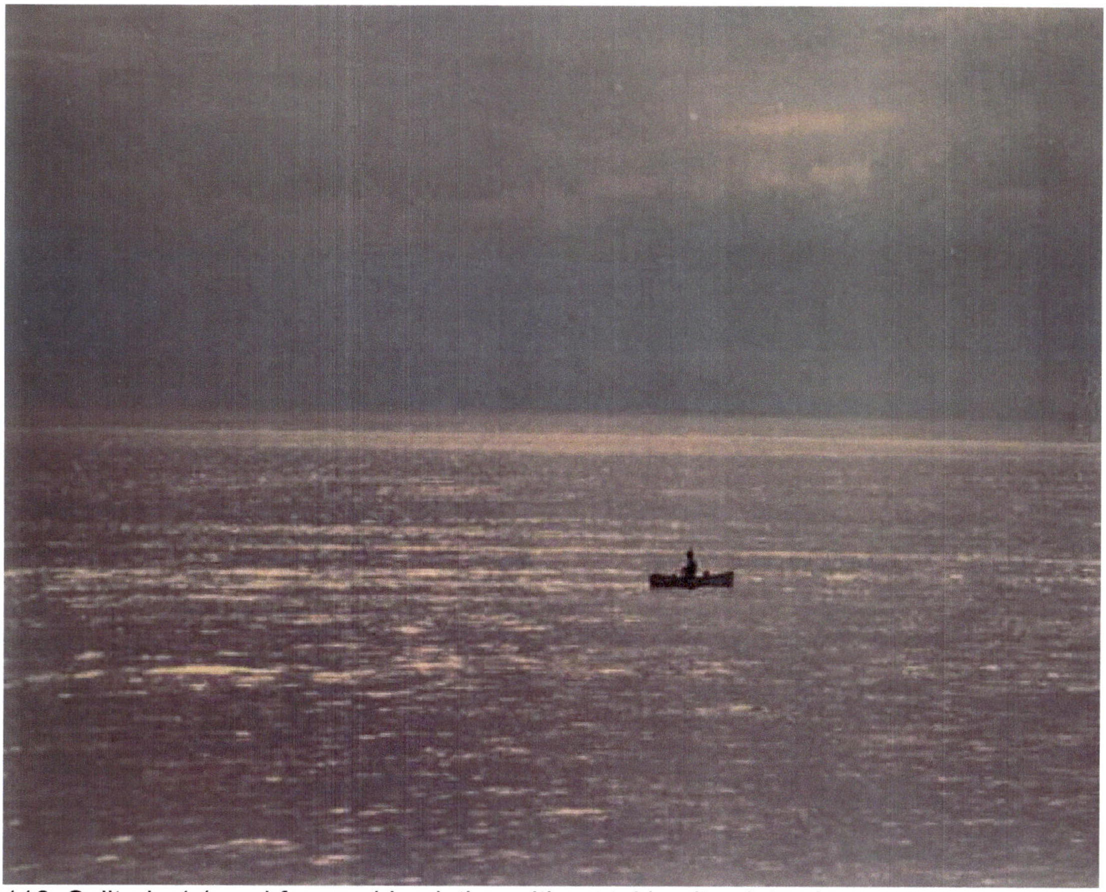

116. Solitude 1 (used for a sold painting without taking its picture)

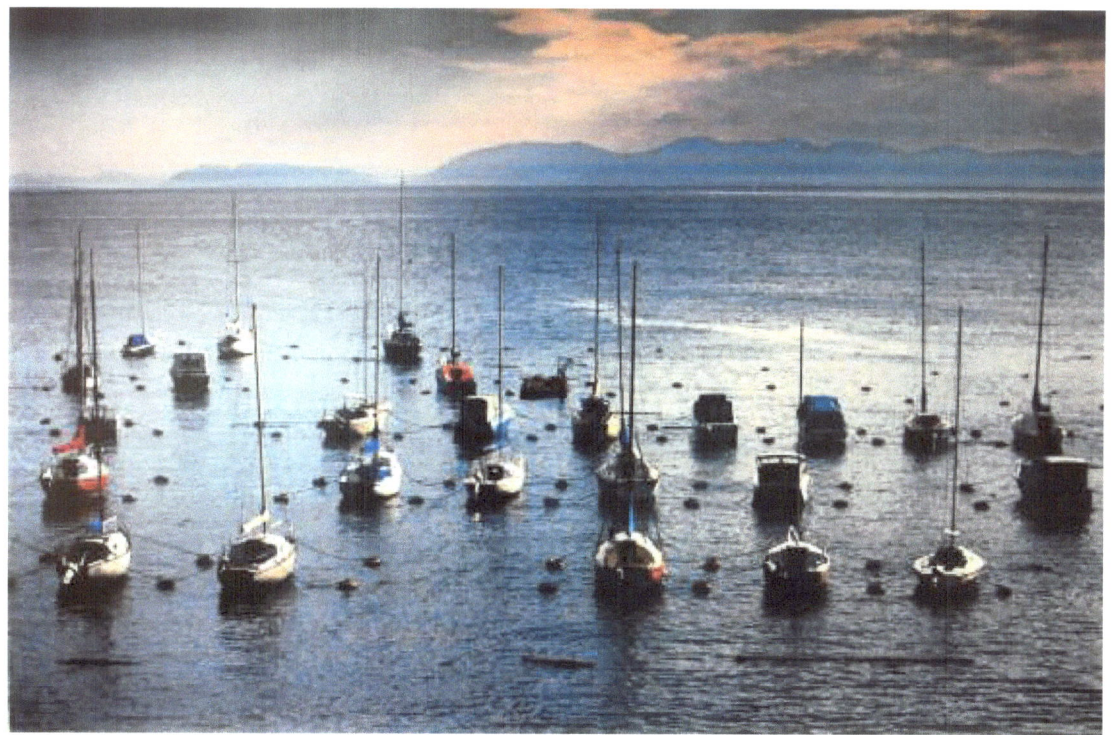
117. Boats Depot at Horseshoe Bay 2

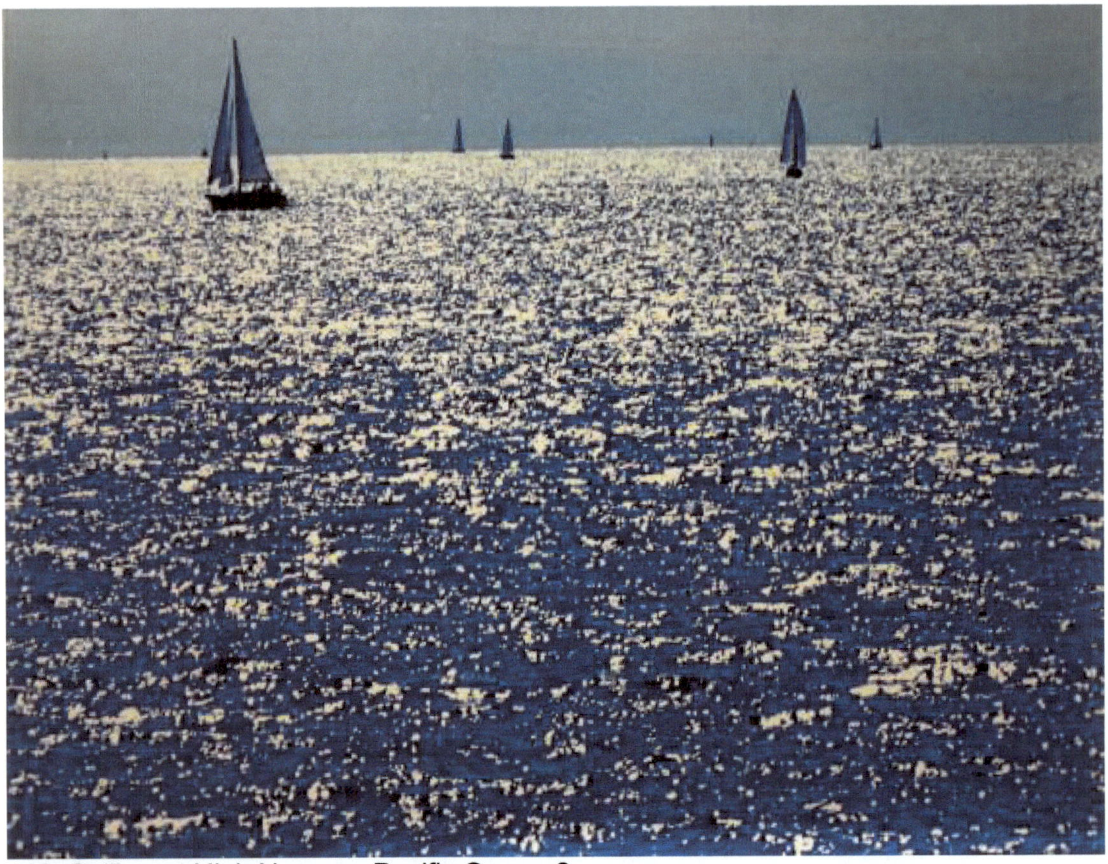

118. Sailing at High Noon on Pacific Ocean 2

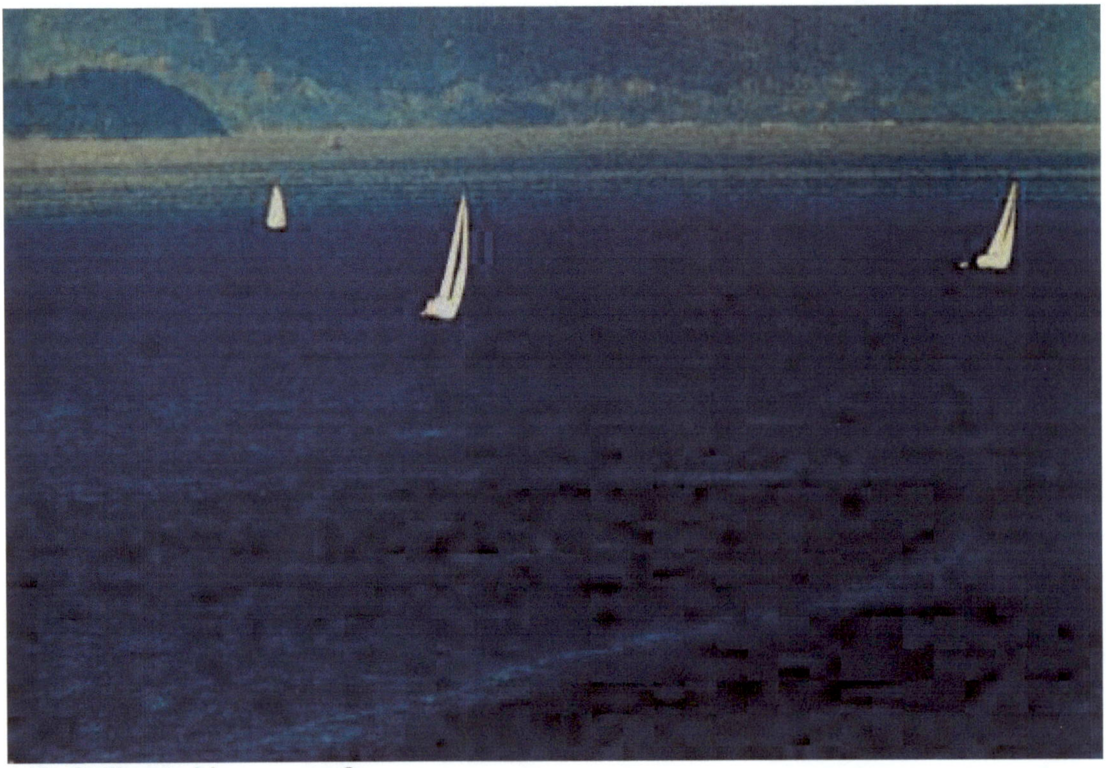

119. Sailboats Manoeuvre 2

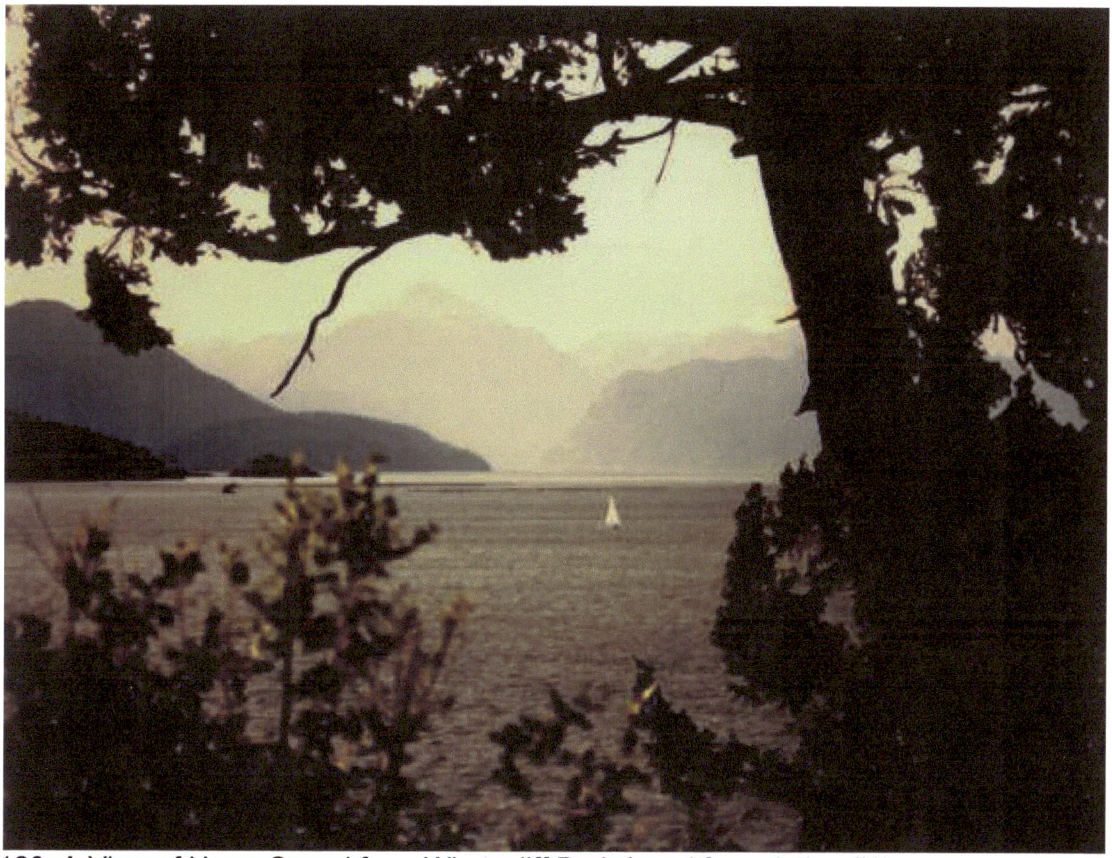

120. A View of Howe Sound from Whytecliff Park (used for painting #6)

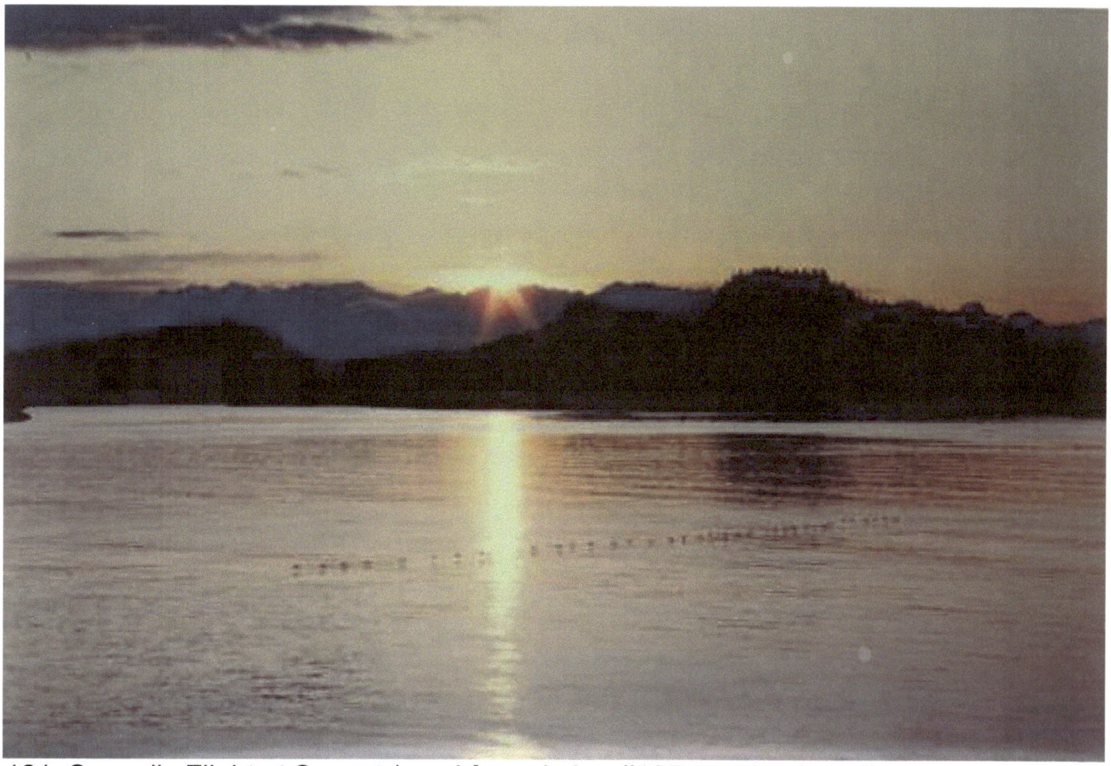

121. Seagulls Flight at Sunset (used for painting #127 as a beginner!)

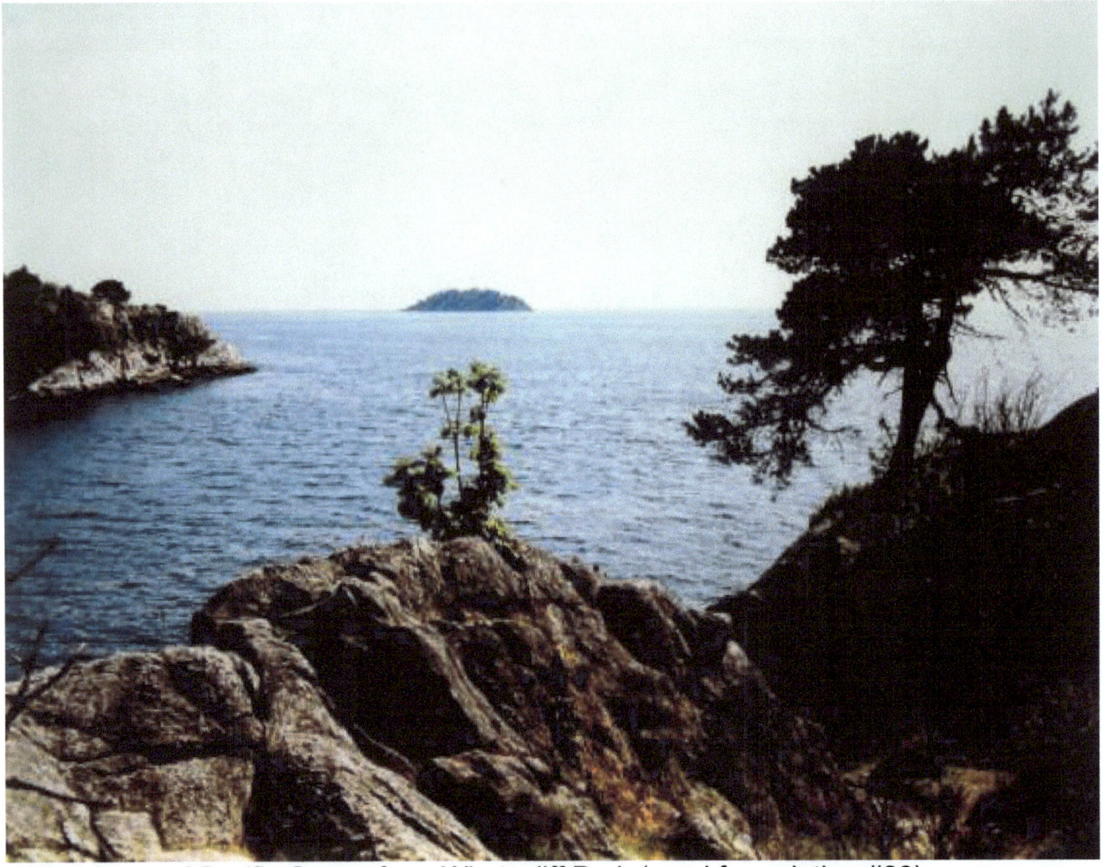

122. A View of Pacific Ocean from Whytecliff Park (used for painting #28)

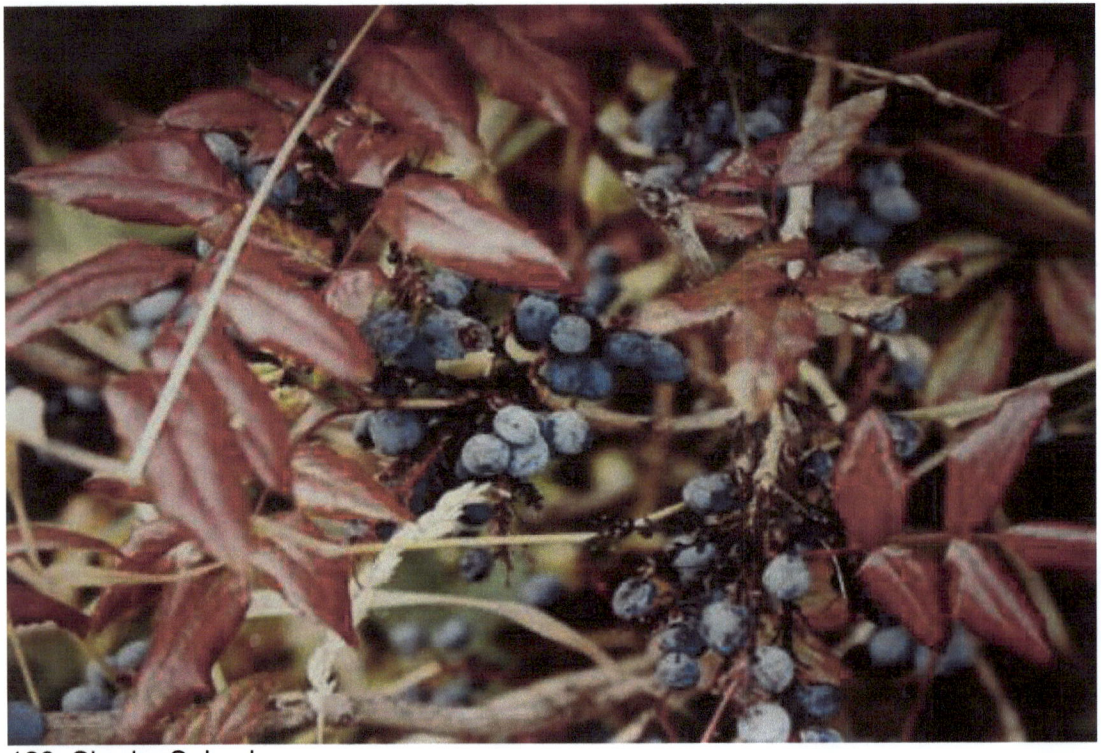
123. Shrubs Splendour

124. Wild Flowers' Splendour 1

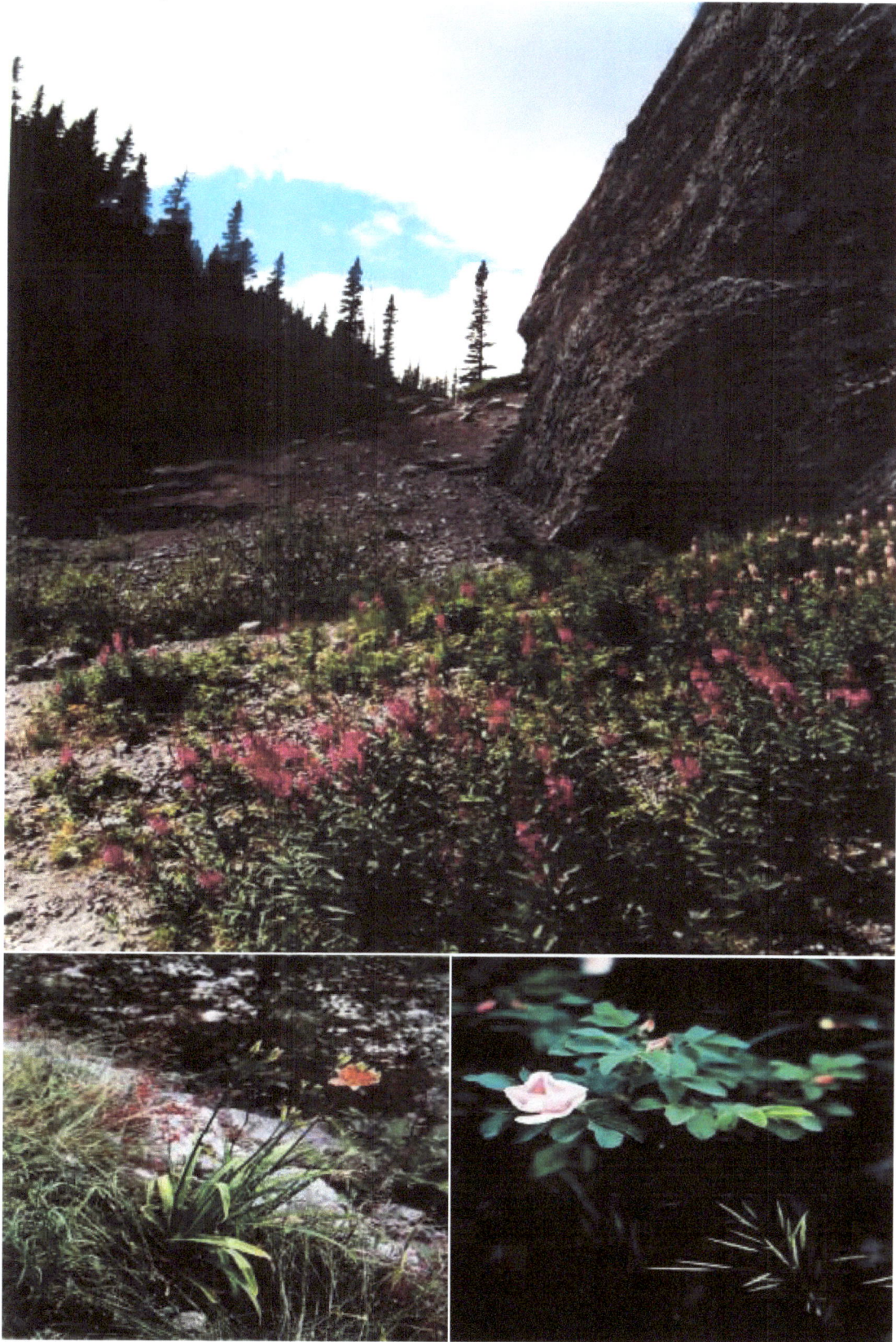

125. Wild Flowers' Splendour 2

126. Wild Flowers' Splendour 3

Wild Flowers and Shrubs

Wild flowers and shrubs exude an inspirational mix of beauty and enigma of their own when we observe them carefully with a subtle urge to learn something about nature and ourselves. Those are spiritual occasions to explore the opportunity of living more naturally ourselves away from the idiotic symbols of civilization that we have embraced naively and made our existence so tough and meaningless.

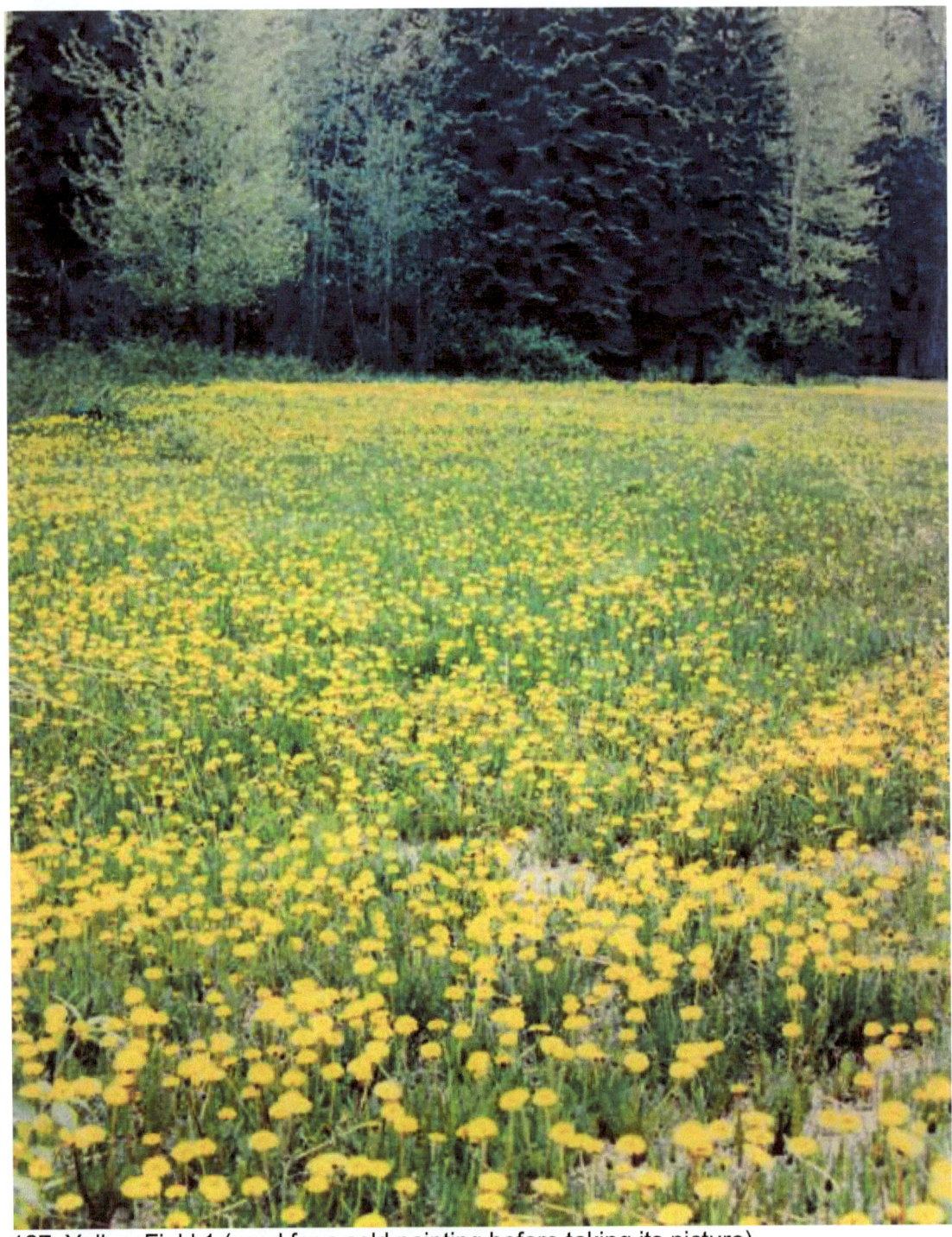

127. Yellow Field 1 (used for a sold painting before taking its picture)

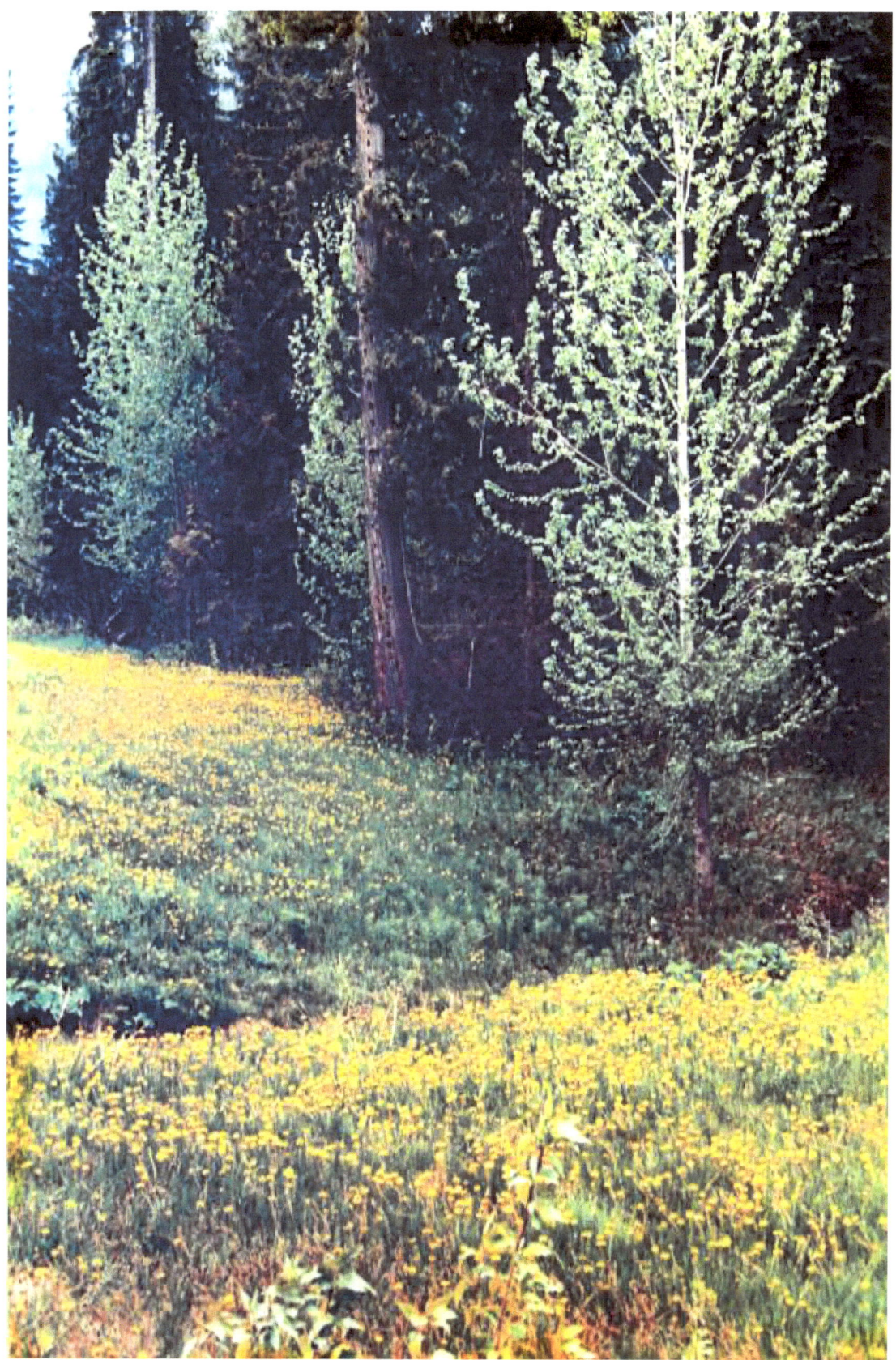
128. Yellow Field 2 (used for painting # 124)

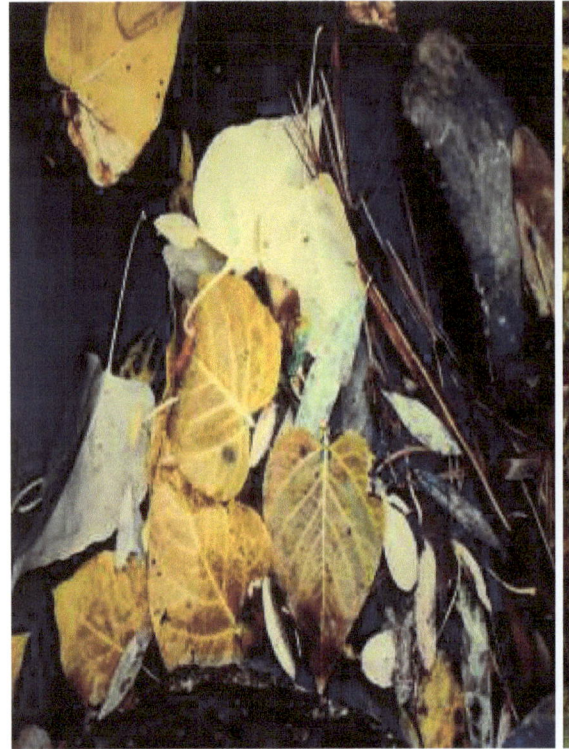
129a. Shrubs and Rocks 1

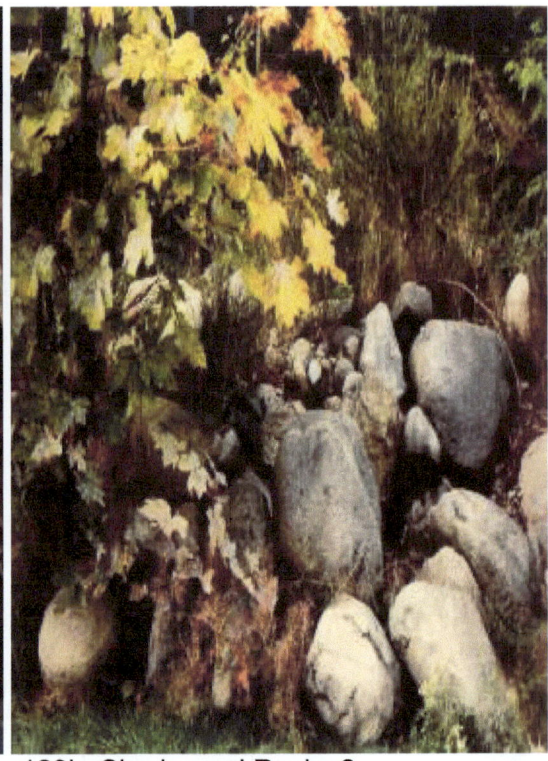
129b. Shrubs and Rocks 2

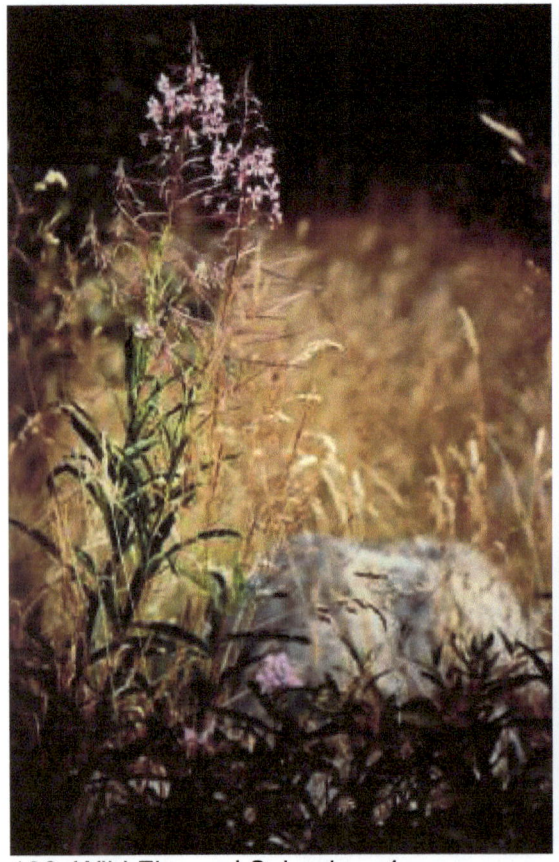
130. Wild Flowers' Splendour 4

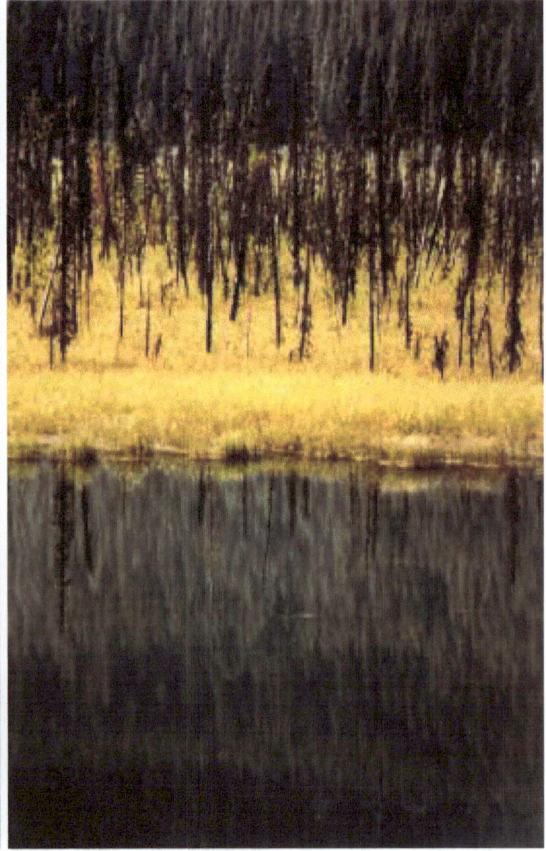
131. Shrubs at Rocky Mountains 2

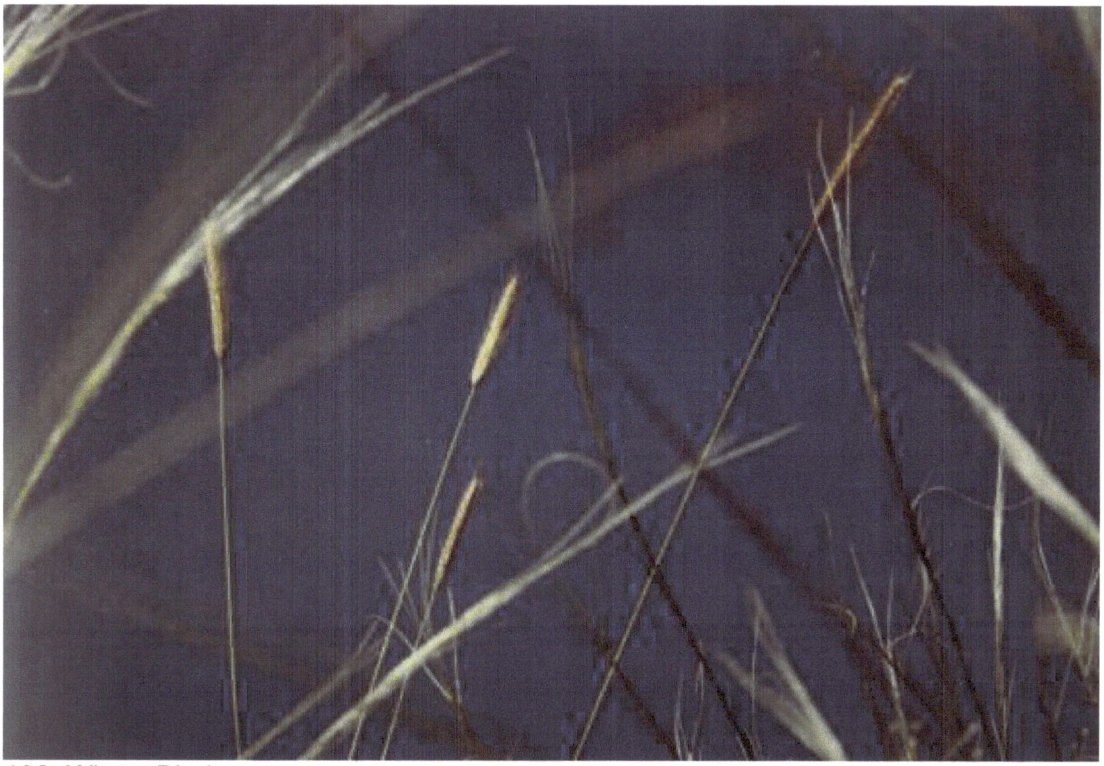

132. Wheat Blades

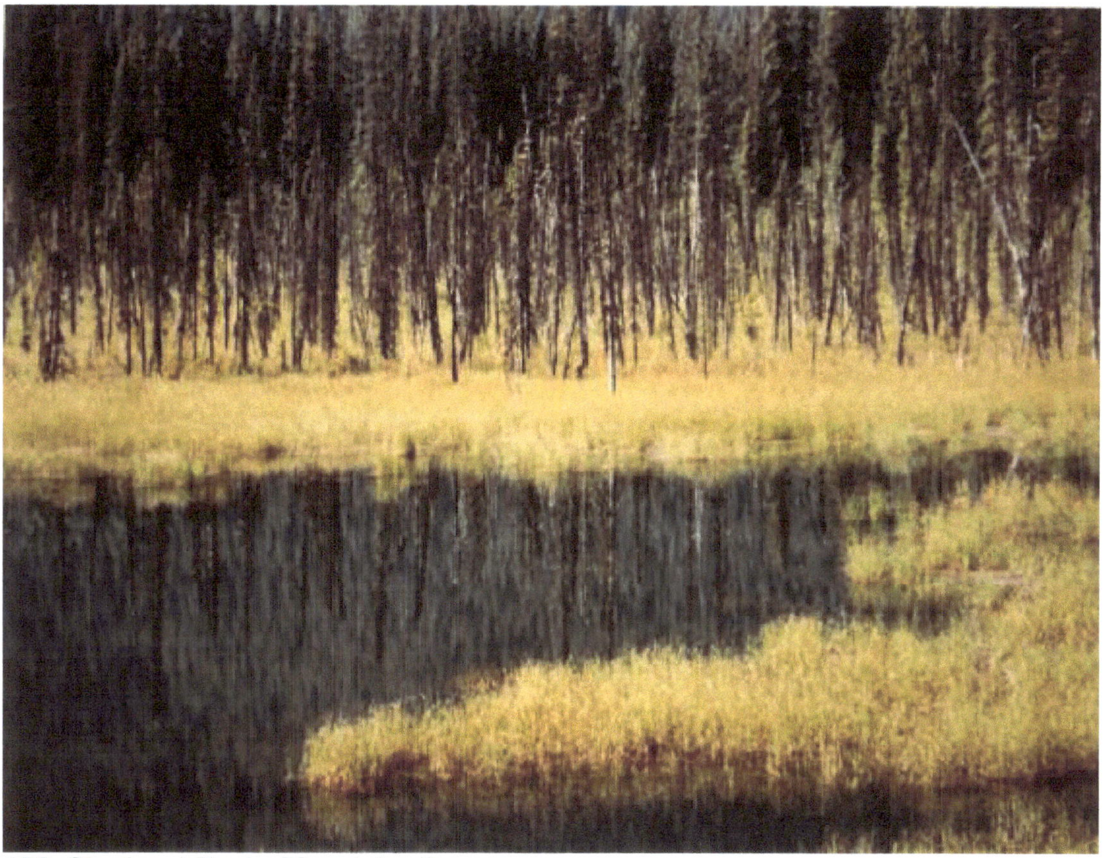

133. Shrubs at Rocky Mountains 3

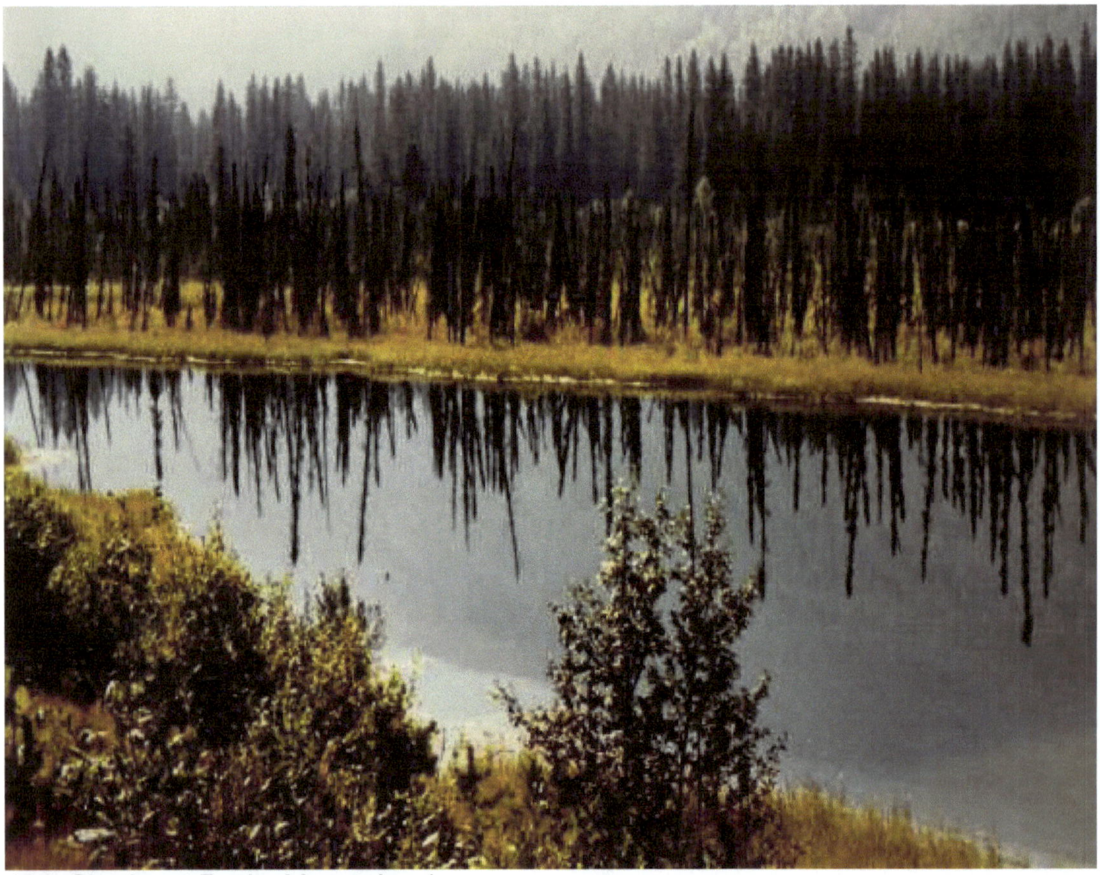

134. Shrubs at Rocky Mountains 1

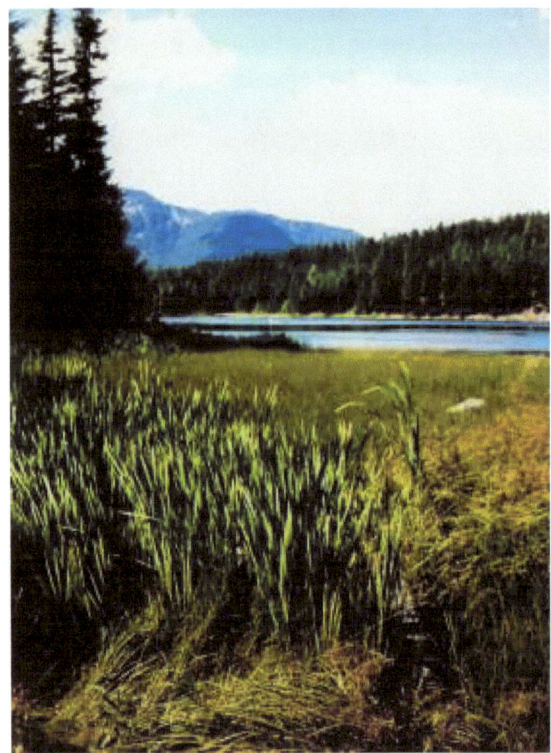
135. Shrubs at Whistler Lake 1

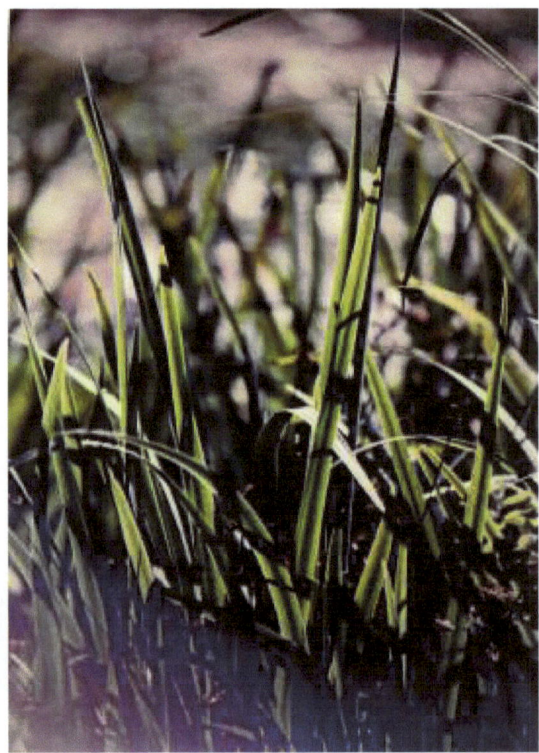
136. Shrubs at Whistler Lake 2

Miscellaneous and Odd Photographs

Besides artistic and sentimental photos, sometimes we take pictures of odd scenes or objects just for fun or out of curiosity. An accident or image might also make us ponder and analyse some dubious features of existence or imagine supernatural messages. Then, often, some mundane objects, such as a single leaf perhaps, give us a deeper sense of nature and connection with our inner self. Naturally, these weird experiences are sacred, personal sentiments in line with one's level of authenticity and self-driven spiritualism outside religious mumbo jumbos. Still, the chance to record the sources of such divine incidents can be viewed as another merit of photography over all other art forms. Sometimes, even one glance at a person can enthral or fool our psyches for good, like when we fall in love swiftly for unexplainable reasons, often with a stranger. How wonderful it would have been if cameras could record those sudden sentiments and momentous moments, too?

I have taken many odd pictures of objects or surfaces that had rather amused me. Luckily, I could elude the temptation of including many of them in this book in fear of appearing too pathetic! If not a sign of inching senility, these bizarre experiences probably show how I miss love and how much devil is teasing me about it, while love also often feels irrational and inane in an era when people's sense of compassion has depleted vastly. Anyway, a few bizarre photos are included in this section only due to mystical sentiments they had triggered in me with possibly no, or different, effect on others. In particular, the three odd pictures on page 101 are included just for fun due to their somewhat enigmatic semblances of heart or the devil.

(Some more odd pictures are offered in Appendix B.)

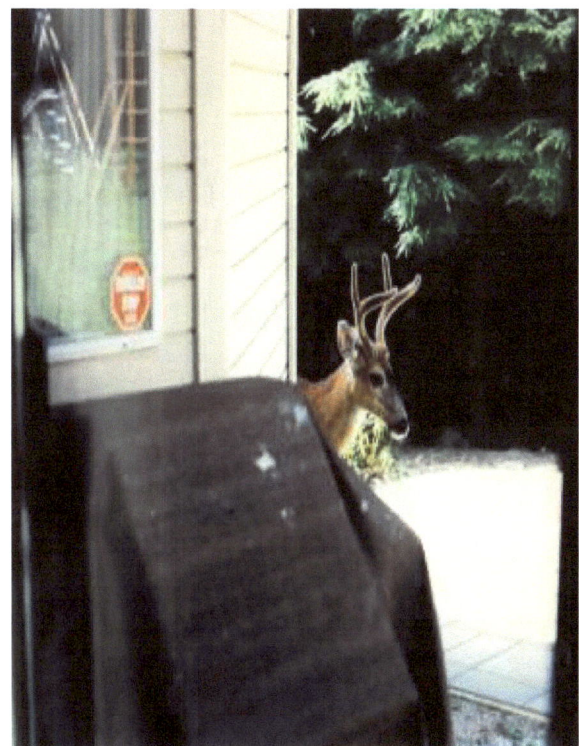

137a. Peek-a-boo in My Backyard 1

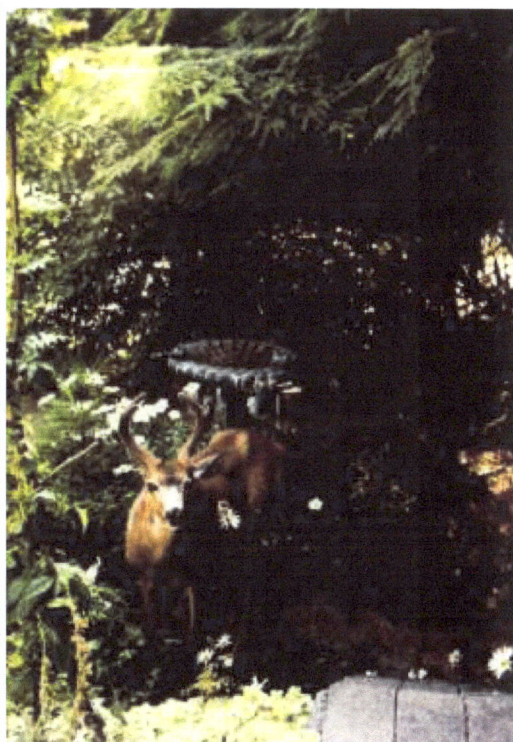

137b. Peek-a-boo in My Backyard 2

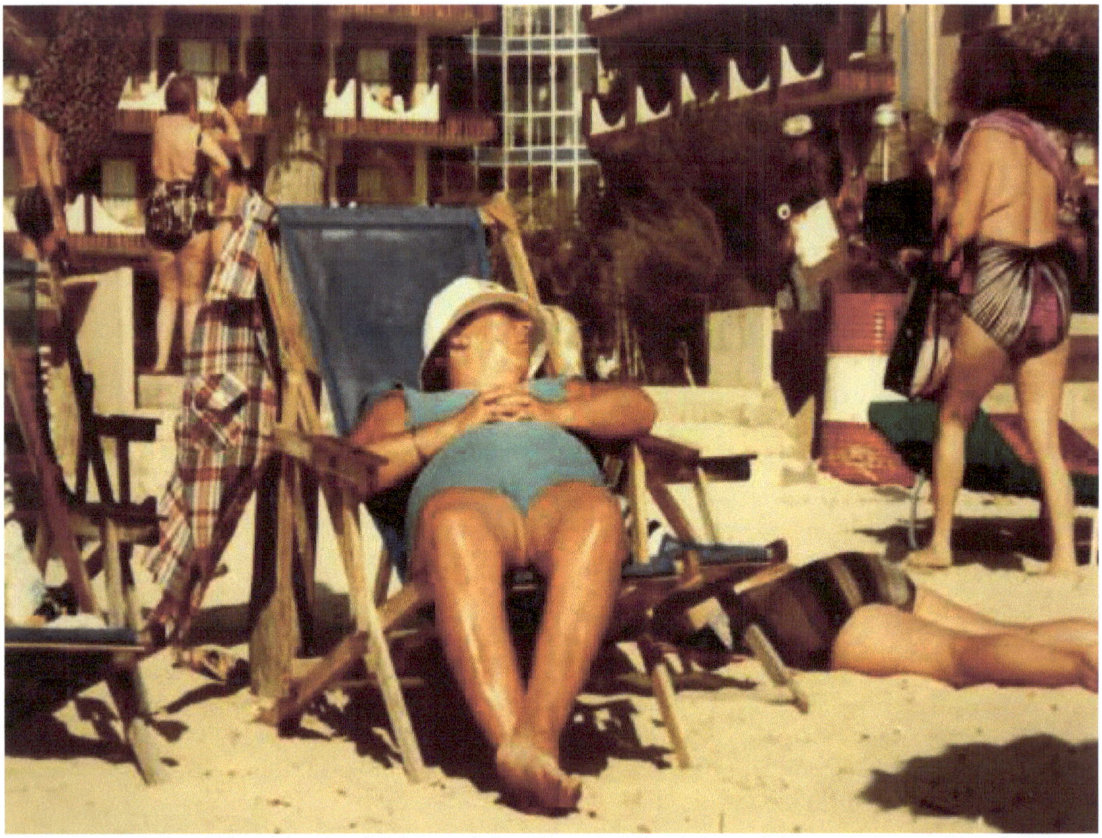

138. Forget the World in the Middle of the Day 1 (Nice) (used for paintings #22 & 97)

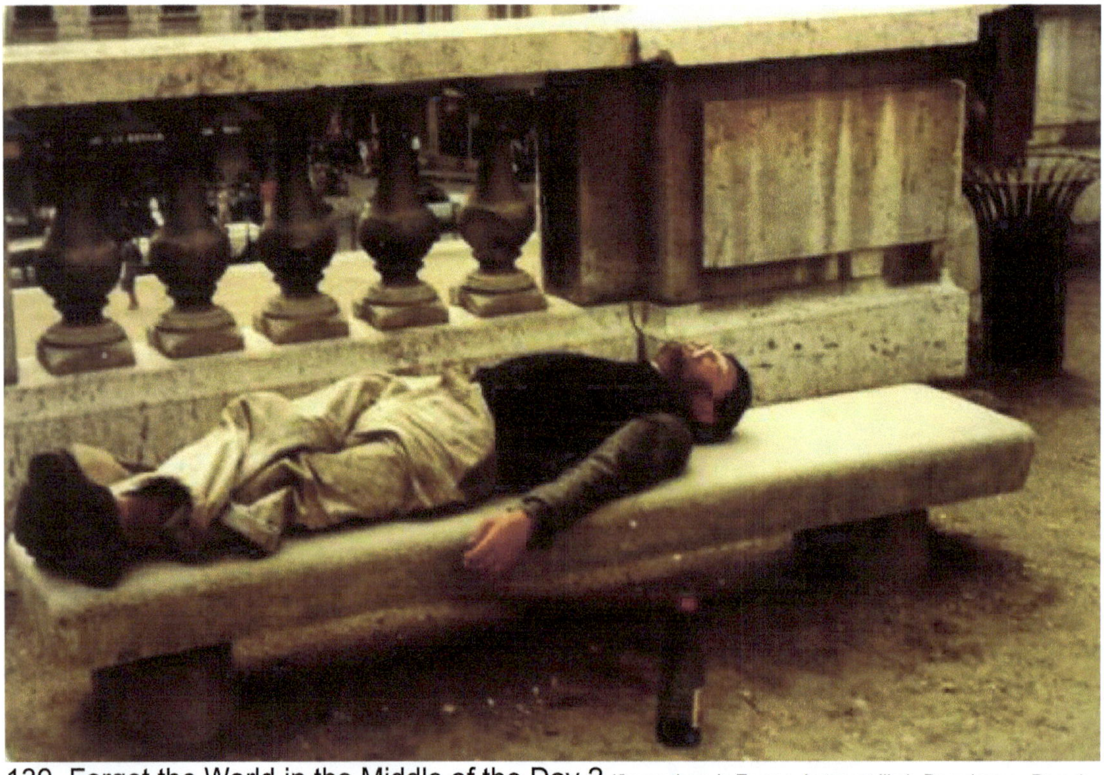

139. Forget the World in the Middle of the Day 2 (Somewhere in Europe, but most likely Barcelona or Rome)

At least we have a few good things in common with animals and birds, such as taking a nap right in the middle of the day in the crowd or doing serious reflections (like those monkeys and seagulls on pages 98-99) before rushing back to our sad lives. Especially, the birds' nonchalance in the Stanley Park about nosy humans disturbing their snooze is admirable, somewhat like the vagrant in the last page *with his cigarette, especially*.

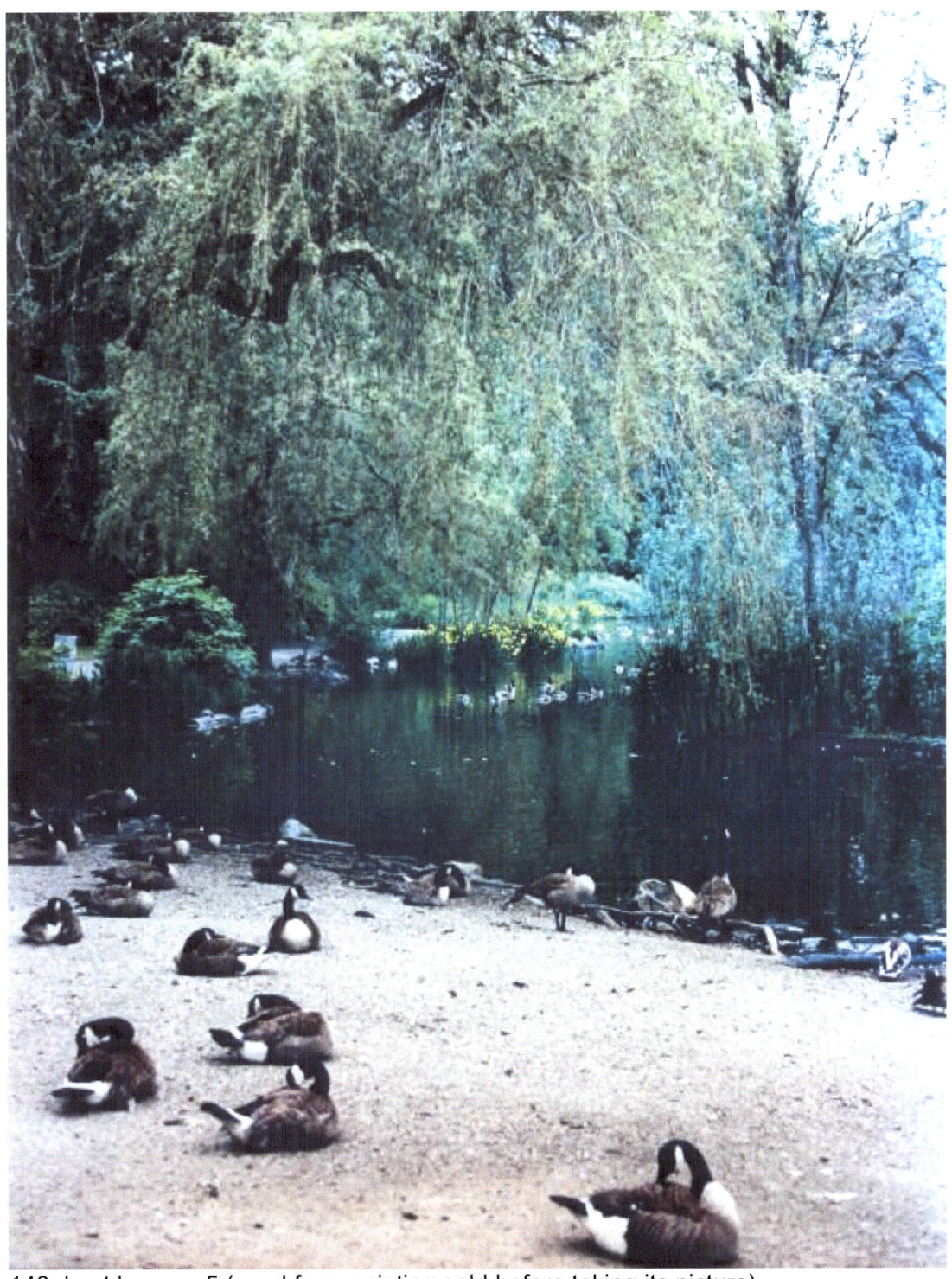

140. Lost Lagoon 5 (used for a painting sold before taking its picture)

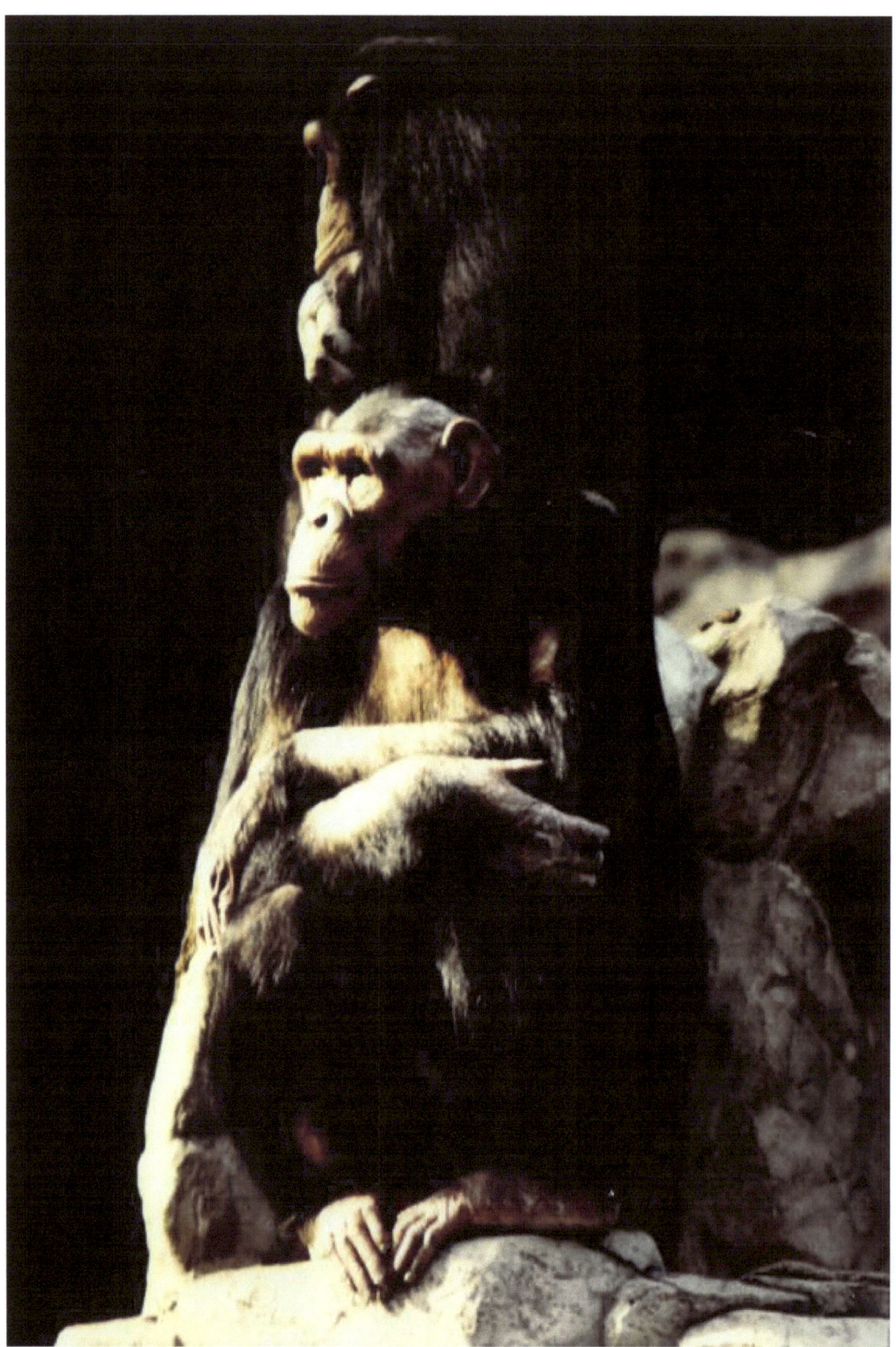
141. Time for a Serious Reflection! (Can you also see that mysterious image on the rock?)

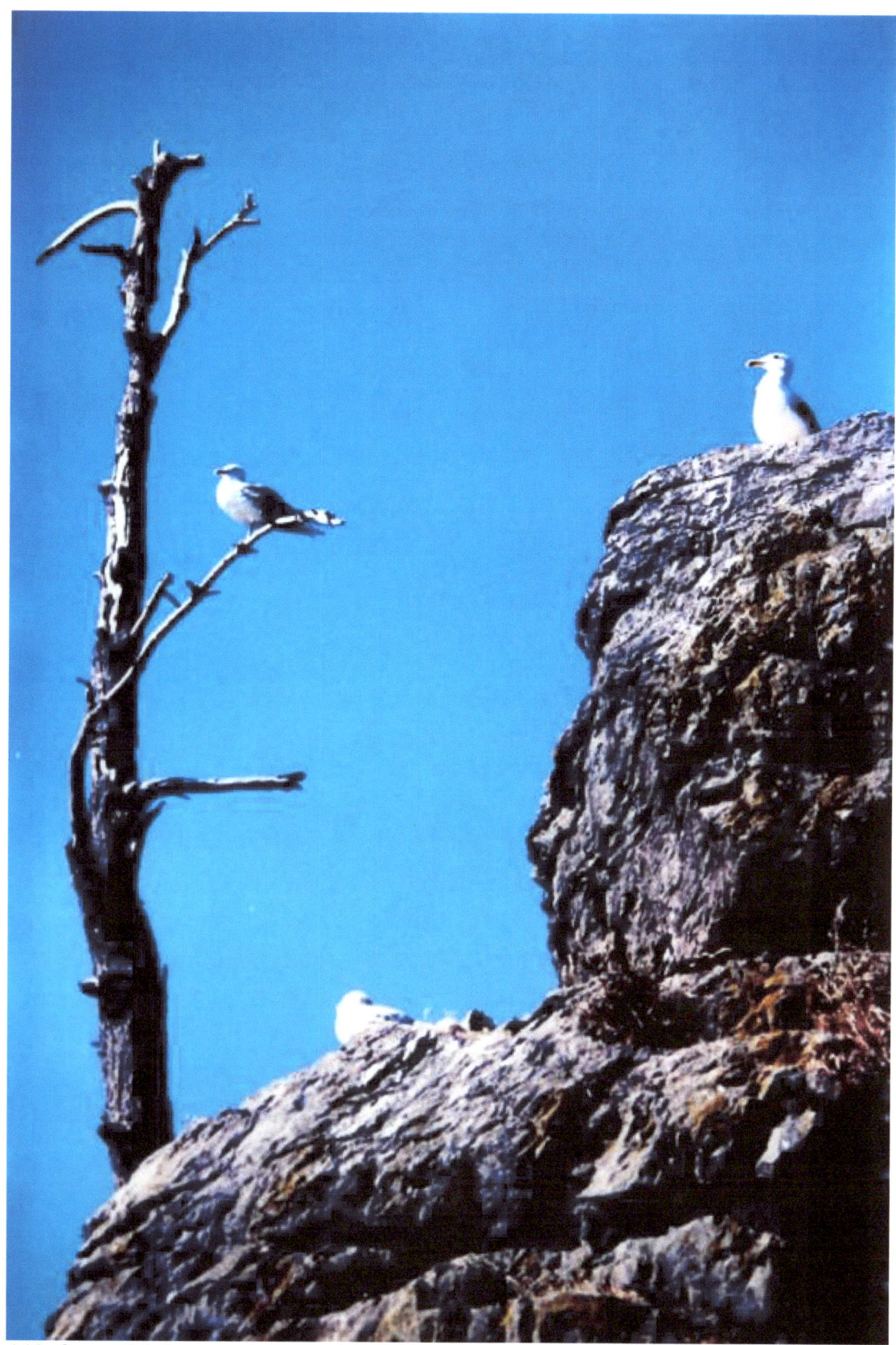
142. Seagulls' Contemplation at Stanley Park! (used for painting #119)

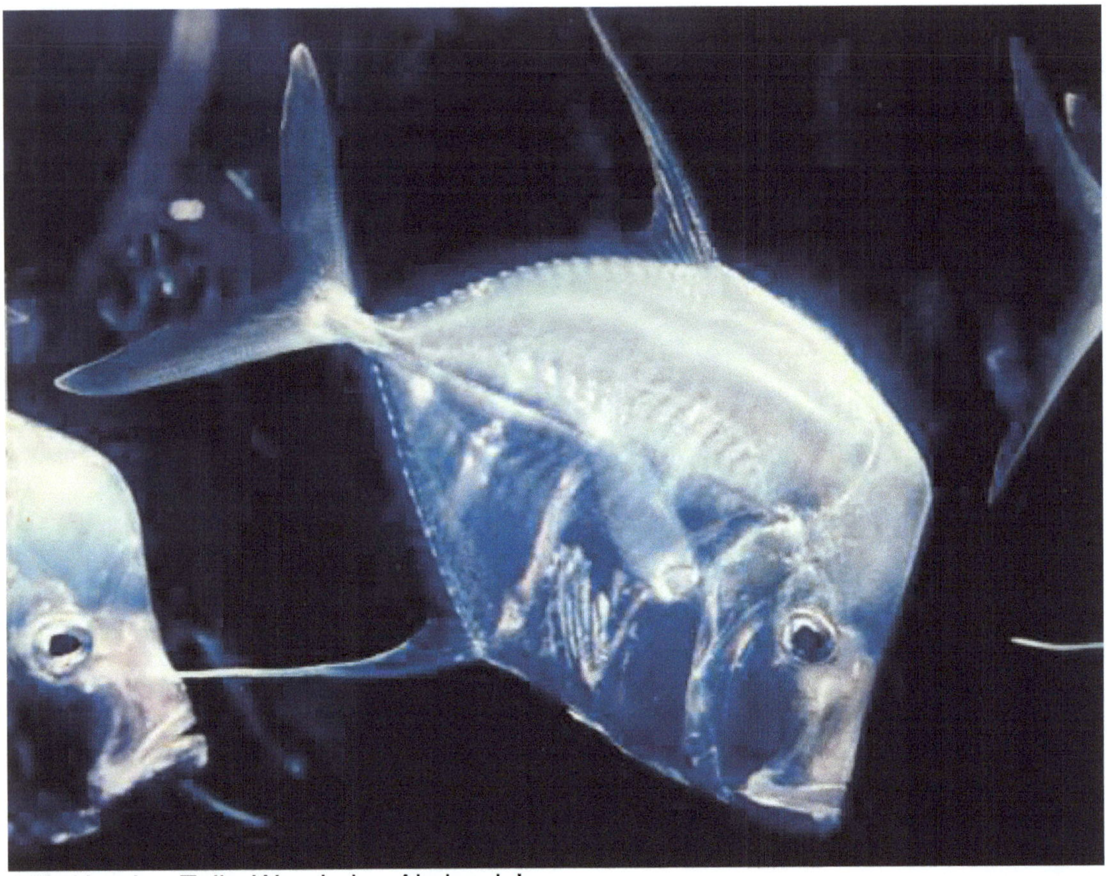

143. Head or Tail—Wandering Aimlessly!

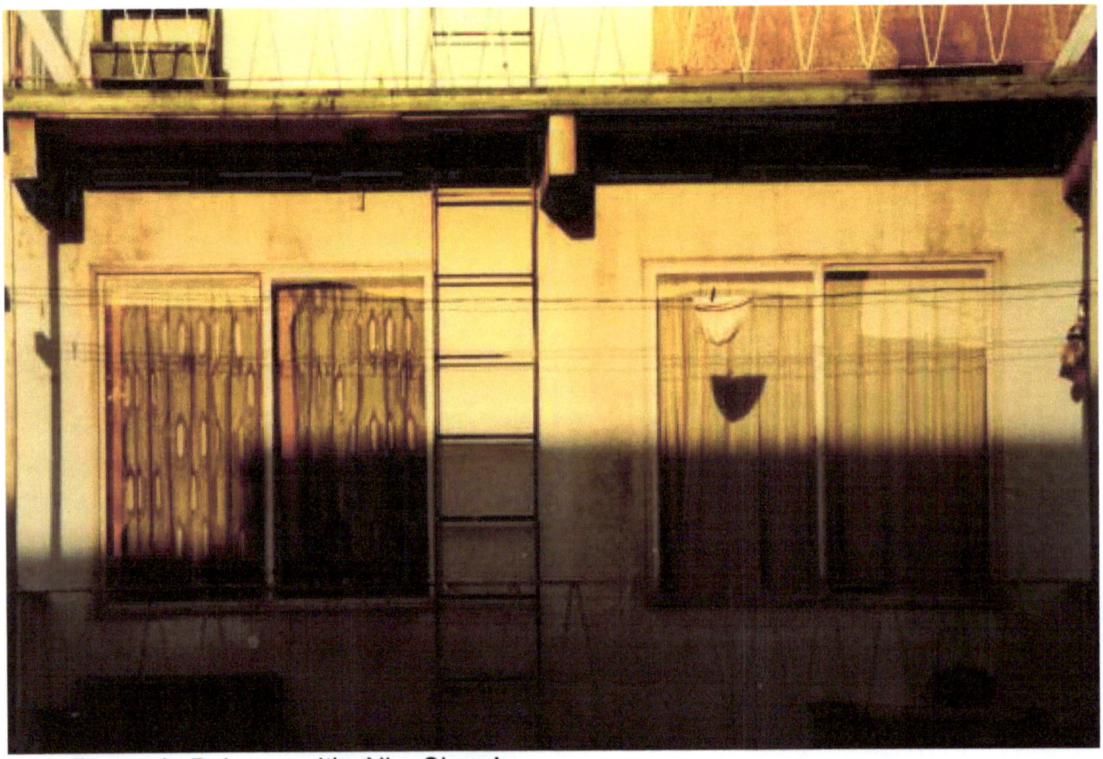

144. Romeo's Balcony—It's All a Show!

I imagine Juliet's balcony had looked like this before all that Romeo's comings and goings had ruined the flowers and the house's general order!

I wonder if she'd ever visited Romeo's house and seen what a mess, especially his balcony, is, as shown in photo #144. *Would she have still loved him and killed herself for him?!*

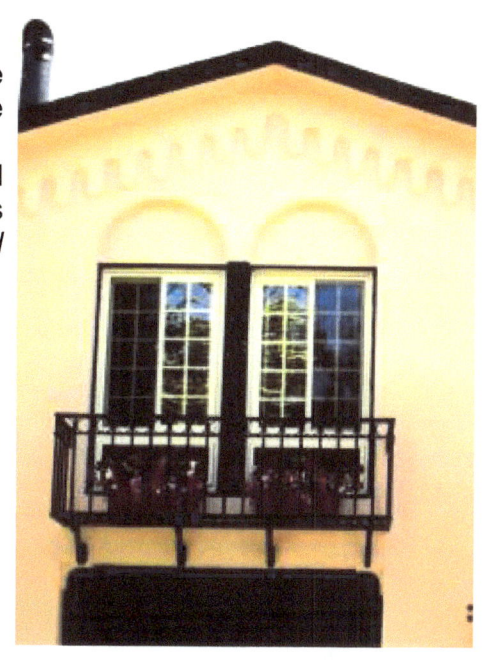

145. Juliet's Balcony—So Tidy!
(used for painting #106)

One day, I saw this odd image of the devil in my sink, while washing the dishes with gloom. This and the next two photos are included here just for fun and testing your imaginations, but I don't even give them a number!

By the way, I can actually see at least 3 images of the devil in this horrible photo. I also see the devil dancing in picture #146b in the upper cloud with a dark heart in its belly and butt! In #146a, I see ET (an alien) in the lower cloud gauging North Shore mysteriously! And I see the nosy devil in the upper right corner of image #86. *So weird, ha? Do you see any of my silly imaginations?!*

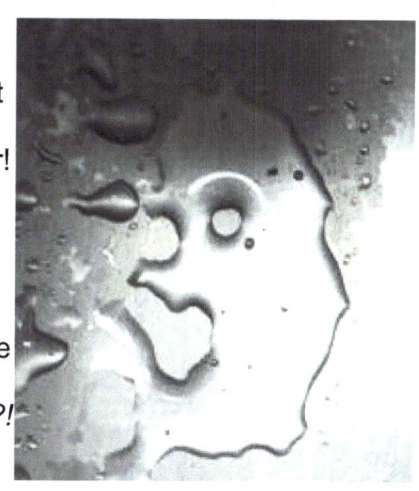

This radish and pebble's semblance of heart had drawn my attention, thus these pictures.

I ate the radish eventually with a broken heart, but the pebble is now a part of my valuable collections, dearer even more than my antique diamonds.

By the way, have you noticed that if we rotate a picture of heart it would look like a cute butt?

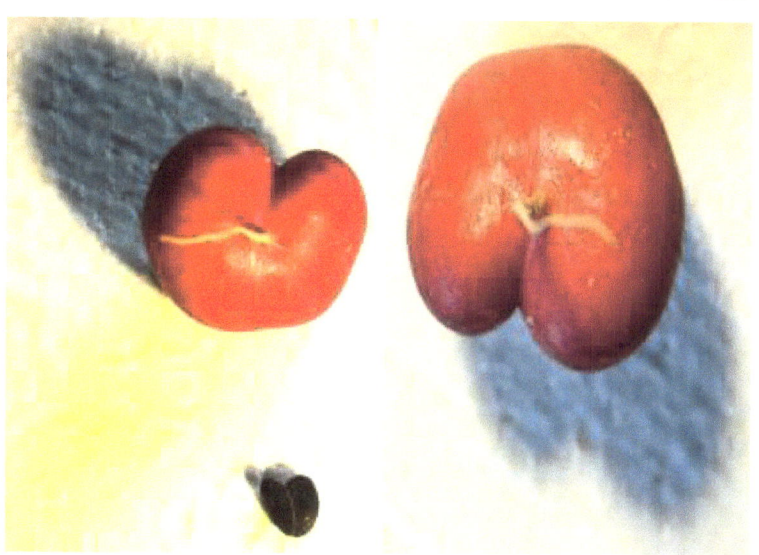

Views of North Vancouver

Most photos of Burrard Inlet and Vancouver downtown were taken from North Shore, thus it feels right to include 4 pictures of that mountainous region itself. Yet, in line with the 'odd photos' topic in the last section, photo 146a shows the devil dancing in the upper clouds and 146b shows an alien, ET, in the lower clouds! *Do you see them, too?*

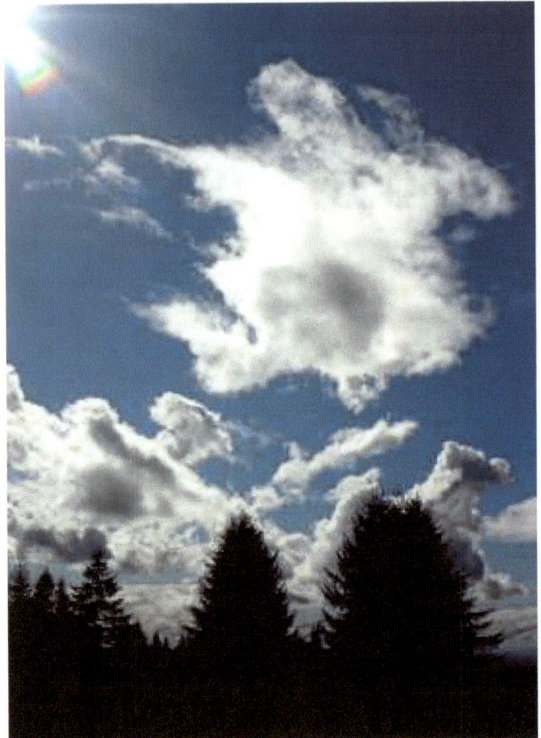
146a. Clouds in North Shore (devil dancing)

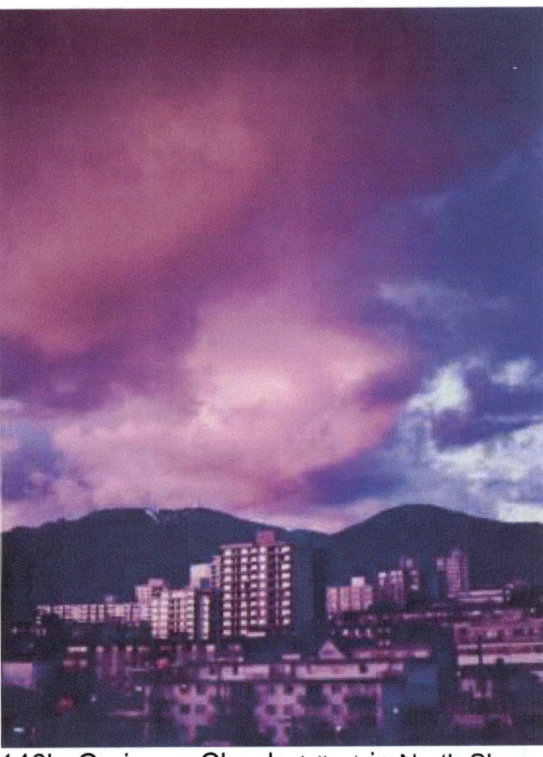
146b. Ominous Clouds (alien) in North Shore

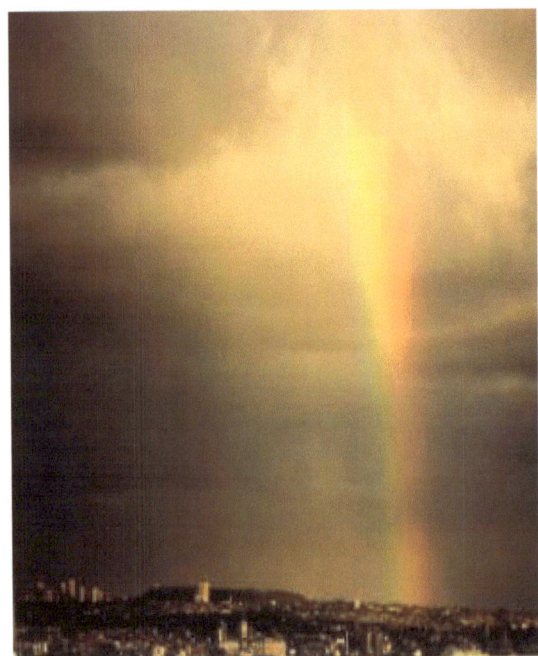
147. Rainbow in North Vancouver

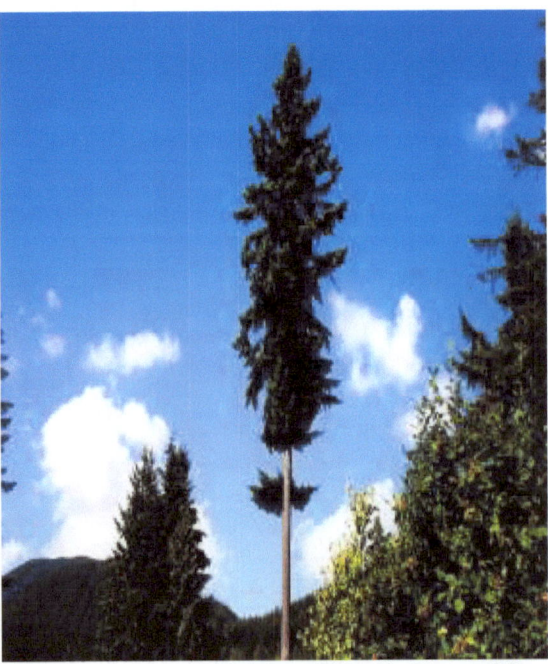
148. My Backyard View of North Shore Mts.

On the One Hand...

My *seemingly sensible* curiosities and urges since adolescence have felt useful for, i) stirring routine reflections and self-analysis, ii) realizing a mix of academic and artistic passions, iii) exploring life's priorities and realities, iv) gauging social norms' validity against the elusive truth in nature, v) finding my place in a falling society, vi) refining my mindset and life path, and vii) soothing my soul. Inconsistent academic interests and degrees during youth also reflect my curiosities and cynicism about my fields of education and living rather hypnotically only according to shallow social/occupational norms, which are built around corporate interests and elites' greed. In fact, listing my university degrees on the title page has been mostly sarcastic about my rather erratic, time-consuming studies in academic and artistic settings, but also a tiny hint about my credentials for expressing basic scientific facts about society and family.

Naturally, the timeliness of our curiosities and urges is also crucial for setting our life priories and getting tangible results. For example, photography during adolescence seems to have been particularly timely and important for me to grow a sacred sense of affinity with nature more than I have ever felt towards humans per se. This inspiring connection with nature has been helpful in shaping my lifestyle and mindset, as well as triggering my passions for painting and writing. In return, those paintings and photos have been vital, especially in the last two decades, in keeping my spirit high for writing books keenly. Switching my passions has also felt logical and useful, maybe even ordained like a divine intervention, to manage my existence rather wisely. *Thus, by this rather positive perspective, I consider myself fortunate and possibly even blessed!*

On the Other Hand...

My life has felt cursed or a bad karma, as I *still* ponder my life's purpose suspiciously! In particular, my naive hope about humans' minute opportunity for salvation has led to endless research, reflections, and writing with no probable practical outcomes. Now, as much as I both love and feel obliged to analyse and write about humanity, my efforts appear too whimsical and a futile sacrifice when my findings merely strengthen my belief about the unlikelihood of humans ever developing the required wisdom for revamping their mentalities and avoiding annihilation. Still, I cannot stop believing in, and propagating, the need for everybody's heartfelt focus on humanity at least during the next few centuries for that minuscule chance of reversing humans' looming fate.

*****

Nevertheless, wrestling with the big paradox delineated above has been too stressful in line with a sense of being too uptight uselessly, while people appear so nonchalant about their lifestyles' impotence for sustaining social health and existence. Pondering radical ideals about humanity with mixed feelings, instead of only enjoying life's basic privileges by following the mainstream's path, has been quite frustrating, considering my cynicism about the possibility of anybody affecting humans' and social mindsets for the better ever. Instead, leaning only on my artistic passions has often felt like a wiser option to forget my curiosity and concern about humanity and raise my social contacts, too, possibly even for a chance to find and love a special woman again.

Ironically, even my artistic efforts for soothing my soul had deepened my addiction to reflections and self-analysis along with more doubts and dilemmas about our daily routines, including the purpose of humans' artistic interests and efforts, as explained on page 68. Despite its power to make us forget life, artistry has just kept raising my cynicism about humans' mindset, wisdom, and long-term goals in such a wicked social setting. Of course, another big obstacle for me to behave more practically—like the selfish majority, mostly by living superficially for today—has been the lack of patience and talent required for handling social and friendships' pretensions, nowadays. Surely, these types of dilemmas also make us cynical about the soundness of our minds and life choices.

Raising these personal sentiments has also been for delineating the odd ways our brains work, as we choose our life paths and passions usually emotionally or illogically, usually painfully, even when our choices feel sound and fulfilling in line with our big hopes and ambitions. Surely, humans think and behave differently according to their odd genetics, rearing, and curiosities. Some become explorers, inventors, or artists to fulfil themselves, yet most of us question our mindsets and life paths regularly, as well as our urges and curiosities, in hopes of justifying our life purposes and choices.

Meanwhile, grasping life's complexity in line with our ideals is becoming harder for our naïve, misguided brains every day. Thus, we doubt the validity of both our social processes and personal efforts frequently, especially as sensitive artists, while our goals and achievements also feel more immature every day in the midst of escalating global disasters and pains. Now, the longer humans fail to recognize their true needs, the more using art as a scapegoat for social survival or mental relaxation feels absurd.

Surely, some of us sense and suffer these fundamental doubts and question our existence more often. Our obsession for self-analyses and reflections mainly about human relations and social values feels like a genetic curse with no amount of wisdom and consolation capable of curbing our yen for a semblance of the truth. Harmonizing one's creative and academic urges or mixing them practically also requires a flexible temperament, while the disparity of physical and mental requirements for following any particular pursuit places its own burdens on us. We envy those who do not sense or worry about such irrational, pitiful features of social living, although we might often feel blessed for our unorthodox ways of seeing things outside the box. Then, we wonder how the relaxed majority, especially our presumed leaders, do not notice or care about humans' natural defects now augmented by societies' vile mentalities stressing only on wealth and happiness along with misleading, incongruent ideologies.

Personally, my brain's persistence to fathom a holistic vision of art and humanity as a life philosophy has contradicted my individualistic efforts to keep my psyche intact through either art or active social contacts! Instead, the convoluted, modern vision of individualism itself feels vastly at odds with our urge for dependence on social living to smooth our existence. It feels very much like our desire to both eat and keep our cake!

Altogether, my erratic interests have sometimes felt like quirks instead of qualities, although they had occurred naturally. Especially, my radical switch to writing, while missing the great joys and serenity of photography and painting, have often felt more like a lack of life purpose, especially considering my long, deep artistic curiosities and plans. Besides my time and money devoted to artistry, those hobbies had felt like a soulful mission to keep my life somewhat purposeful and amusing despite my family's apathy and a boring career in government, while people and experts had also kept encouraging me to exhibit my paintings more actively. The emotional reason for a swift switch to painting after forty years of delightful photography and printing large images in my colour darkroom are outlined in my novel, *My Lousy Life Stories*, and analysed briefly in *About My Paintings* book, too. Then, my passion for painting being dampened itself after ten years by another sudden urge to write novels and academic books has been both questionable and necessary for the reasons mentioned all along. By the way, I had stopped exhibiting my paintings very early on after missing them gravely when sold—a kind of nostalgia possibly amplified in the absence of a family.

Appendix A
Common Pictures Inspiring Good Paintings

Any artistic photograph should raise people's appreciation of a point or a message it exudes often in line with nature's inert glory. Yet, even common pictures can inspire paintings that grab our attention. Most of my paintings have been based on simple photos that are not particularly artistic or special, yet a bunch of them are printed in the following pages merely for offering references to the paintings depicted in *About My Paintings* book, possibly along with stories about the sources of those paintings, such as photographs #157 and 158 included in this section (used for paintings #37 and 38 respectively.)

Six ordinary photographs (#172-7) are also included at the end of this Appendix as good candidates for interesting paintings that I envision, although the chance of doing any more paintings myself is quite remote. Therefore, I do not mind if anybody uses that set of unused pictures to create inspiring paintings. All the credit belongs to them, of course, although mentioning the source of the picture they use would be nice, too. A big prize might also be awaiting the person who does a very special painting from those unused ordinary images. Good luck.

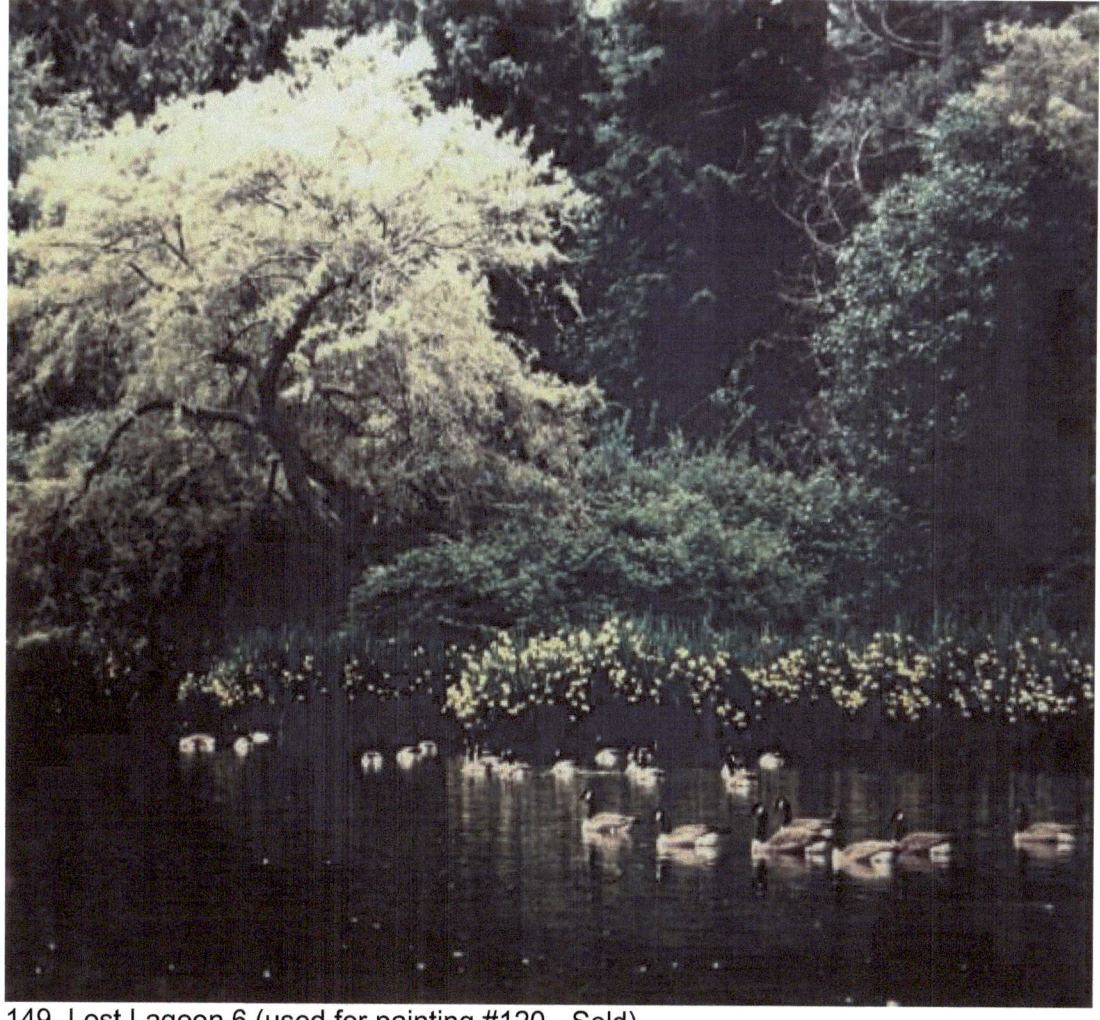

149. Lost Lagoon 6 (used for painting #120 - Sold)

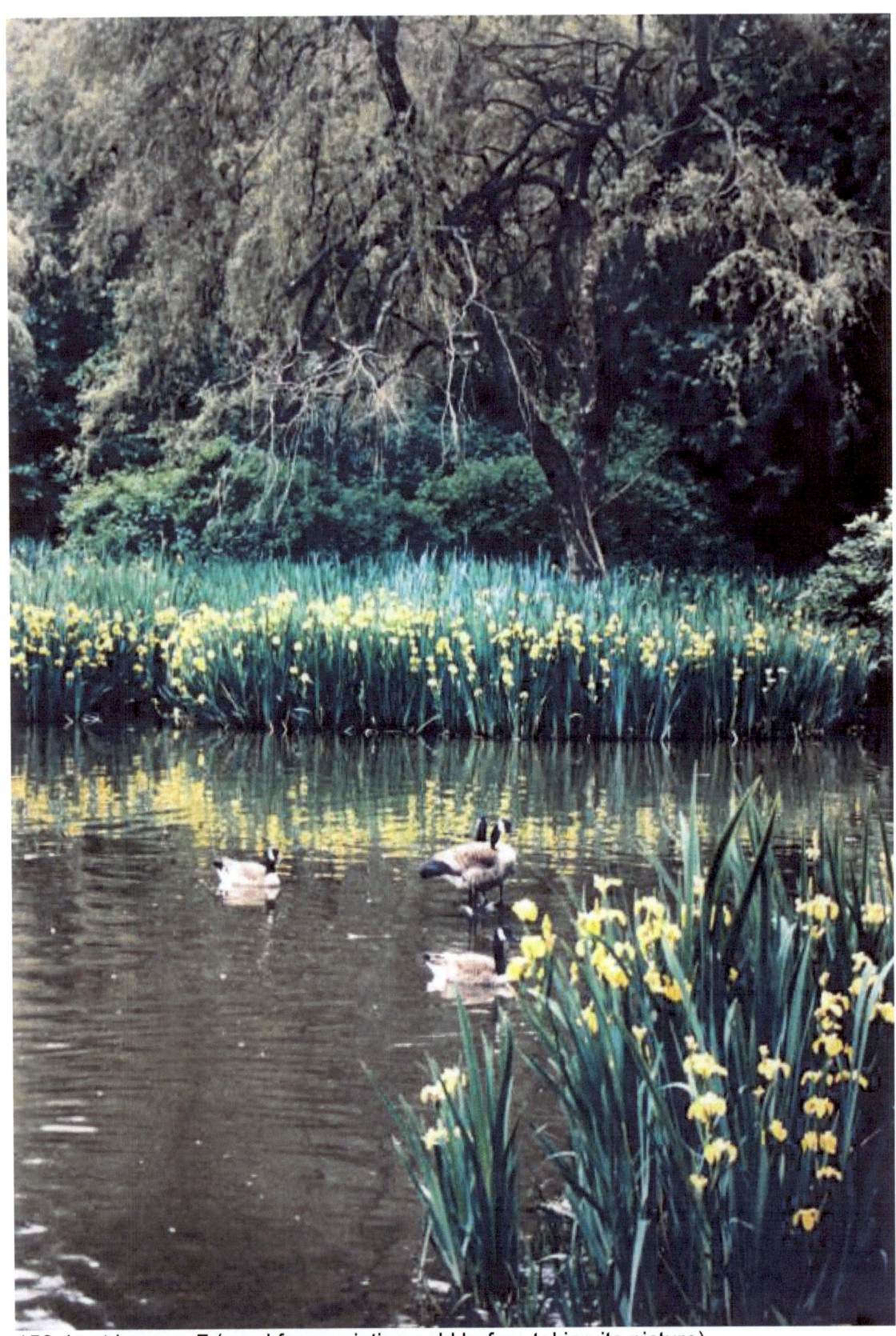

150. Lost Lagoon 7 (used for a painting sold before taking its picture)

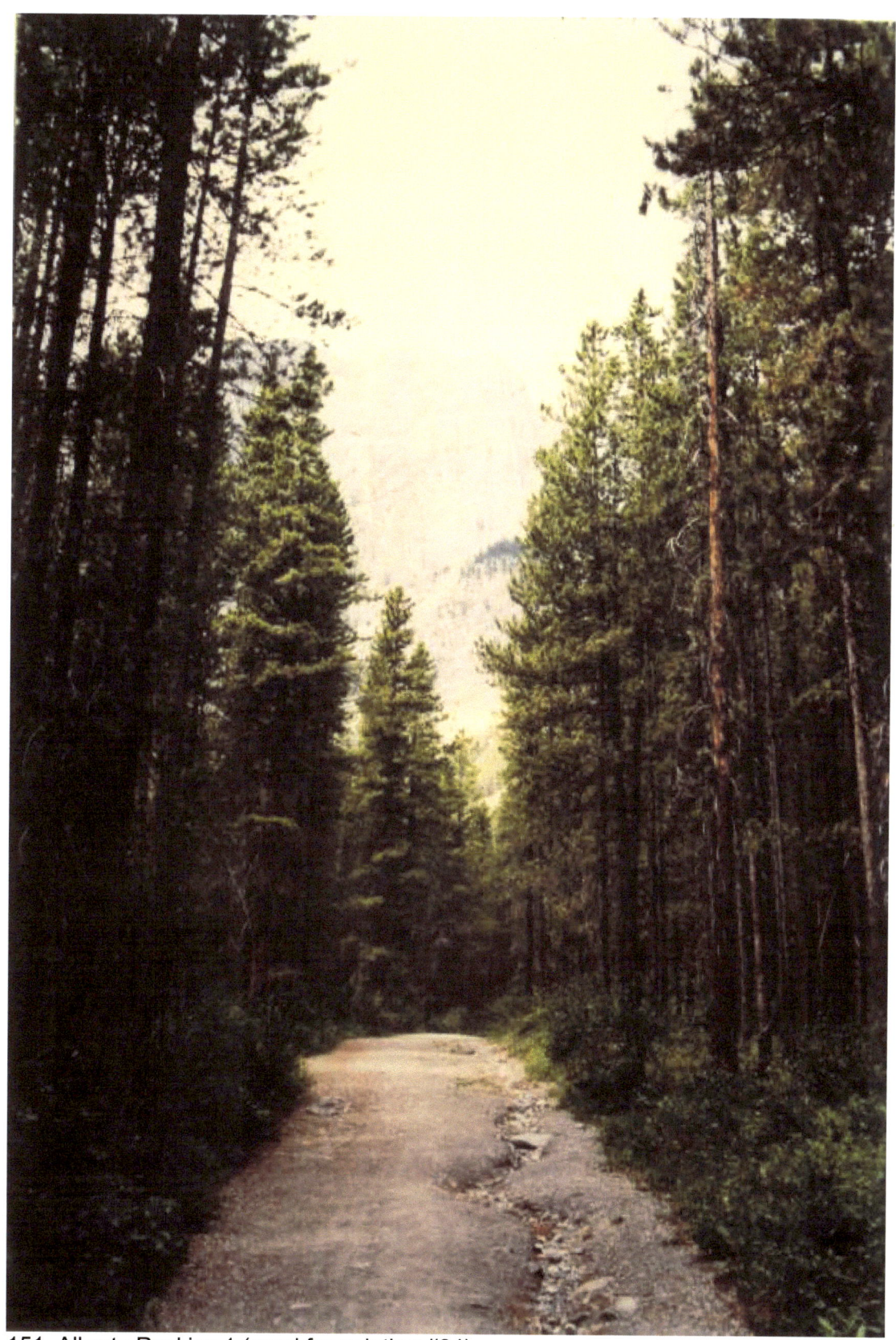

151. Alberta Rockies 1 (used for painting #34)

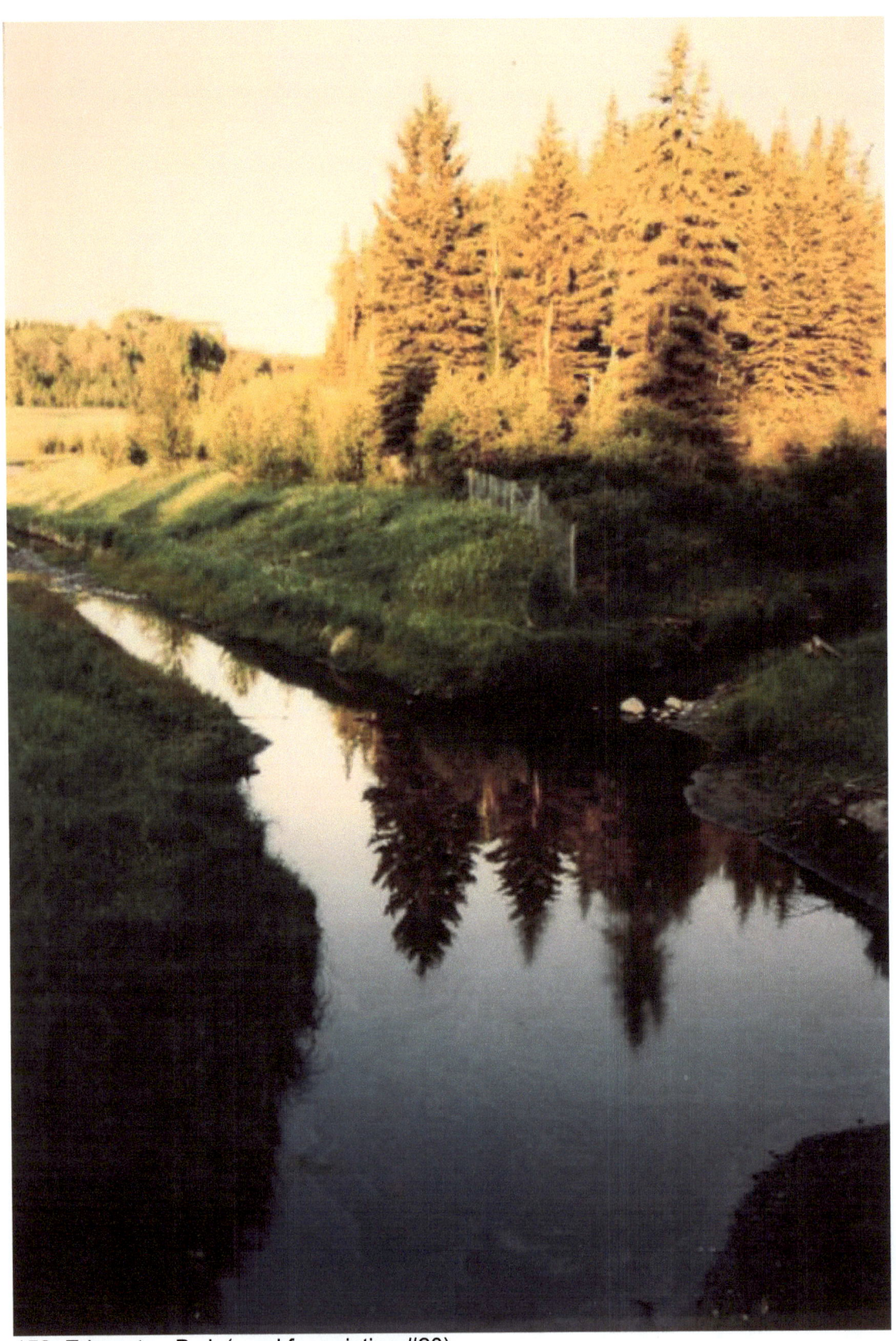
152. Edmonton Park (used for painting #20)

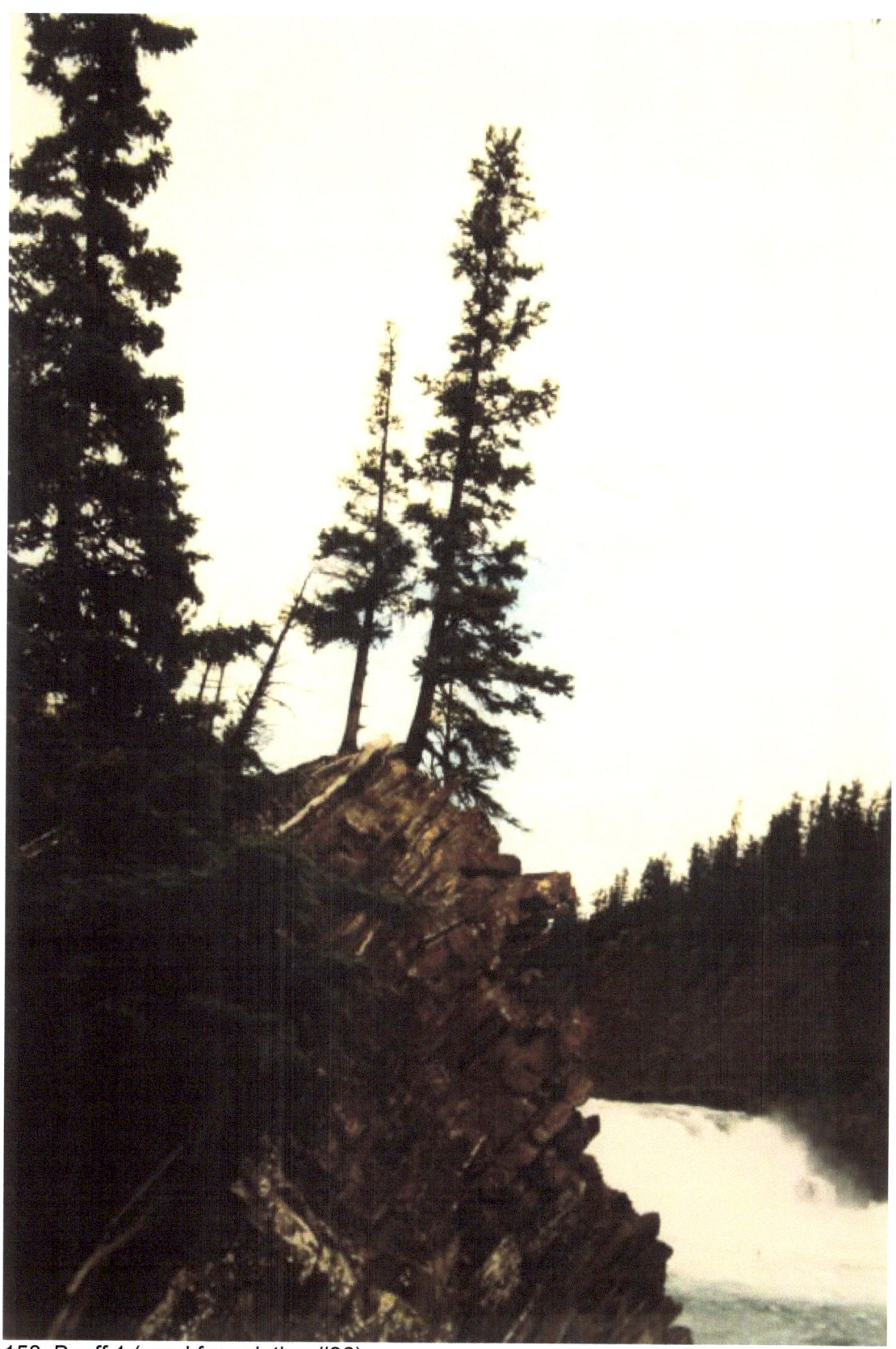

153. Banff 1 (used for painting #36)

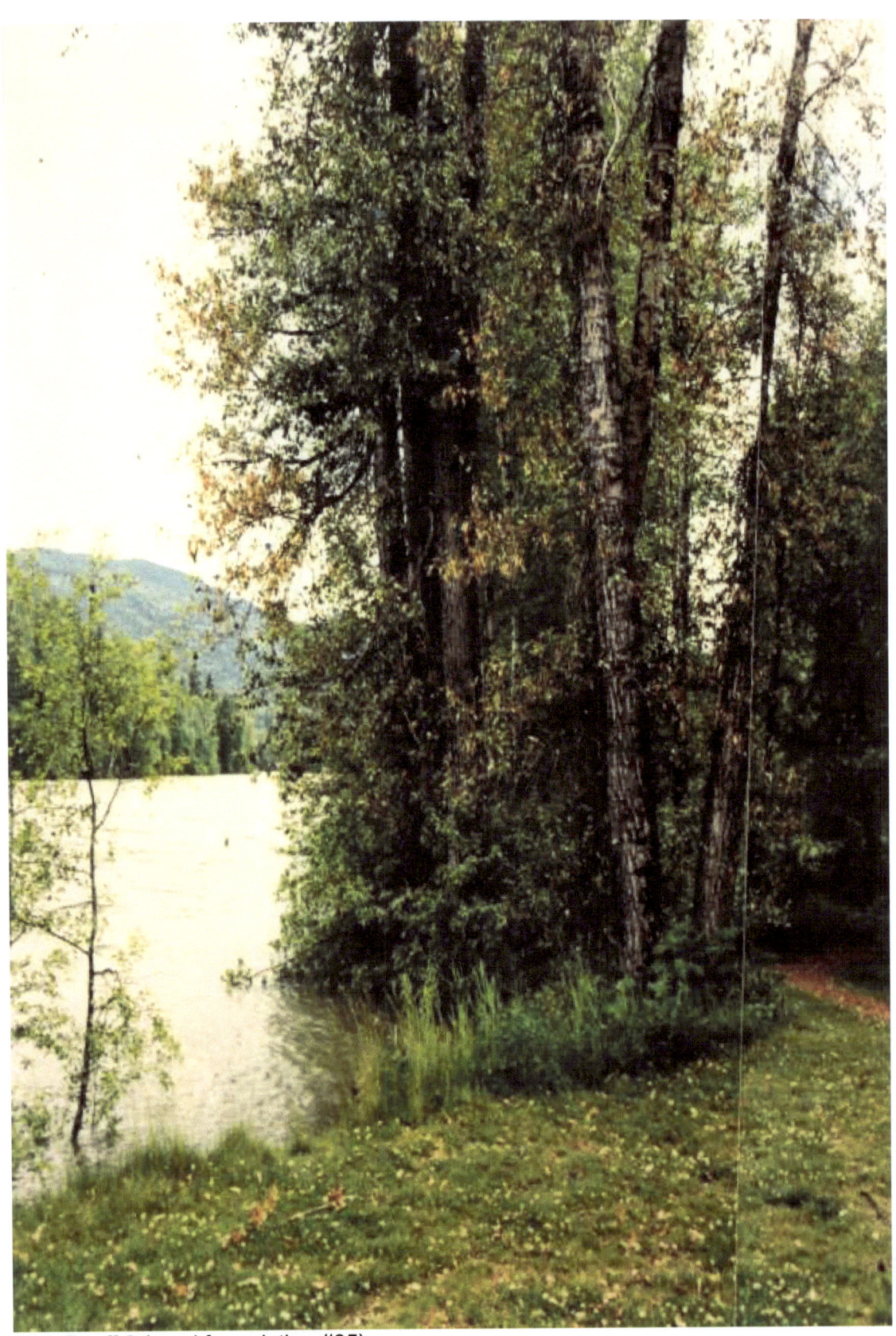
154. Banff 2 (used for painting #35)

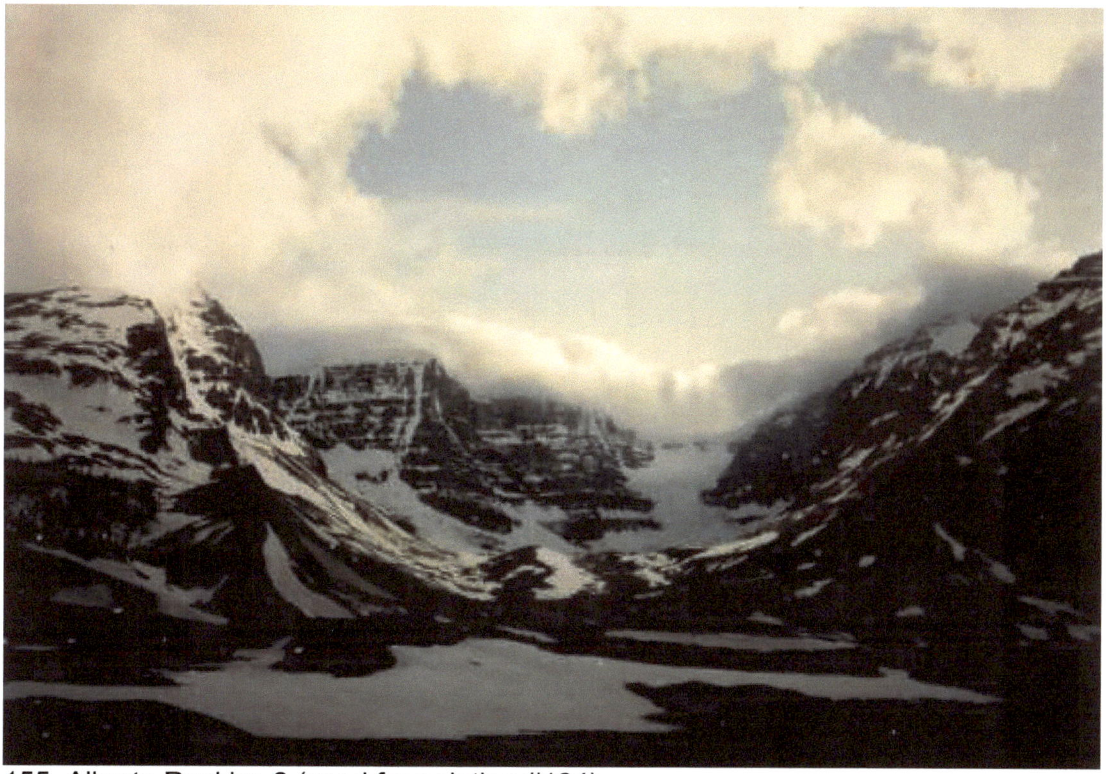

155. Alberta Rockies 2 (used for painting #124)

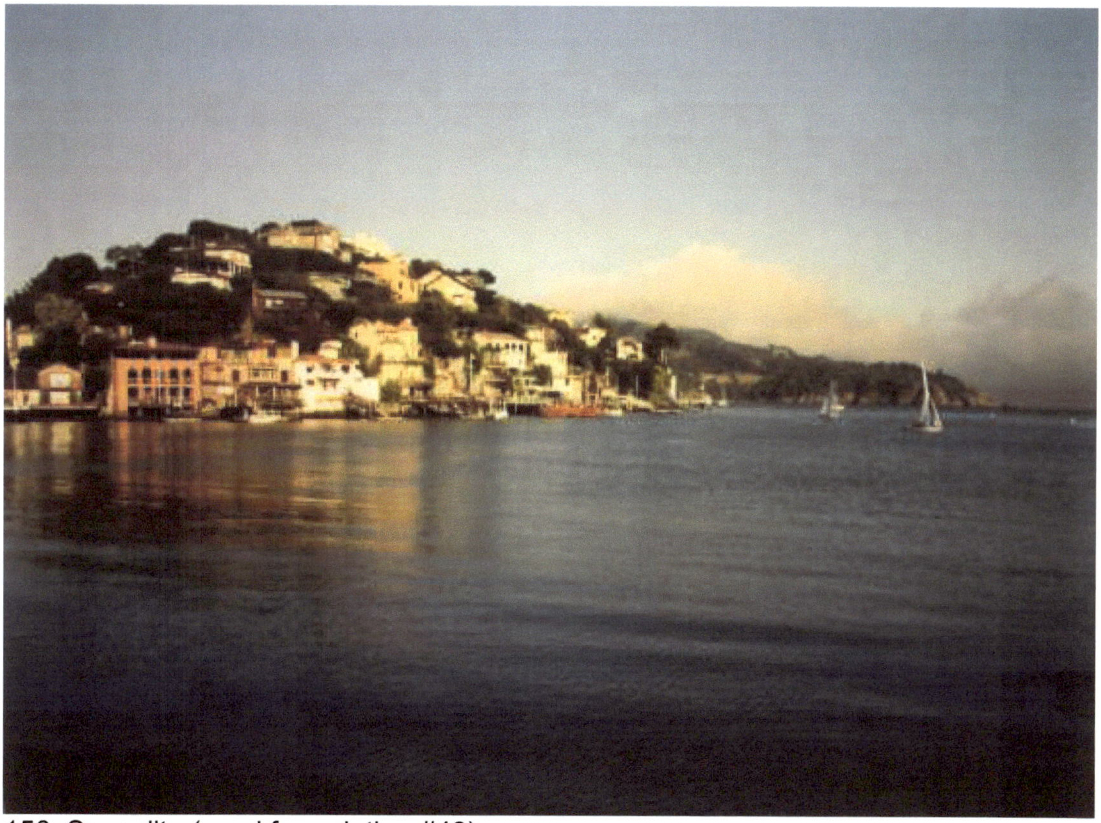

156. Sausalito (used for painting #48)

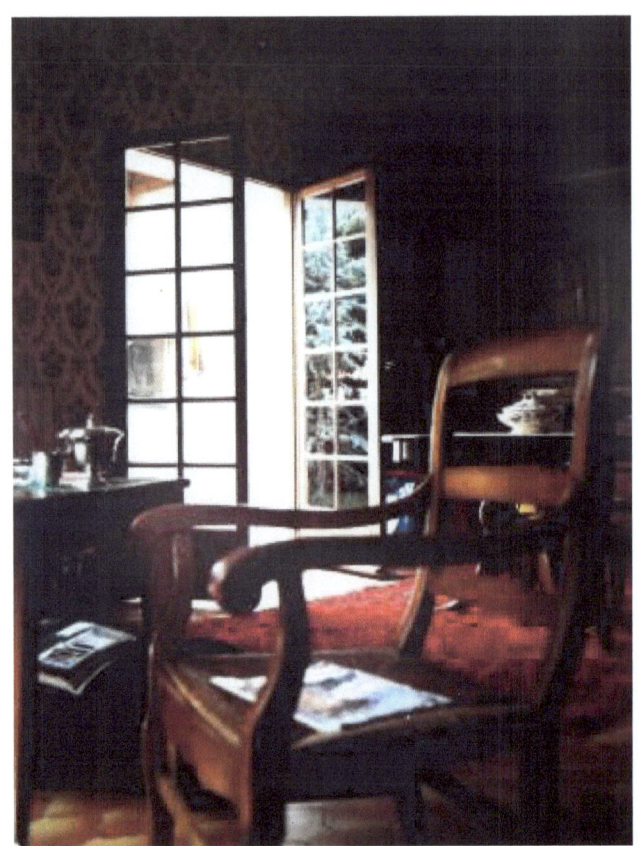

157. Jean Pierre's Living Room (used for painting #37)

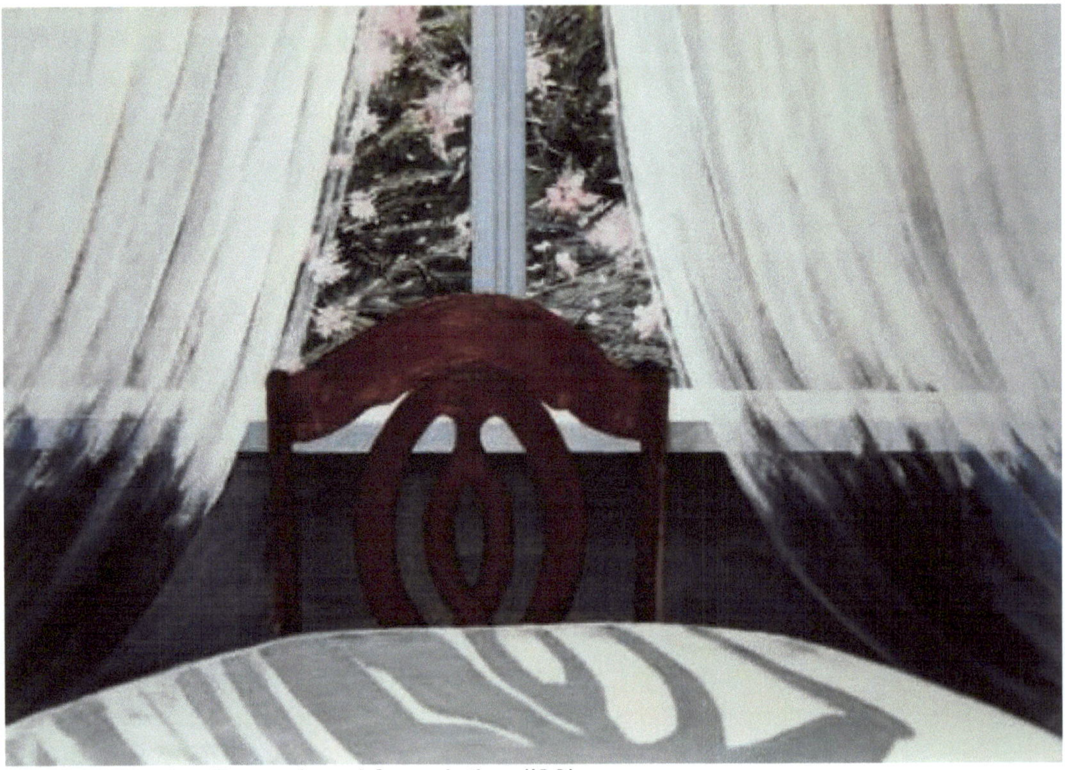

158. My Dinning Room (used for painting #38)

159. Sneaky Tulip (used for painting #33)

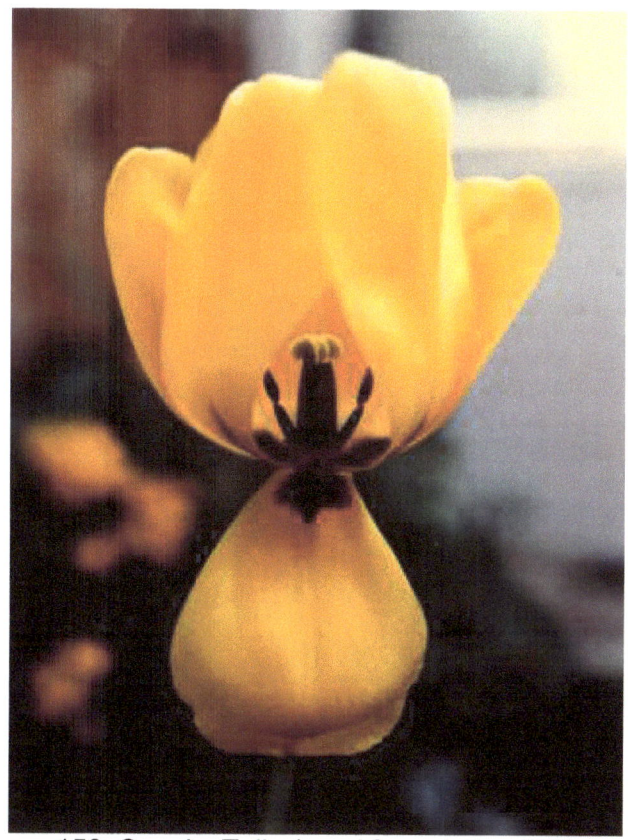

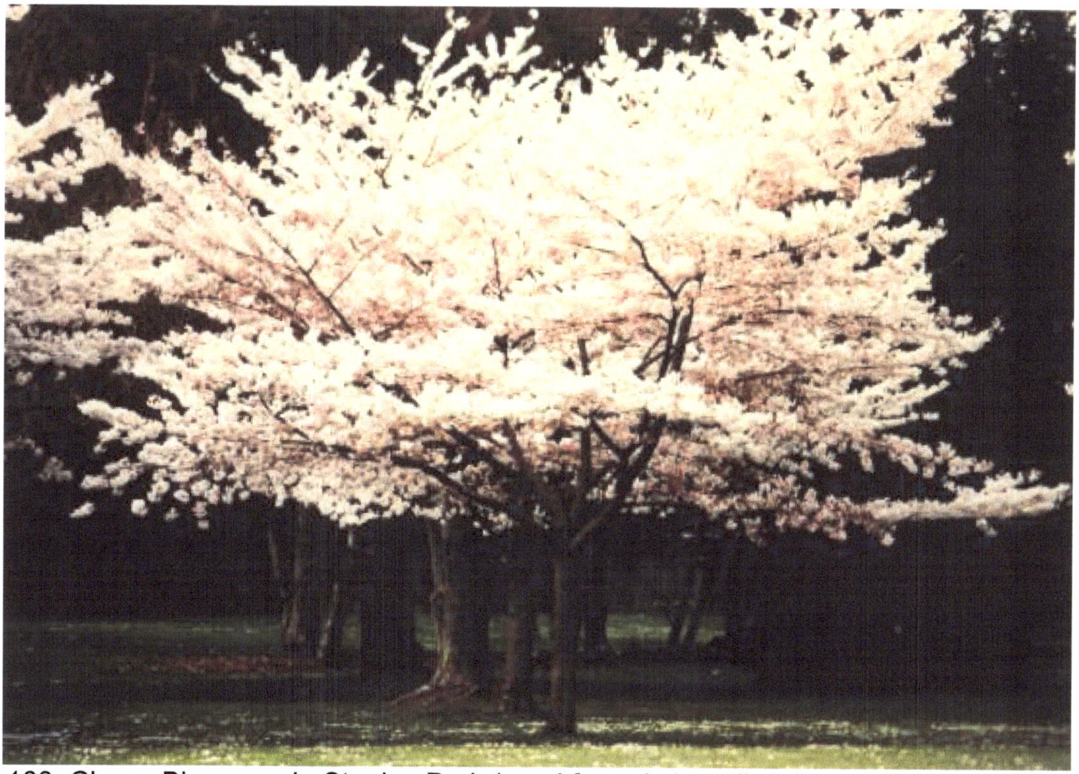

160. Cherry Blossoms in Stanley Park (used for paintings #50 & 123)

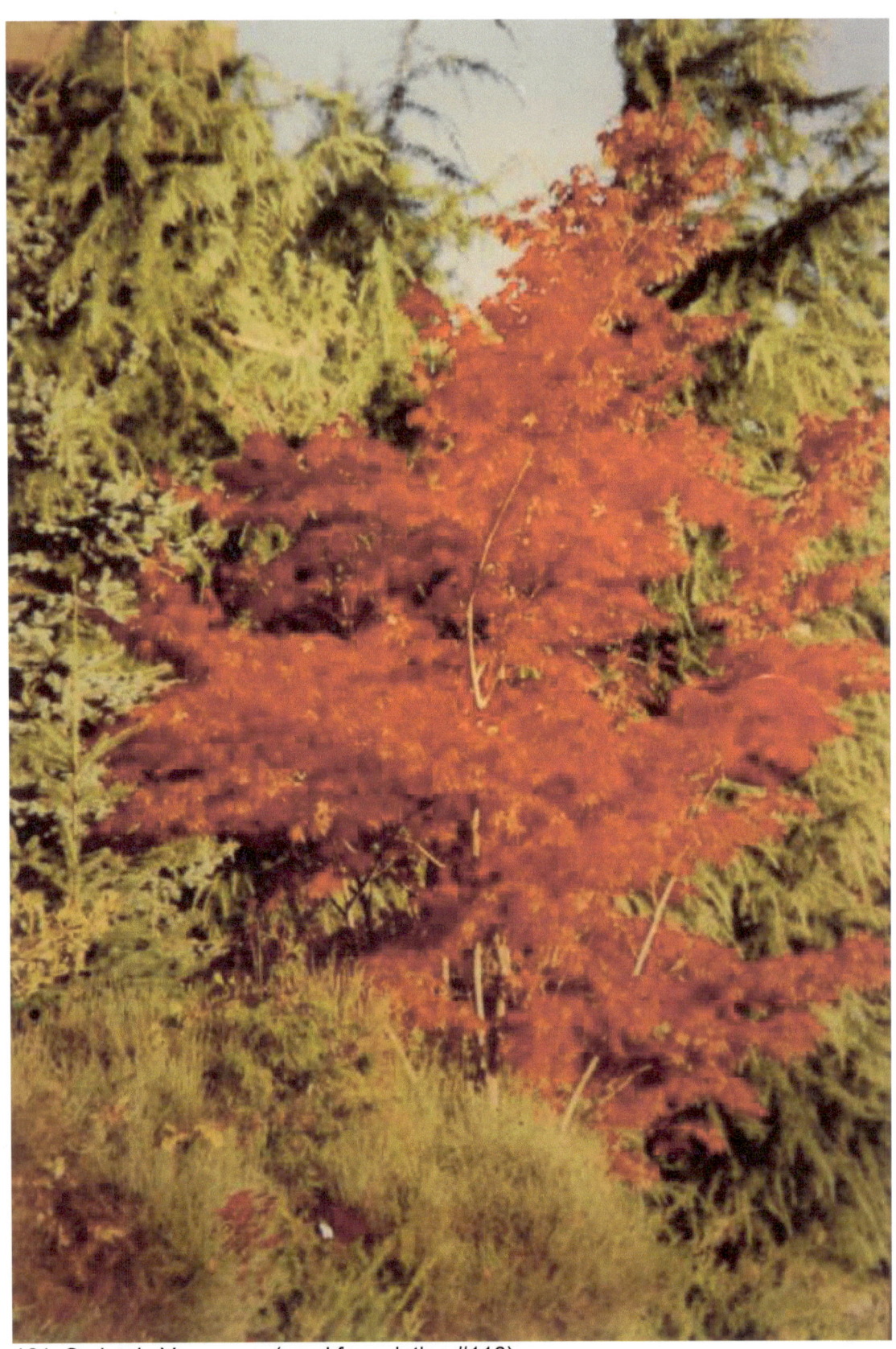

161. Spring in Vancouver (used for painting #116)

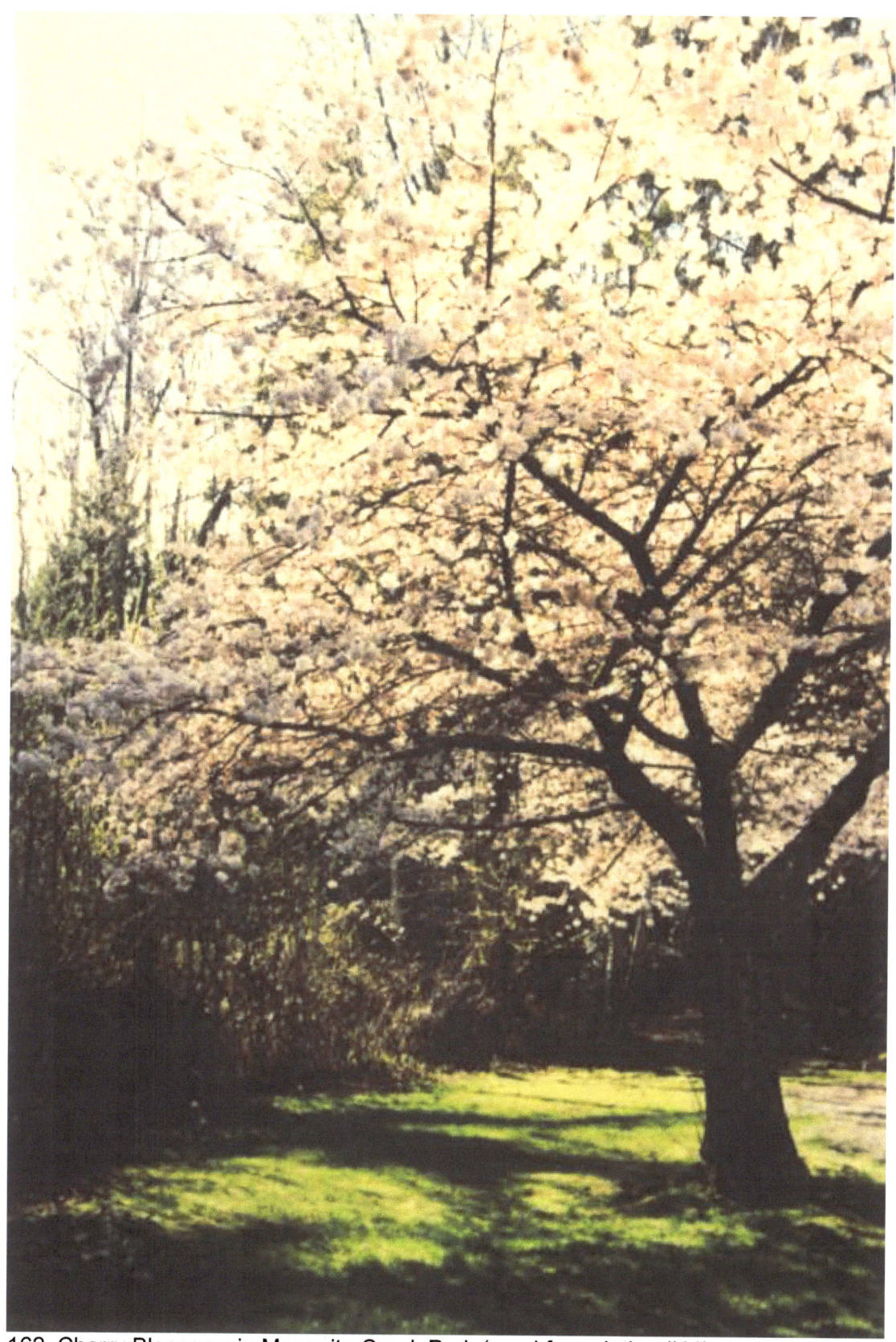
162. Cherry Blossoms in Mosquito Creek Park (used for painting #44)

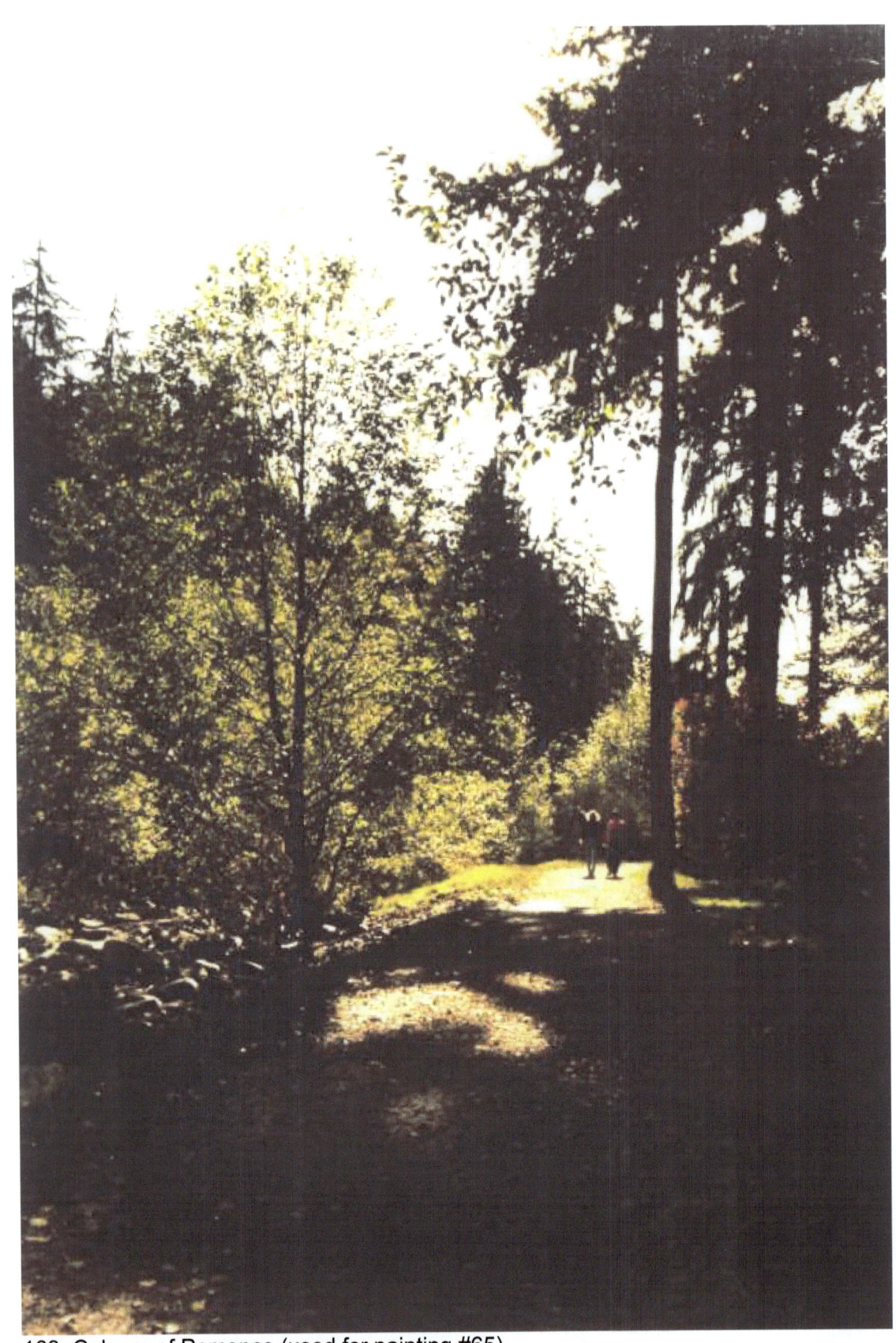

163. Colours of Romance (used for painting #65)

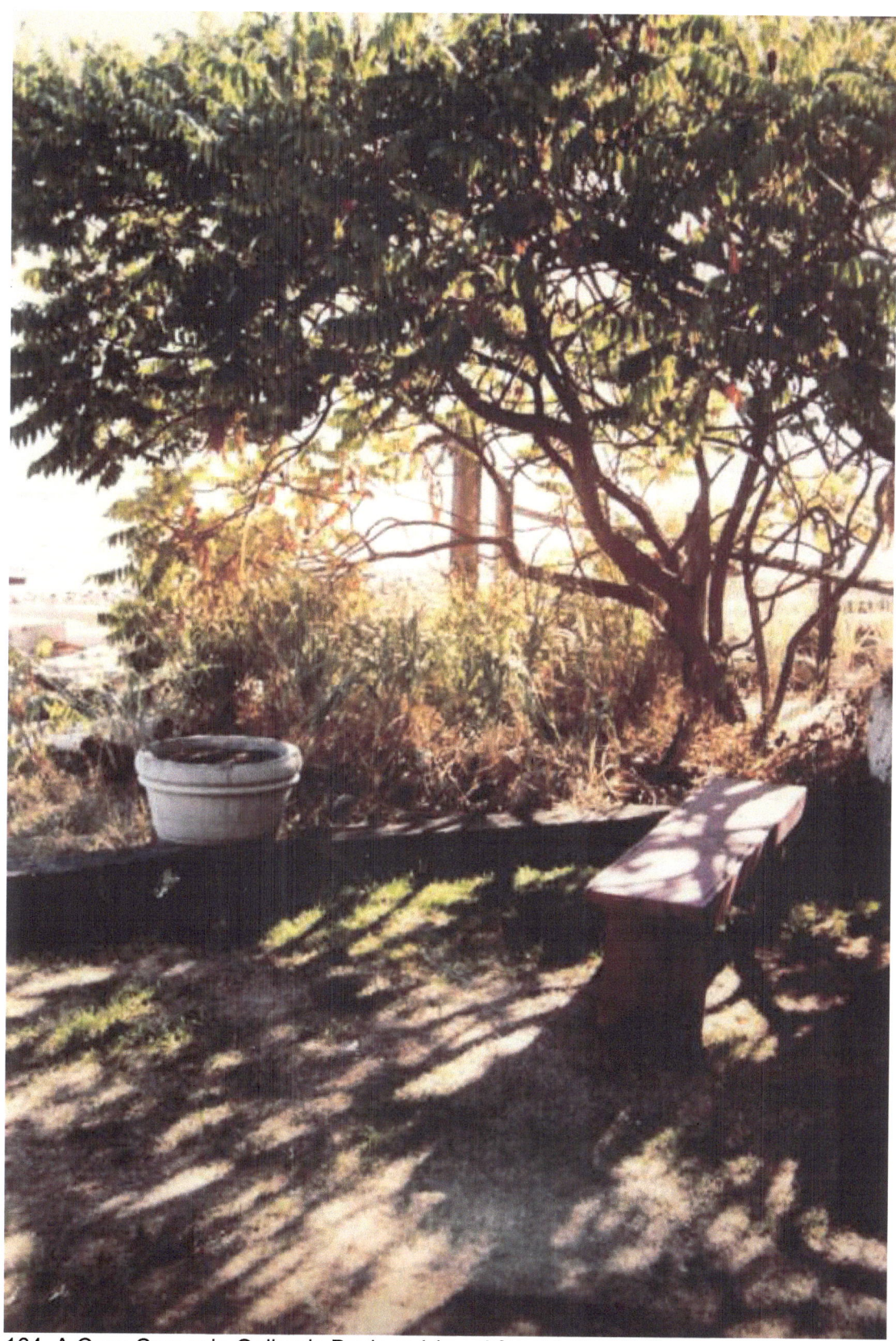
164. A Cosy Corner in Gallery's Backyard (used for painting #32)

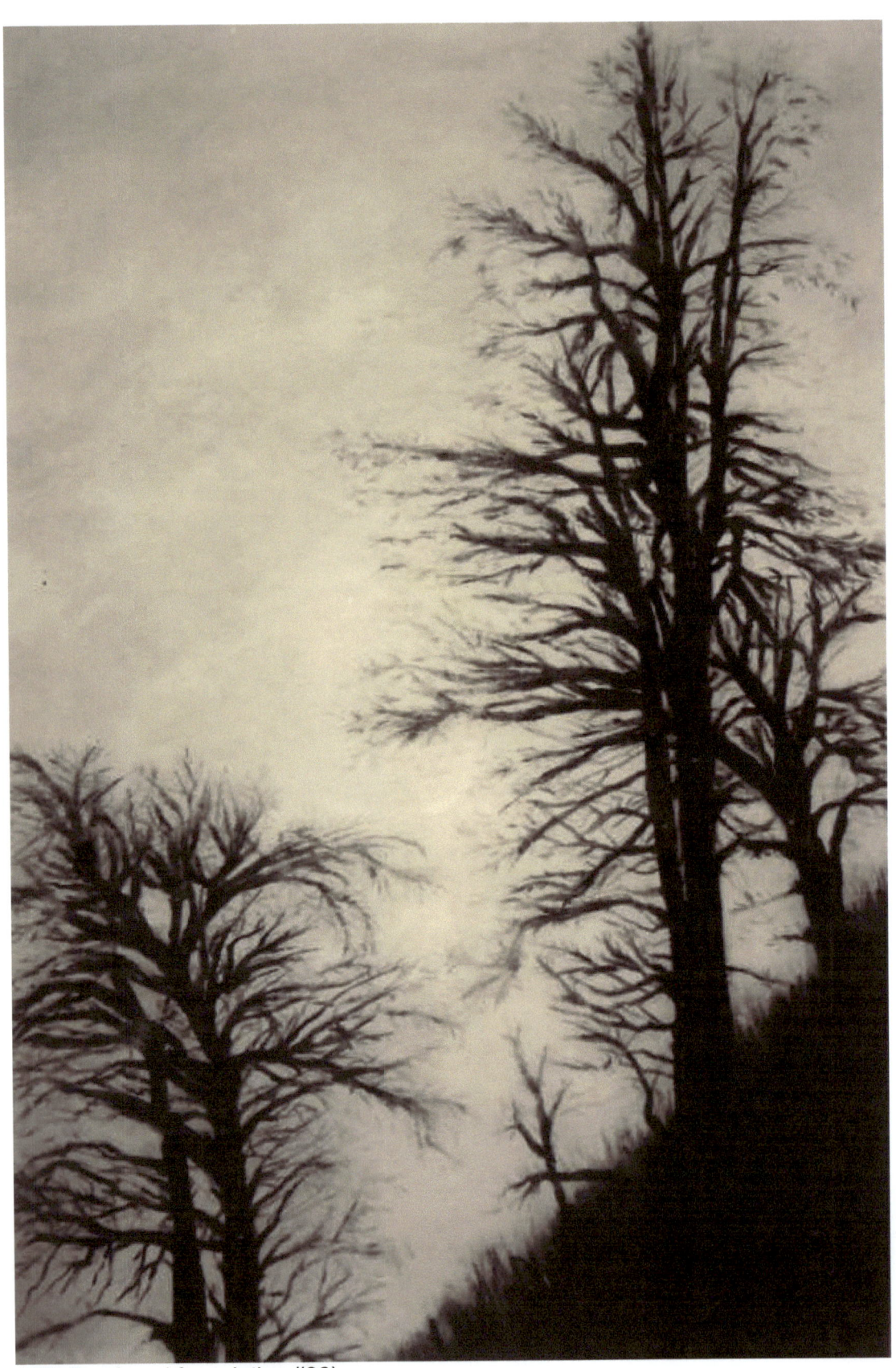

165. Fog (used for painting #96)

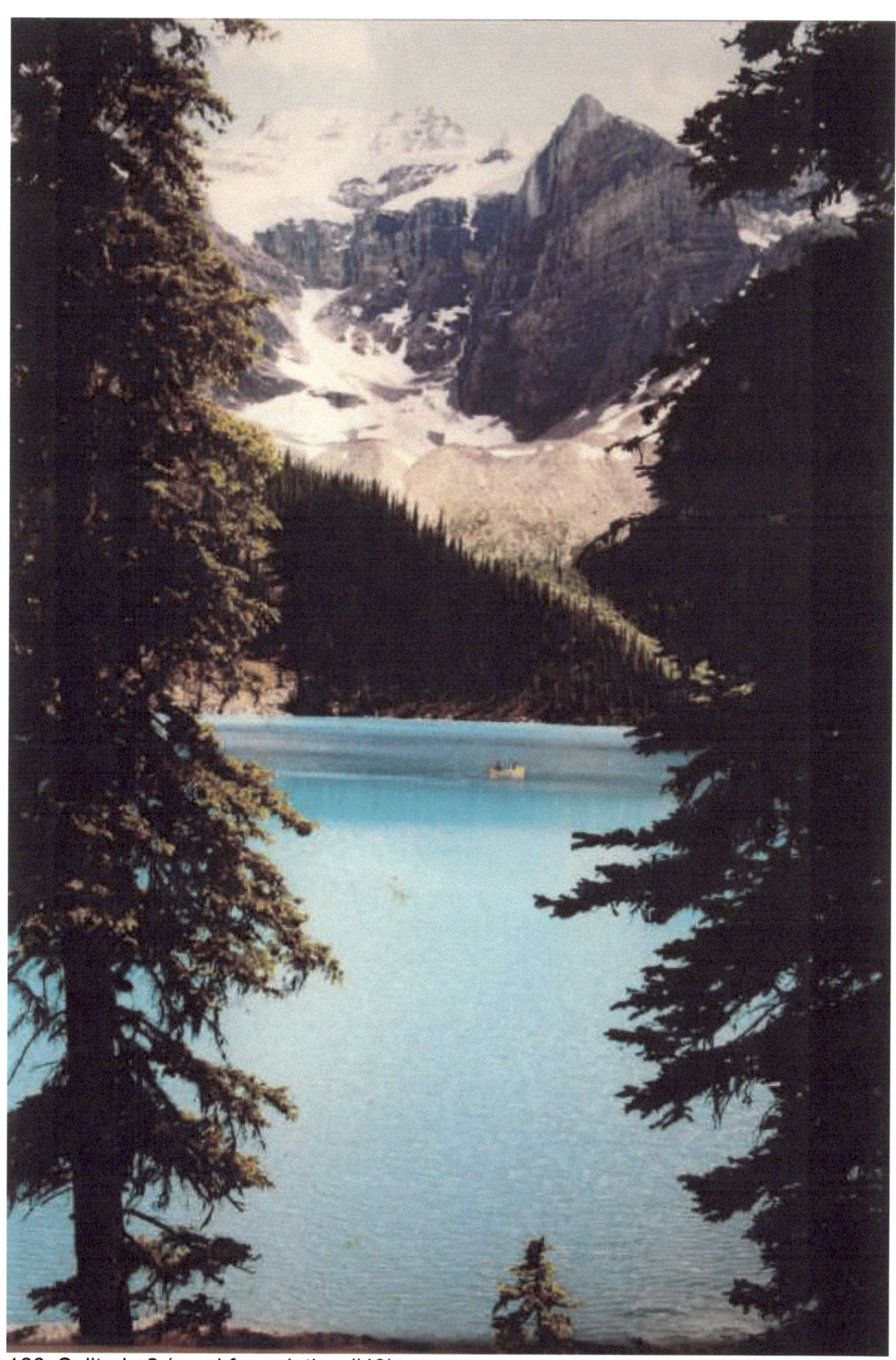

166. Solitude 2 (used for painting #49)

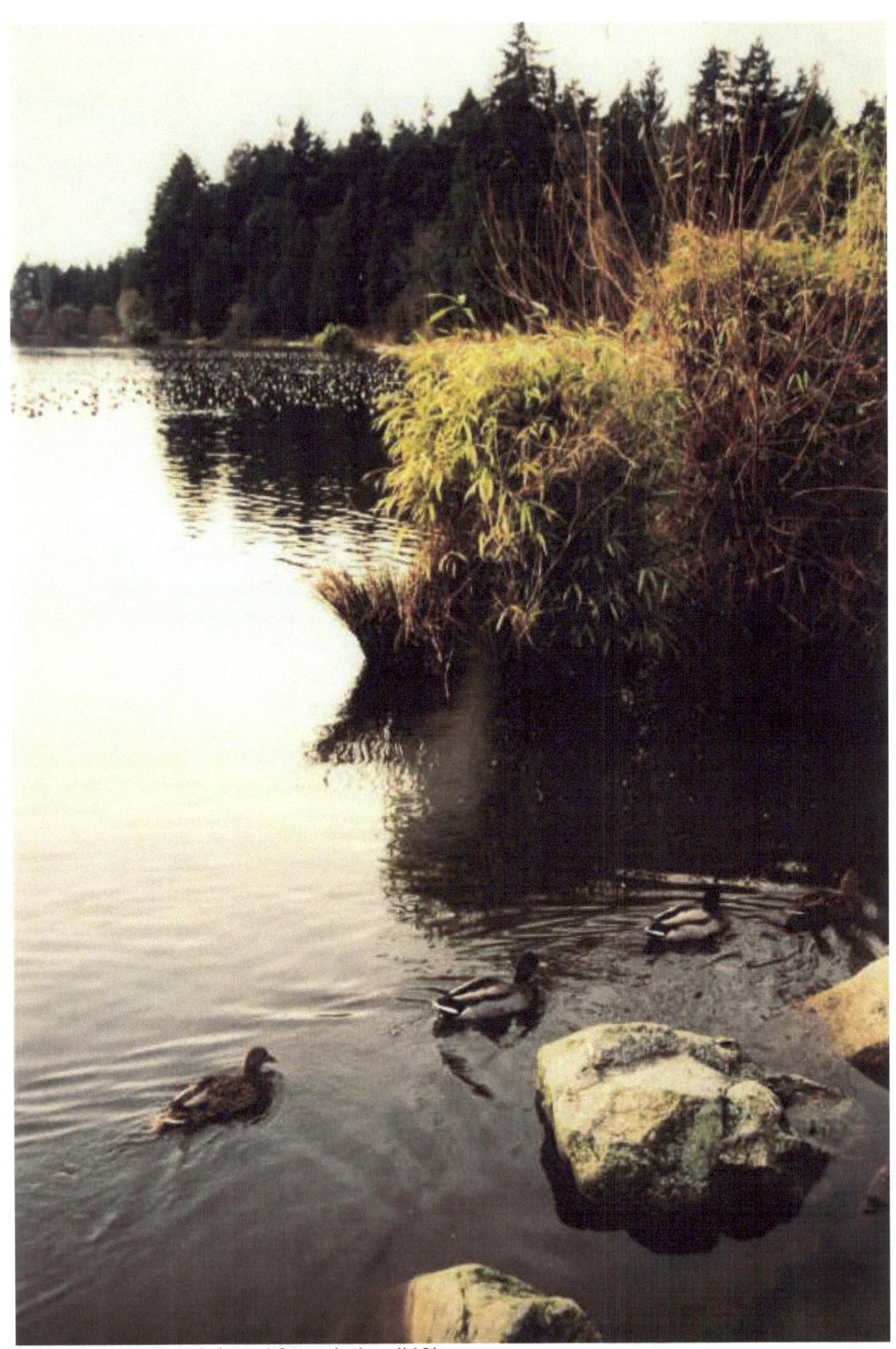
167. Lost Lagoon 8 (used for painting #43)

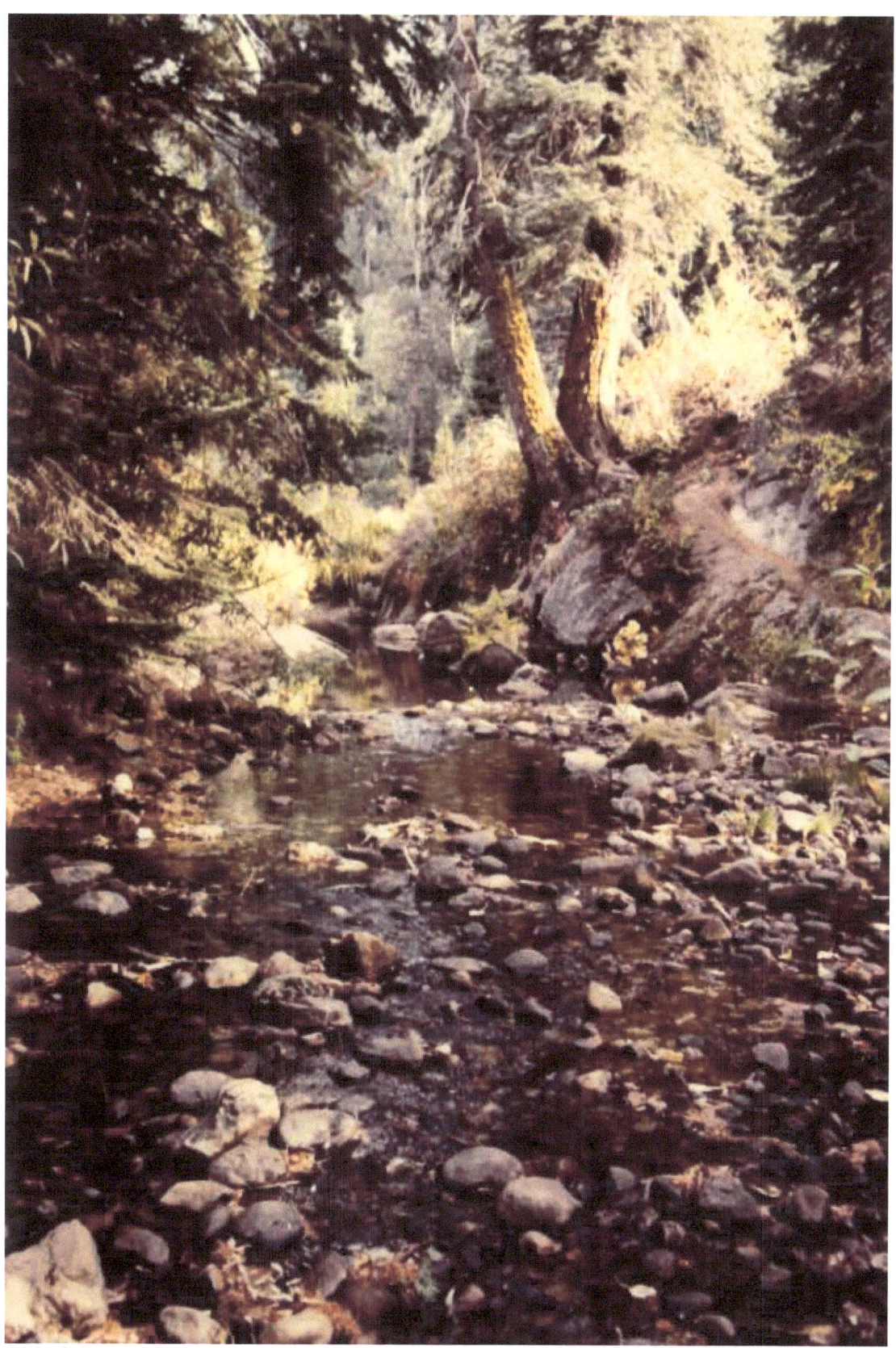
168. Colours of a Creek (used for painting #98)

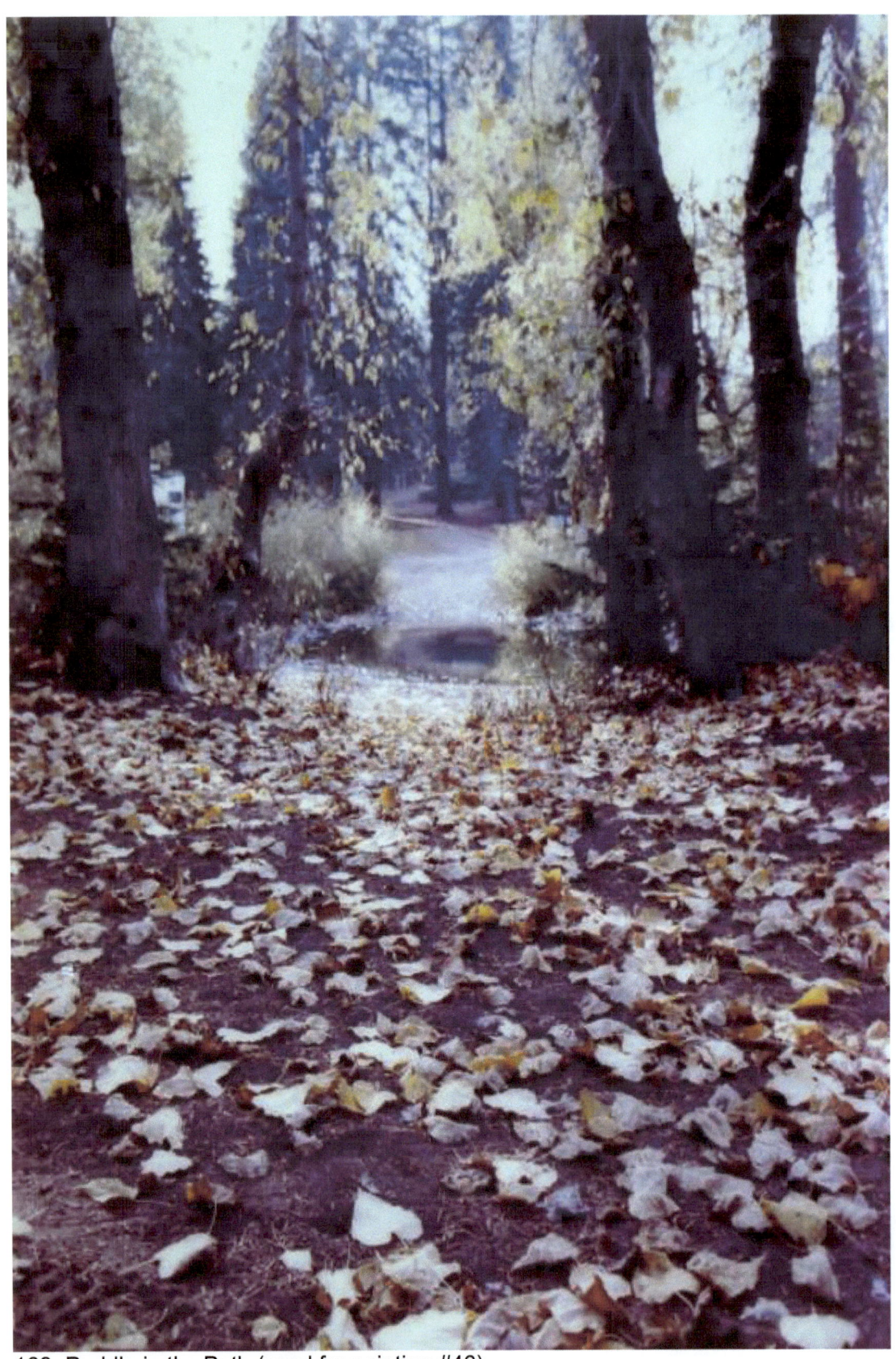
169. Puddle in the Path (used for painting #46)

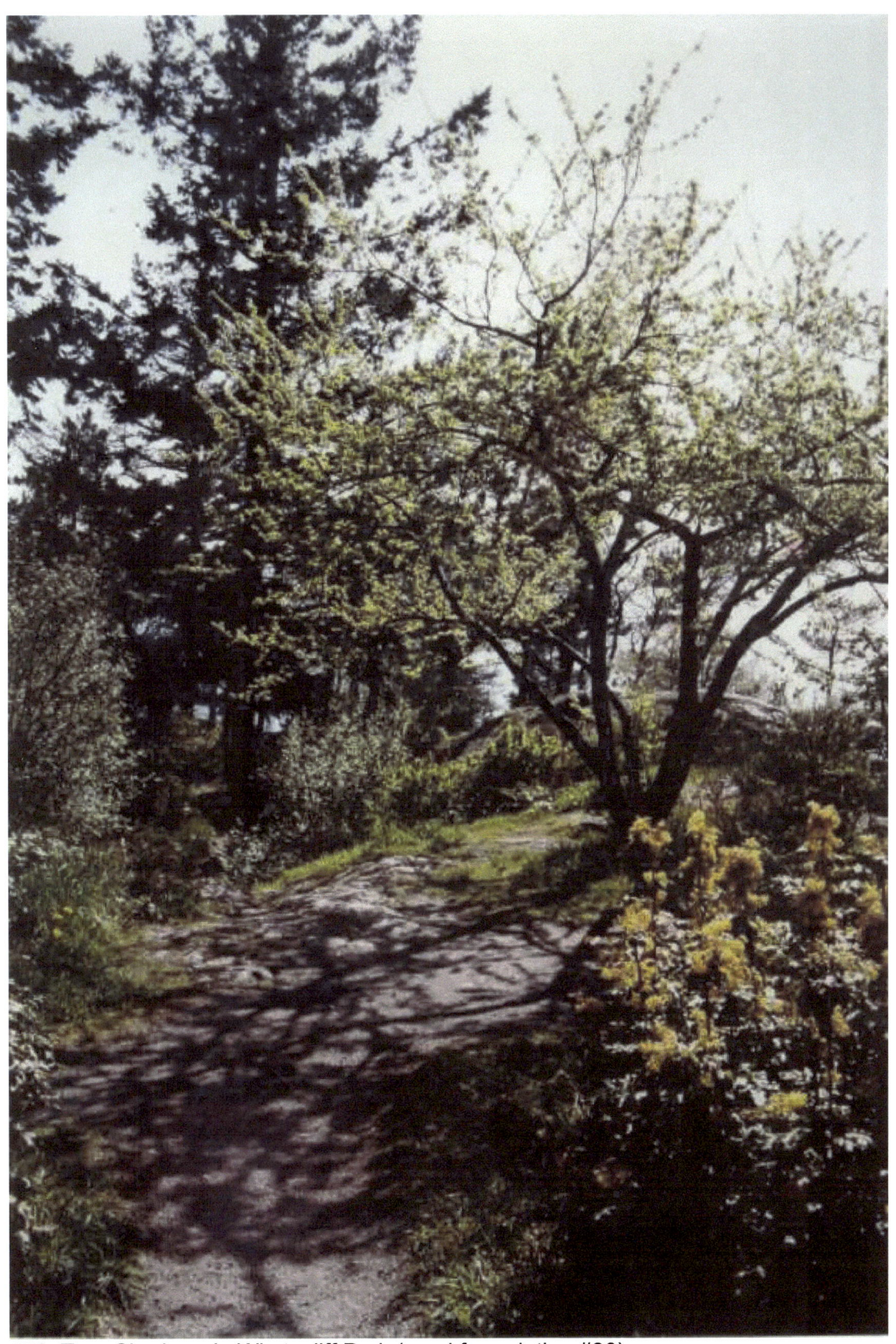
170. Tree Shadows in Whytecliff Park (used for painting #80)

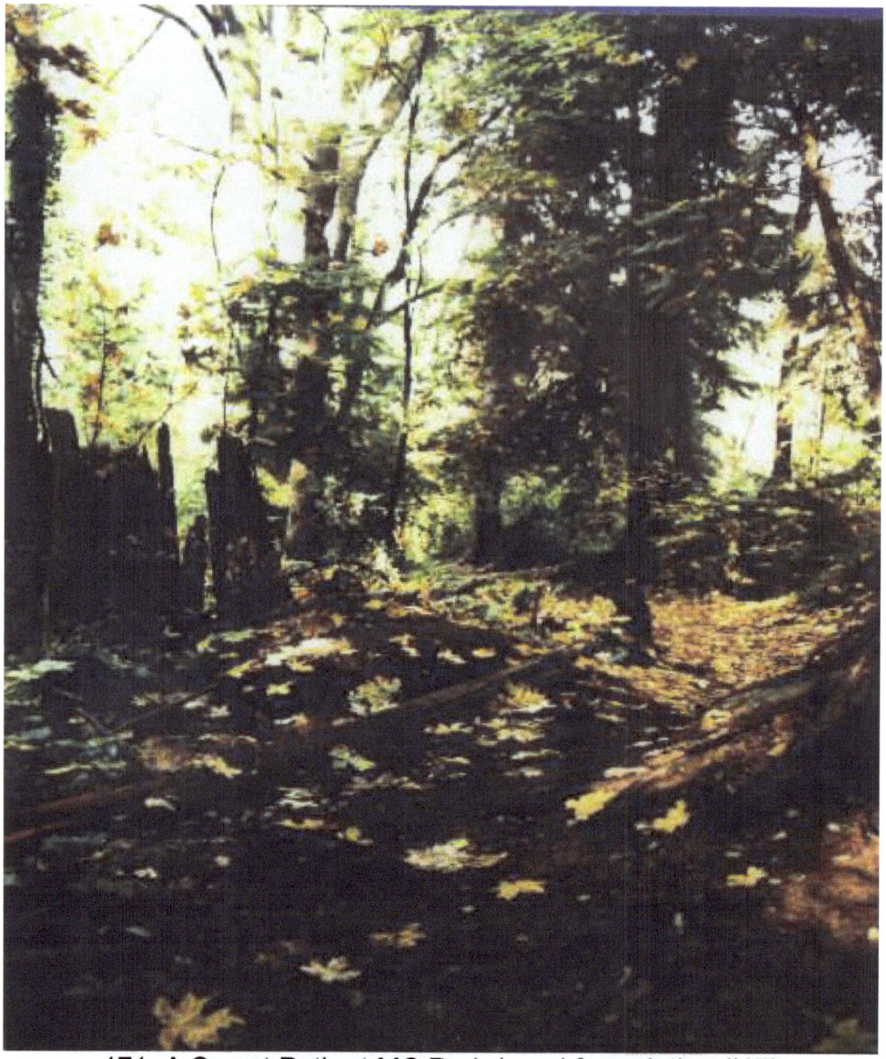

171. A Secret Path at MC Park (used for painting #17)

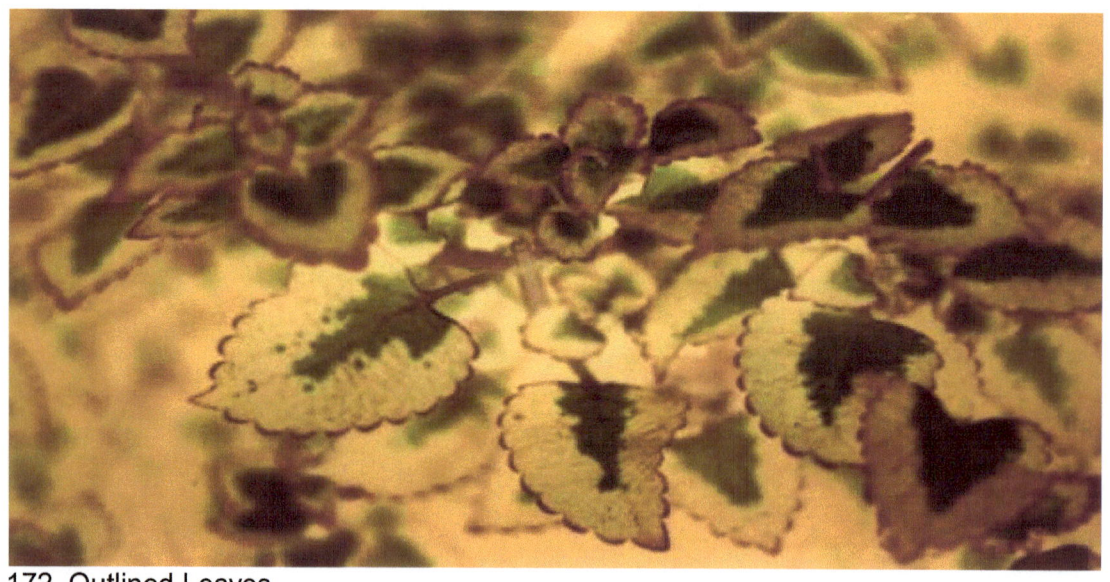
172. Outlined Leaves

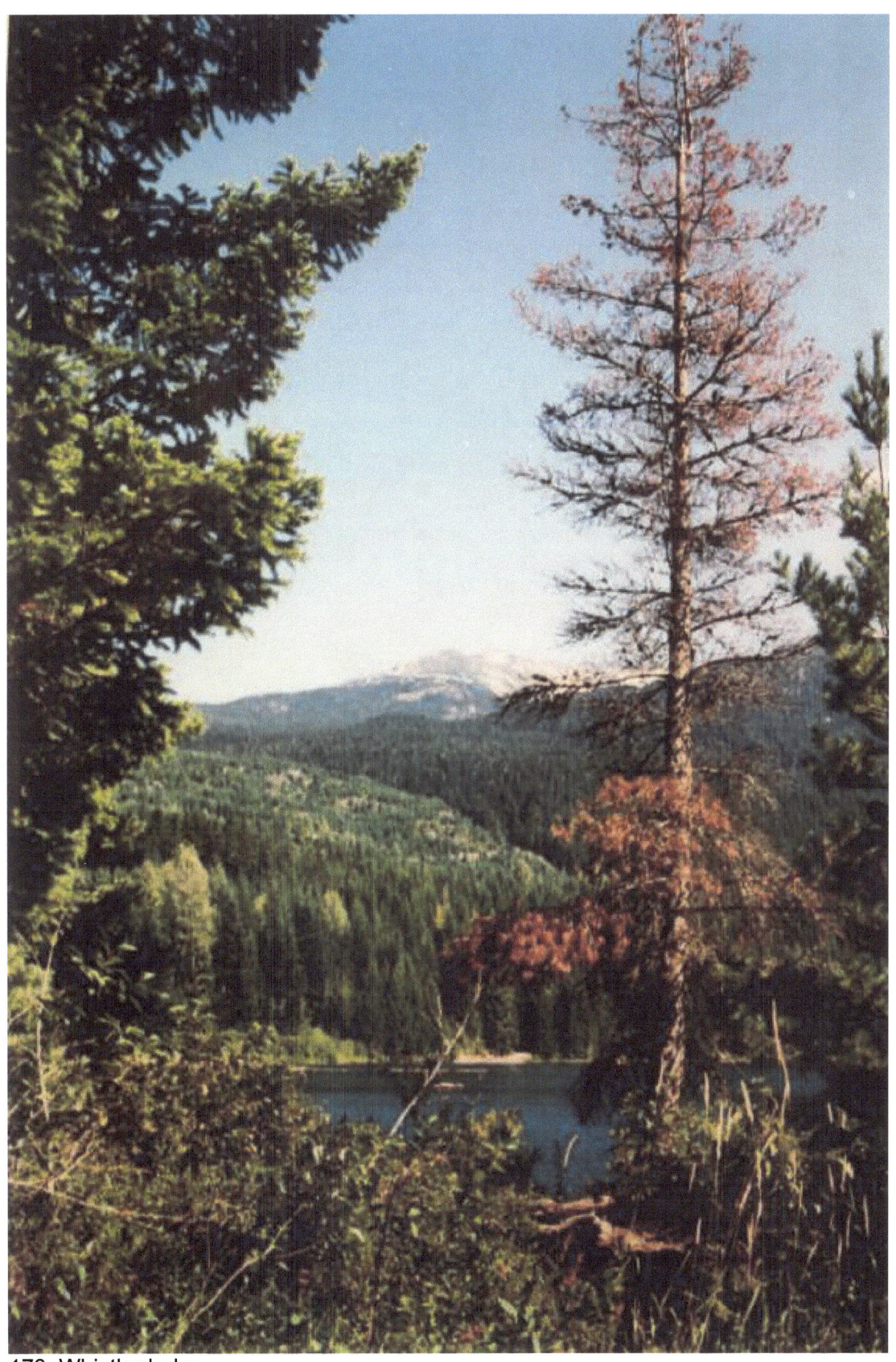

173. Whistler Lake

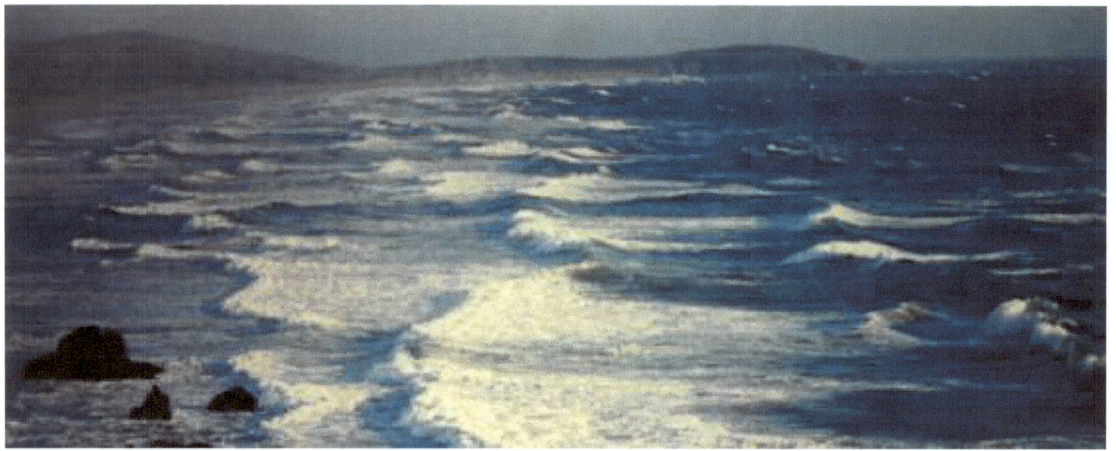
174. Nature's Romantic Rhythms

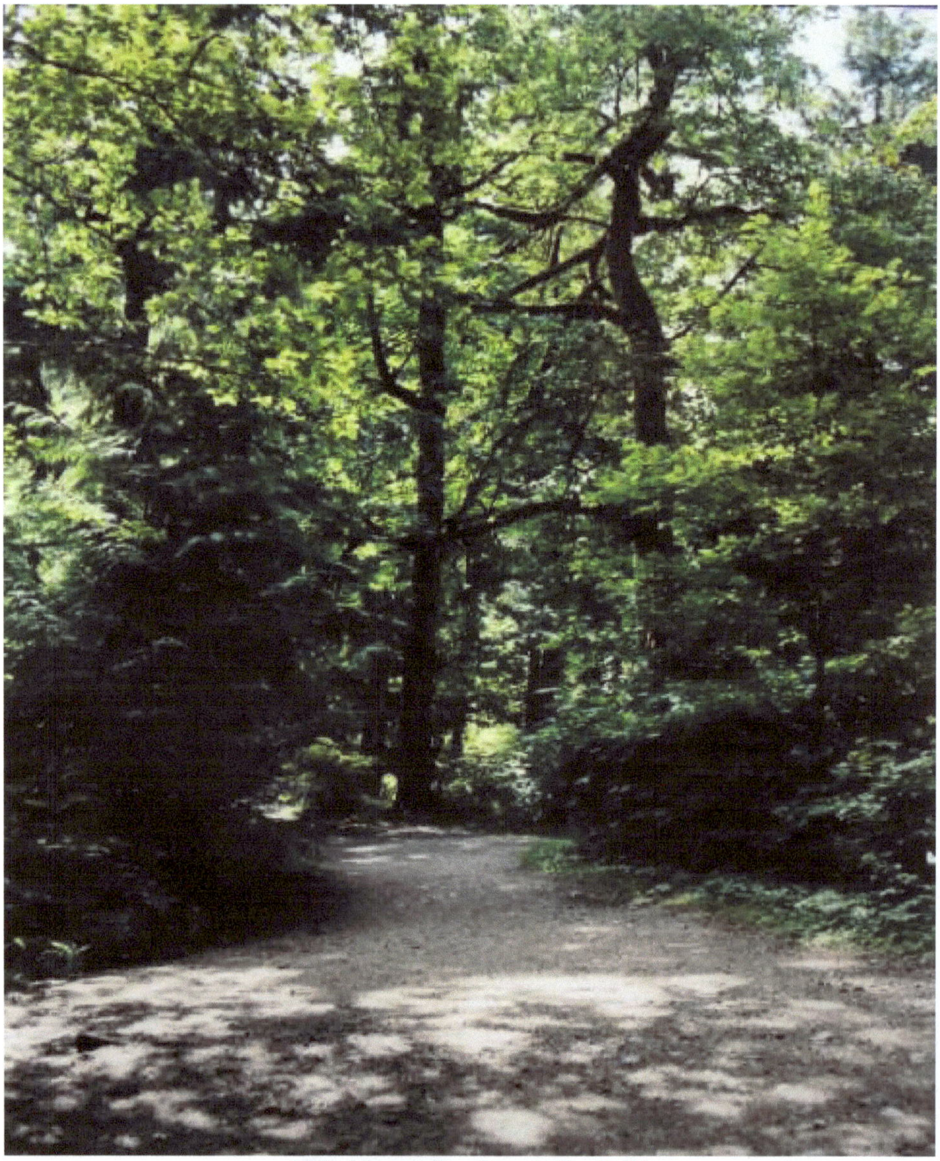

175. Mosquito Creek Trail #4

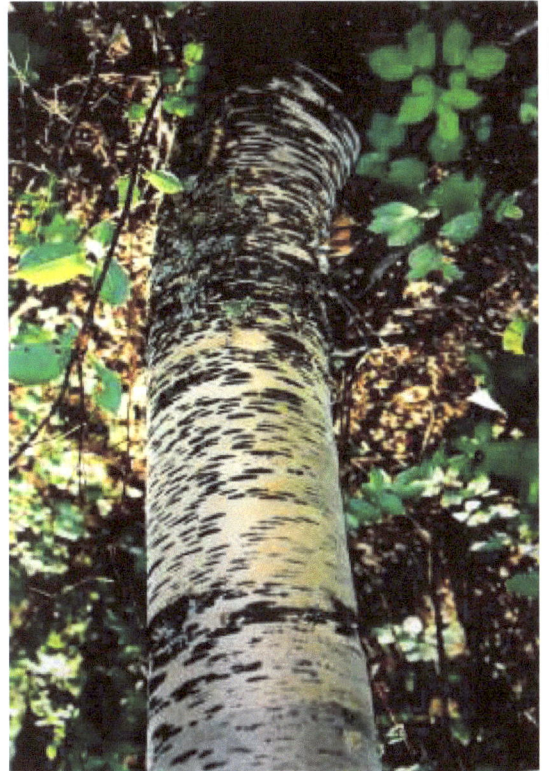
176a. Delicate Patterns of a Trunk

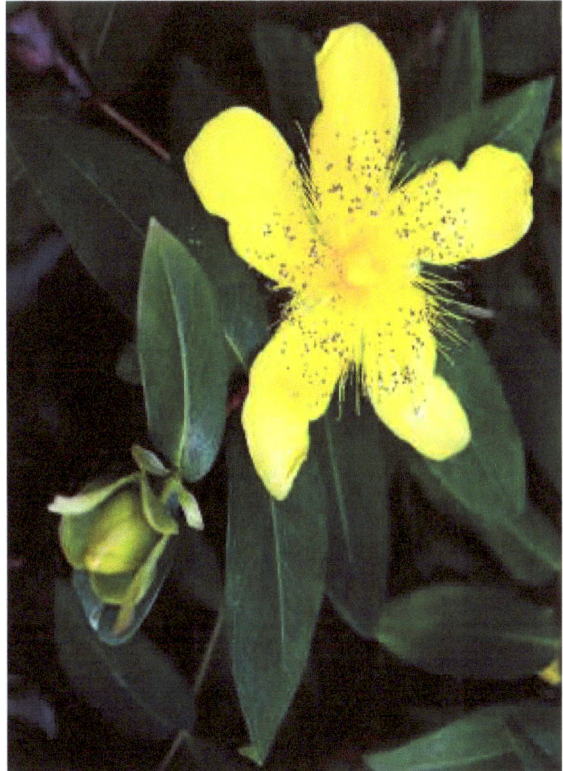
176b. Delicate Patterns of a Flower

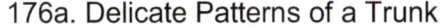
177. Total Peace

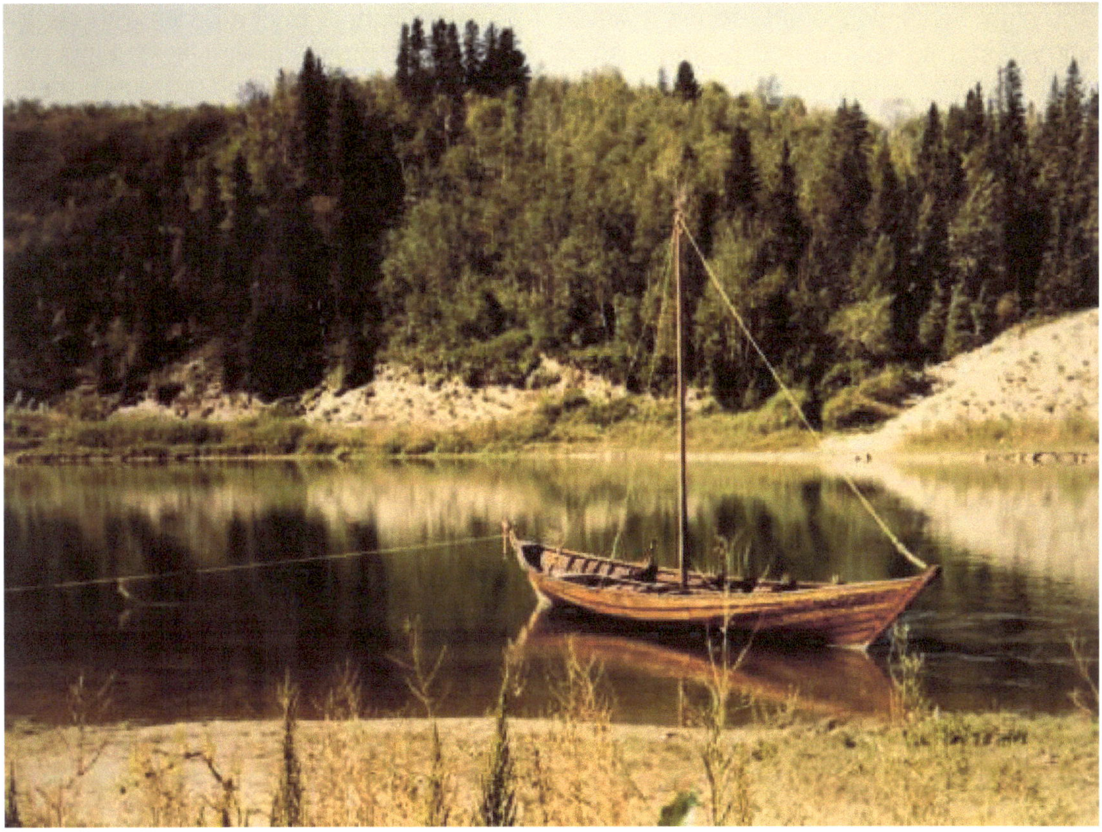

Appendix B
Odd Urges to Photograph (A supplement to odd photos on pages 95-101)

A big variety of urges drive our adventures in photography, as partly noted in this book. Still, some of these odd urges to photograph, including so many selfies these days, are particularly interesting to analyse, including the three personal experiences noted in this appendix just for fun without even numbering the pictures.

The Awakening Moonlight

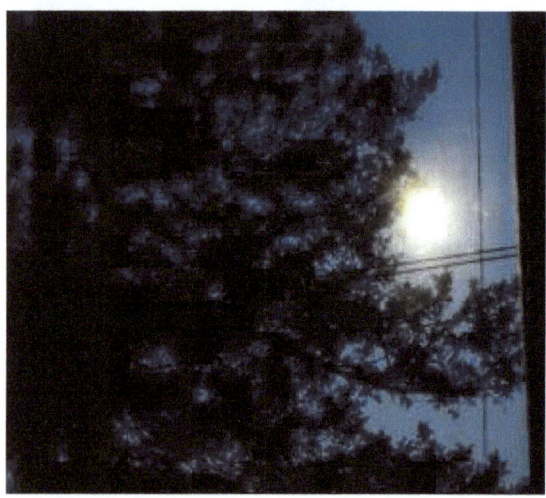 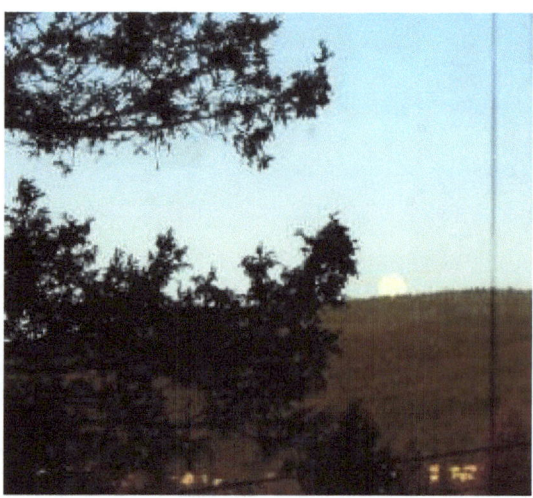

One night I was awakened around 4 Am by an intense light in my bedroom with some worry about its source and possible attack by aliens. Instead of simply shutting the blinds and go back to sleep, I decided to go find my camera and tripod, put the battery in the camera, and spend ten minutes to adjust everything for taking a decent picture before going back to bed and trying for an hour to fall asleep again. I wondered not only about the moon's nerve and power to disturb my sleep, but mostly the weird urge goading me to go thru so much hassle and depriving myself of a chance to fall asleep quickly again just to record moon's intrusive beauty. Then, as I woke up and went to the washroom at 6:30 AM, I noticed how that arrogant moon had lost all its annoying luminance and was now fading shamefully behind the mountains in North Vancouver.

The Cougar

Although I have kept hiking a portion of the Mosquito Creek trail for exercise once or twice a month, I have not been carrying my camera after getting serious about painting and writing over two decades ago. Then, one time, about 3-4 years ago, I saw the sign printed on the next page at the entrance of the trail. Thus, I returned to the trail with my camera the next day just to take a picture of the sign before the officials possibly realized its absurdity and removed it for all the good reasons that boggled my simple mind, especially about the necessity of closing the park until the cougar could possibly be captured—*if my idea was not silly or too much inconvenience for park authorities*?!

At the time, I was reediting the last chapter of my novel, *My Lousy Life Stories*, with hints about the protagonist's witty mindset trying to find an innovative, refined way of suicide. Thus, the following excerpt (protagonist's words) from that novel is quoted below for fun. *He is fooling around about his clever plan for ending his dismal life.*

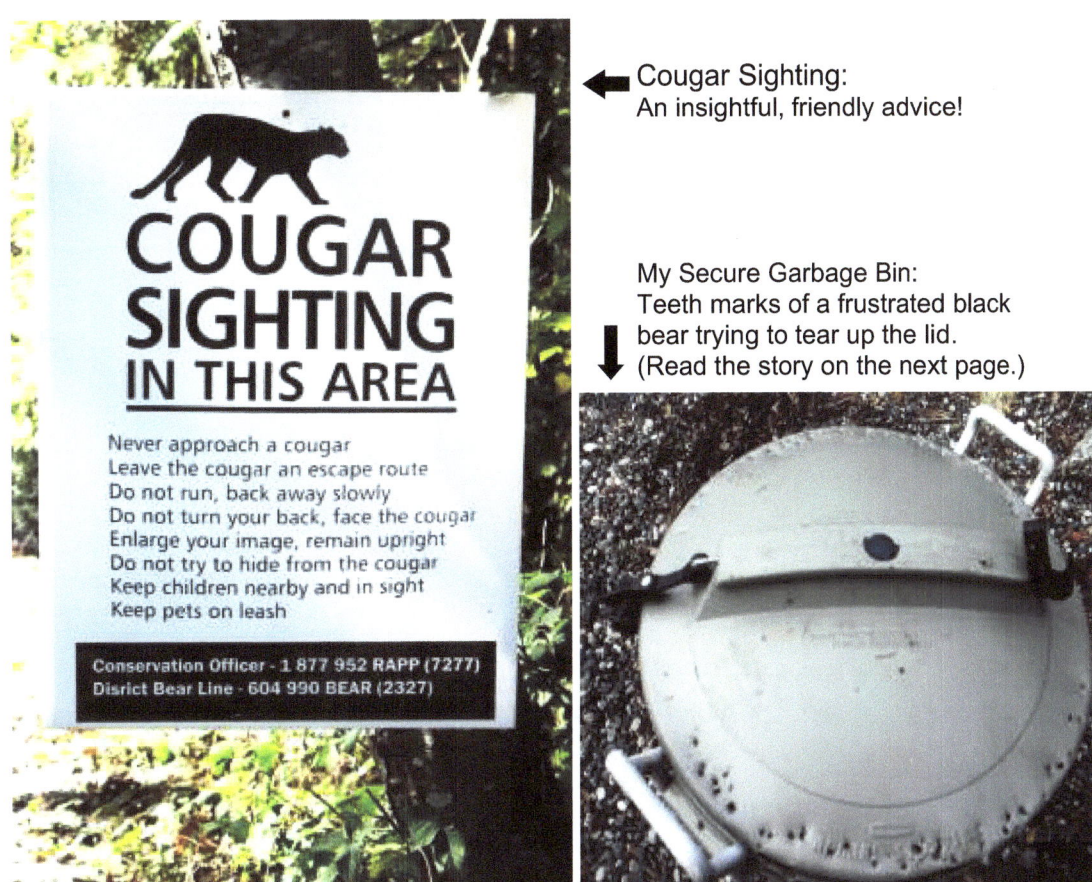

From *My Lousy Life Stories, An Abstract Novel,* pages 366-7:

"I listed the following crucial steps, in line with the meticulous advice on the sign, to be prepared: Approach the cougar and try to block its escape route with absolute tenacity. If it did not work, I would turn my back and wait a while to see if it gets my drift and excited. If not, I would start running away, but make sure not too fast or far. If still alive, I would cringe as much as possible to look as small as the cougar might like. If the damn animal is still standing there and only yawning, then I would go hide behind a rock or a tree to stir its curiosity or frustration about all the silly games that I have been playing uselessly to get its attention and entice its appetite for an old man's flesh. Sadly, my children are not small enough anymore and I do not have a pet to take with me as baits or maybe even as hors d'oeuvre. If none of my elaborate gimmicks works, then the stupid cougar deserves to die of hunger and I must go find a dense forest, after all. *I did not know these wild animals are so fussy or it is so difficult to get their attention!*

By the way, I truly admired Conservation Officer's priceless concern, foresight, and advice! I have been meaning to call the good officer and thank him/her for *everything* on behalf of people using that trail every day! The only reason for my hesitation has been that he or she may get confused or misunderstand my words or think I had sounded sarcastic. But do not let me stop you from calling him or her yourselves and expressing your gratitude for his/her scrupulous life-saving efforts. Tell her/him I said hi, too, without mentioning my sentiments. Of course, I would definitely call him/her myself to complain about the warnings' impotency if the cougar refused to move a finger to eat me after I disobeyed all those instructions to the dot."

Later, I took pictures of other official signs about loose black bears, coyotes, etc. all over my neighbourhood with the intention of writing funny stories about these carefree animals, too. I also photographed my garbage bin in the backyard after a frustrated bear had tried tenaciously to bite apart its secured lid to have a fiesta (see last page.) A few times, a bear had been just taking a nap in my front yard quite nonchalant about the noise that either I or neighbours made to make it move away. Still, my few direct encounters with bears had shown their passive timidity as long as we did not disturb their sauntering and crushing the garbage bins in the neighbourhood. One time, I came face to face with a bear at the top of the stairs connecting the lower and upper levels of W. Balmoral Rd. near my house. It just emerged out of the bushes and stared at me for 5-10 seconds with surprise—either about my courage or stupidity to disturb whatever it had been doing in a neighbour's yard. Then, it looked away tiredly and walked in the opposite direction, leaving me still frozen in shock. *You see, the whole point of this story is that bears seem to regain their dignities and composures after a shock much faster than we humans can, although I might've looked more arrogant to it!*

I have also taken a few pictures of flyers posted everywhere in the neighbourhood about so many cats suddenly gone missing, while *only some* of their anxious owners mentioned rewards for finding them. I wondered if all those cats had finally become fed up with their possessive owners and decided collectively to go rebuild their dignity and lives. Posters about missing dogs were common, too, but in much lower volume. *This possibly proves that cats are much more arrogant than dogs, as we had all suspected!!* All along, I was pondering to write a short story about a useless, witty character trying to tease these owners in different ways, for example by claiming that he had found the cat and needed a larger reward to deliver it. Or simply calling to ask about the amount of the reward before starting to look for a lost cat—"Just to ensure it's worth my time looking for it," he might tell the owner. Or he might even start haggling about a fairer reward amount before or after finding the right cat or a look-alike (or stealing one). Yet, my preoccupation with the humanity book has hindered this and many other precious projects, too. *Gosh, all my futile sacrifices just to write about humans feel too pathetic!*

<u>My Indoor Plants</u>

After admiring and photographing so many trees and bushes in nature, my indoor plants that I have created from scratch and now reaching the high ceiling in my foyer deserve a quick mention as well. After all, they have played a big role in keeping me amused and also being envied by people who have been surprised regularly by the sheer size and health of these 25-35 year old plants. Someone asked me once rather rudely, "Is this a house or a jungle?" I just ignored him. I trim the plants sometimes, while also not minding to let them grow to break the Guinness World Records for the tallest and oldest indoor plants. Certainly, keeping them alive and healthy according to a very well-preserved secret has not been easy. Actually, the taller these plants have grown, the more cynical I have become about sharing my *simple* secret with people who had been trying hard or sneakily to drag the secret out of me; and then, as they have failed, they have just said testily, "You have the greenest hand, then." I have realized my meanness about this particular issue, while always insisting that it is only a matter of watering them properly! Then again, I have nurtured a kind of legitimate reason for keeping the secret, which I *might* reveal (the reason only or the secret, too) in my upcoming humanity book after making enough points about humans' general laziness to use their brains even for their very basic needs and survival, let alone keeping their plants healthy.

For now, the necessity of offering proofs of my claims about my indoor plants had stirred the odd urge of photographing a few of them to include in this book. Hopefully, you will get a chance to read my upcoming book about humanity and learn at least about my reason for being secretive regarding my plants, besides minimizing anybody else's chance of breaking the Guinness World Records for the tallest indoor plant.

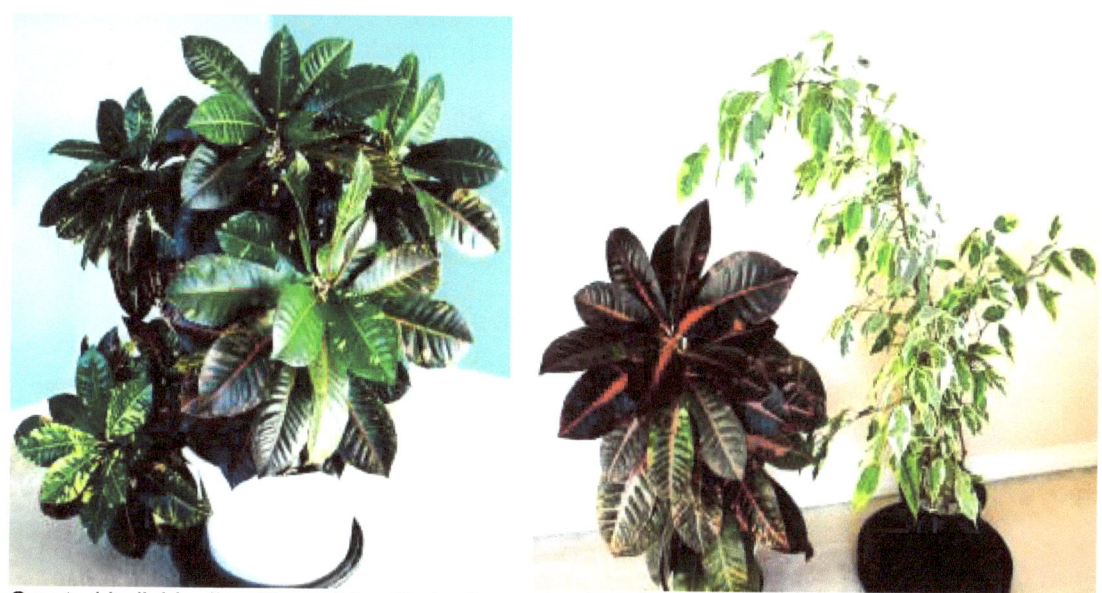

Created individually with my big efforts, they grow together with hopes for some general unity.

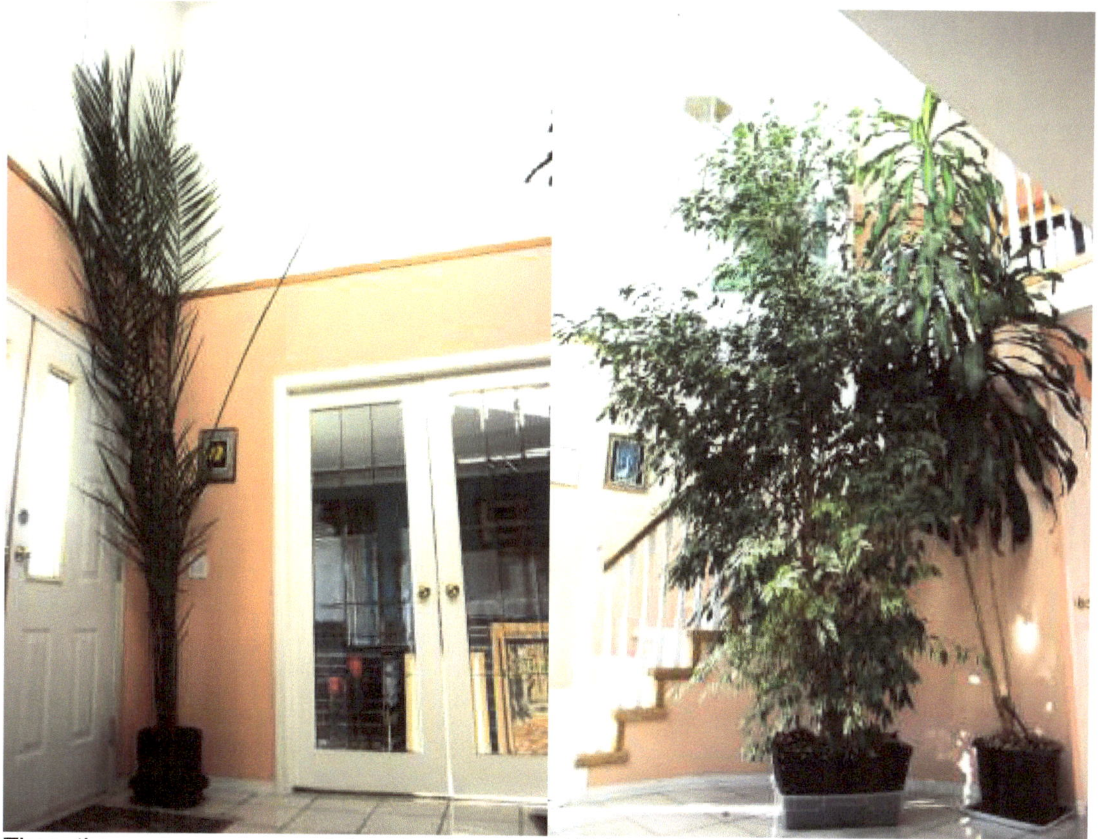

Then, they cause us so much hassle, like our real kids, as they try to occupy our whole world.

Appendix C
Three Sentimental Photographs in Three Life Phases

While inspecting my boxes of photographs, three pictures had stirred my nostalgia in line with my thoughts about life's three ironical phases. Together, pictures #178 below (my parents and I) and #2 on the back cover had reminded me of my naïve planning and dreaming during childhood and adolescence, while worrying about my future—*life' phase one attribute*. Picture #179 had made me nostalgic about my good times around my family along with lots of reflections about *the meaning of life* and how to elude its inherent turmoil, especially for keeping my family together—*life's phase two attribute.* Picture #180 shows my immense puzzlement, along with a sense of resignation, about my life's value and purpose, despite a lifetime of planning and reflections—*life's phase three attribute*!

These three photos also prove the privileges of photography compared with other arts merely for inciting deep reminiscences. In particular, #180 shows the magic of a simple click and the jargon 'Every picture says a thousand words' in the way it depicts my absolute puzzlement and resignation in the last phase of my life.

These sentiments have also goaded me to include these three personal pictures in this book, especially #180 for ending the book with that funny, ironical picture. Photo #178 is also a tribute to my parents for being the only persons loving me selflessly.

During life's three phases, humans fight with a variety of fundamental questions consciously or subconsciously, especially now that social and family relationships are getting more out of hand and humanity is facing its demise.

Why have we failed so embarrassingly to use our brains for our long-term welfare and thus become the saddest species in this *possibly* wonderful universe?

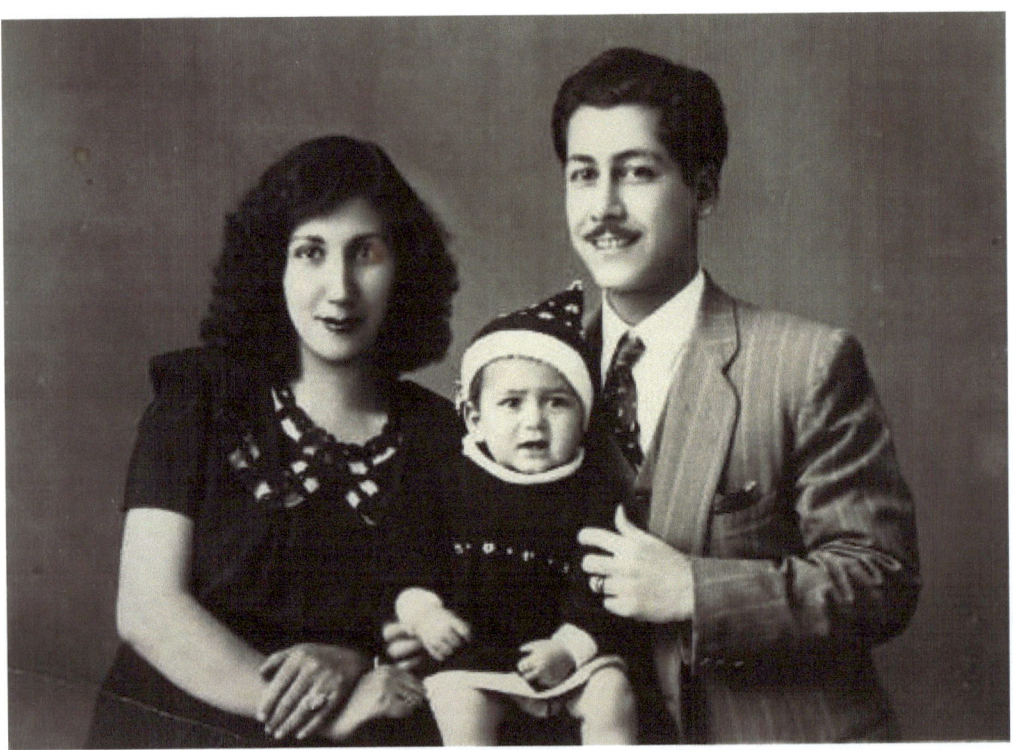

178. Hopes and Anticipations! **Life's Phase I…**

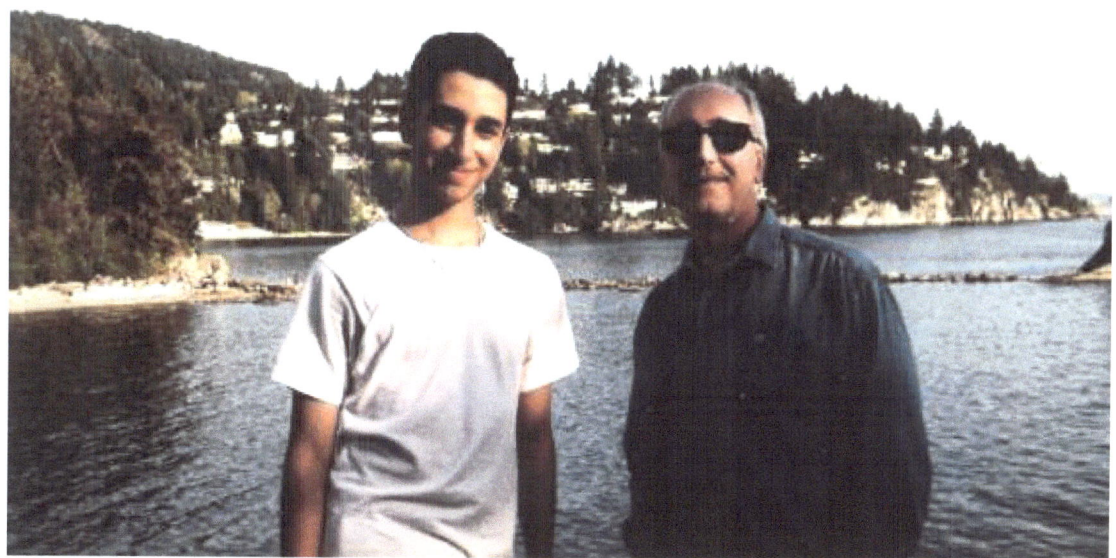
179. Smiles and Reflections! **Life's Phase II…**

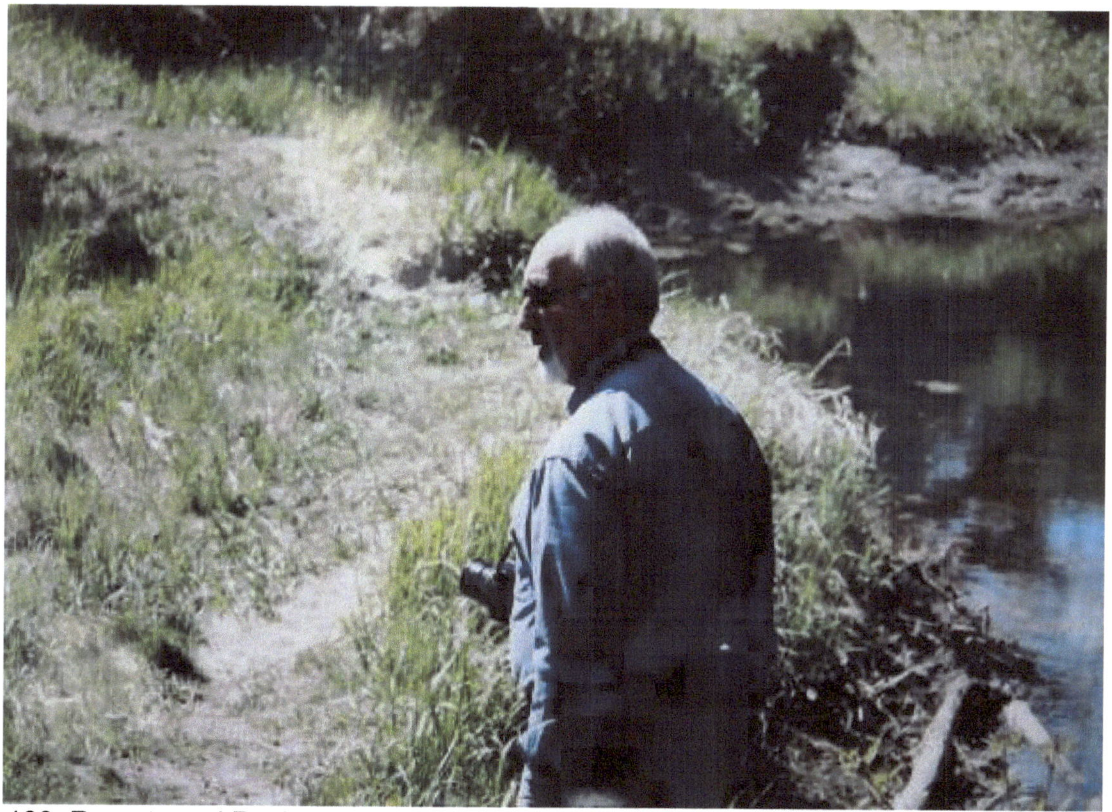

180. Regrets and Resignation! **Life's Phase III…**

www.ingramcontent.com/pod-product-compliance
Lightning Source LLC
Chambersburg PA
CBHW051149220526
45473CB00003B/705